玩转TOPPER
从入门到大师

THE TOPPER BOOK
TOPPER SAILING FROM START TO FINISH

摄影：Simon McIlwaine

摄影：Simon Mcllwaine

玩转TOPPER

从入门到大师

THE TOPPER BOOK

TOPPER SAILING FROM START TO FINISH

[英] 戴夫·柯克瑞尔　约翰·凯格／著
(Dave Cockerill & John Caig)
王　欣／译

英文版作者 Dave Cockerill 给中文版的前言

有了正确的指导，学习帆船是简单的事情。每次你在水上航行都可以一如既往地体会到那种快乐、兴奋与自由，而这种感受可以持续一生（我父亲一直到86岁都在参加帆船赛）。帆船给我的收获如此巨大，因此我非常高兴把对帆船的热情分享给大家。

过去的很多年我非常荣幸地指导了成百上千的帆船选手。其中有的人获得了奥运奖牌，并在世锦赛中取胜。而最让我高兴的并不是他们取得了这些骄人战绩，而是看到这些年轻人通过从事帆船成长为更优秀的人。我观察到孩子们不断提高自信心，解决问题的能力也明显提升，更加敢于担当。我也听到很多家长讲述孩子们在练习帆船之后学习成绩明显提高。这些都是孩子们获得成功人生所必需的基本技能。

我的儿子通过Topper爱上了帆船。从他八岁开始练习Topper一直到他转到更大的帆船，这期间我逐渐获得了大量的知识，并构成了本书的基础。

我从事帆船比赛已经有50年了，其中结合了在中学任教的25年，我逐渐地把教授帆船竞赛发展成自己的职业。我会把这两段经历相结合所产生的奇妙成果带给大家。这本书将指导你掌握基本技能直到赢得比赛。开始的部分指导你如何装船并作为初学者下水航行。对于想提高竞技水平的选手这本书也能提供帮助。通过练习和艰苦努力，你一定会实现目标。

我非常荣幸地指导了很多中国的少年帆船选手，并参与了中国休闲航海运动的快速发展。通过在中国各地具有专业资质的帆船俱乐部学习帆船，你会发现帆船非常有趣、安全，并且容易掌握。我可以预期在不远的将来一定会有成千上万的优秀中国选手来享受这个非凡的运动，毫无疑问会有很多人在世界舞台上获得巨大成功。

我要特别感谢John Caig对本书的贡献。他对Topper船型的发展做出了巨大推动，我很高兴能够把他的杰出工作延续到21世纪。我还要特别感谢来自北京航海中心和万航帆艇的Rick Pointon、李小桓、叶小明和王欣，他们独具慧眼致力于Topper的普及并推动中国休闲航海运动的发展。

很多年以来，我从Topper设计者Ian Proctor的儿子Roger Proctor那里获得了非常多的帮助。他和我与Topper International（制造商）合作持续地对作为竞赛船型的Topper进行改进。他的支持和睿智的见解具有无法估量的价值。

Dave Cockerill 简介：

- 1972 – 2000 年先后在三个中学担任设计技术课老师,成为学科负责人
- 2004年RYA全国代表队最佳教练
- 2001 – 2014 RYA Topper国家级教练
- 2009 – 2011 RYA奥林匹克残奥会教练
- 2000 – 2014 共14年成功的航海工作经历
- 对Topper进行了一系列成功的改进，包括中置式主缭和4.2级别帆
- 国际Topper级别协会ITCA负责训练的副总裁

Topper专利所有人 Roger Proctor给中文版的前言

Topper是个不可思议的故事。

我父亲Ian Proctor（皇家工业设计师）在1960年代后期设计了Topper。他在职业生涯中设计了很多高性能的竞赛船型和奥运级别船型。他设计Topper的目的是制造一艘价格低廉而令人兴奋的船，让各年龄阶段和各种能力的人们都能从事帆船运动，掌握技巧，强健体魄，磨练意志，提升耐力，自立自强，最重要的是享受乐趣。

在1970年代他重新设计了Topper并采用了新的注塑技术，使这种船结实耐用，坚不可摧。到目前为止，Topper可能依然是世界上最大的聚丙烯注塑产品，它不仅是一艘超级棒的帆船，也是一件工程设计杰作。

结果是显而易见的，这种便宜而“友好”的帆船让所有年龄段的人爱上了帆船这项运动。

但是设计和技术仅仅是Topper故事的一个方面，另一方面则是与它有关的人。世界各地的帆船选手和推广者，培养出了各种船型的国家级和世界级冠军，还包括那些环游世界的大帆船水手以及奥运会冠军选手们，都使用Topper进行训练和比赛。

Dave Cockerill和John Caig 是Topper训练和竞赛领域的传奇人物。多年以来，他们两位为Topper投入了大量时间和热情，因为他们坚信对于投身并热爱帆船运动的年轻人来说，Toppper是一种非常理想的船型。

Dave Cockerill对于把Topper发展成为领先的训练和比赛用船做出了突出贡献。帆船比赛永远是充满挑战的，但在Dave的帆船哲学中，首要因素是享受乐趣。没有人比他更了解Topper，也没有人比他更能够挖掘出Topper的妙处。在过去的20年中，Dave的哲学与智慧令他享誉世界，他还领衔训练了很多奥林匹克未来帆船之星。

现在，Dave的知识财富也在帮助中国的新一代水手发现、享受Topper并爱上这项伟大的运动。如果你要向大师学习，这本书就是秘笈。如果你想问Dave为什么对Topper 训练如此痴迷和投入，我想一定是因为他非常享受Topper选手脸上洋溢的笑容与快乐。

享受帆船吧！

Roger Proctor 简介：

- 国际Topper级别协会ITCA执行委员
- Proctor+Stevenson设计公司董事长
- 英国帝国勋章获得者 (MBE)
- 前 Topper英国冠军
- Topper船型设计者Ian Proctor的儿子

Copyright © 2014 Fernhurst Books Limited：
版权所有：

This second edition first published in 2014 by Fernhurst Books Limited
62 Brandon Parade, Holly Walk, Leamington Spa, Warwickshire, CV32 4JE, UK
Tel: +44 (0) 1926 337488 | www.fernhurstbooks.com
英文版权：Fernhurst 图书有限公司，中英文双语版版权：万航帆艇。
Some of this material was previously published as Topper Sailing.
Previous edition published in 2006 by John Wiley & Sons Ltd.
本书部分内容于2006年由 John Wiley & Sons公司作为“Topper航行”一书出版。
All rights reserved. No part of this publication may be reproduced, stored in a retrieval system or transmitted, in any form or by any means, electronic, mechanical, photocopying, recording, scanning or otherwise, except under the terms of the Copyright, Designs and Patents Act 1988 or under the terms of a license issued by The Copyright Licensing Agency Ltd, Saffron House, 6-10 Kirby Street, London, EC1N 8TS, UK, without the permission in writing of the Publisher.
版权所有，侵权必究。

Designations used by companies to distinguish their products are often claimed as trademarks. All brand names and product names used in this book are trade names, service marks, trademarks or registered trademarks of their respective owners. The Publisher is not associated with any product or vendor mentioned in this book.
本书出现的各种品牌标识、商标等与本公司无关。

This sport has inherent risks and injuries could occur. Do not rely on this work as your only source of sports training information or advice. Do not attempt any of these activities without the proper professional supervision and safety equipment.
帆船运动伴随着风险和受伤的可能，请勿把此书作为唯一的训练信息来源。帆船运动必须在专业人员的监督下并使用相应的安全设备才能进行。
Acknowledgements：
The authors and publishers would like to thanks Liz Mansell for taking the majority of the photographs and Dave Cockerill and Tim Davison for additional photographs.
Robert Spencer and Rachael Scarfe for sailing in front of the camera and the Royal Lymington Yacht Club for hosting the two day shoot.Also, Nick Marshall for sailing for us in Fournells, and Minorca Sailing for hosting the one day shoot there.
鸣谢：作者和出版商感谢 Liz Mansell提供了大部分照片，除特别标注作者的照片，其他照片由 Dave Cockerill和 Tim Davison提供。 Robert Spencer和Rachael Scarfe进行示范操作。

中文版译者：王欣
中英文双语版出版社：哈尔滨工程大学出版社

Contents 目录

Introduction 绪论 **8**

Part 1 Sailing the boat 第一部分：航行 **14**

1 Parts and rigging 组件和装船 15
2 The centre mainsheet 中置主缭 26
3 Sailing theory 航行原理 30
4 Reefing 缩帆 34
5 Launching 下水 36
6 A first sail 首次航行 38
7 Reaching 横风航行 43
8 Beating 迎风航行 49
9 Tacking 迎风转向 56
10 Running 顺风航行 60
11 Gybing 顺风转向 65
12 Taking a penalty 受罚 71
13 Capsizing 翻覆 72
14 Landing 上岸 76
15 Care and maintenance 保养和维护 78
16 The International Topper Class Association 82
国际Topper级别委员会ITCA

Part 2 The Topper 4.2 第二部分：Topper4.2级别 **83**

Part 3 Racing: the basics 第三部分：比赛：基本技巧 **87**

Part 4 Masterclasses 第四部分：大师级别 **101**

1 Preparing yourself for success 做好准备获得胜利 102
2 Preparing your boat for success 装配好船以获得胜利 110
3 Advanced control lines 加强版控制索具 118
4 Boatspeed and boat handling for success 124
提高船速并控制船只以获得胜利
5 Tactics and strategy for success 制胜的战术与策略 140
6 Preparing for an event 赛事准备 150
7 Dave Cockerill's guide for parents 给家长的建议 152

And finally- silly games 终结篇——趣味游戏 **155**

Introduction 绪论

The Topper has a special place in sailing. Thousands of people learn the basic skills in Toppers every year.But it’s not just a beginner’s boat as you will see by reading the later chapters of this book. Topper fleets are established at many sailing clubs, and the class association organises a programme of open meetings and championships for Topper enthusiasts.The Topper Book is for beginners and racers, and is organised into four parts:

Topper在航海界有特殊的位置，每年有成千上万的人使用Topper学习航行的基本技能。但看完本书后你会发现Topper不仅仅是适用于初学者的船，很多航海俱乐部都在使用这种船，Topper国际级别委员会每年都会为爱好者们组织一系列公开的活动和锦标赛。本书主要针对初学者和竞赛爱好者，分为四个部分：

Part 1 is for beginners and teaches sailors to **rig and sail the boat.**

第一部分是为初学者讲解**如何装船和航行**。

We have also introduced the centre mainsheet here, because most sailors now use it. All the photos show the boat with gear in race configuration, but to keep things simple at this stage the race control lines are shown later in Masterclass 3.

我们也将介绍现在大部分水手使用的中置式主缭。所有照片中的船只都是竞赛型配置。但为简便起见，竞赛时的索具控制将在后面的大师级别3部分进行讲解。

Part 2 details the new **Topper 4.2** rig. This is a boon for light sailors (<45kg) and for strong wind sailing for the less experienced.

第二部分讲解新款的Topper4. 2船型帆索具。这是适用于体重轻于45公斤的初学者在大风时航行的船型。

Part 3 is an **introduction to racing.**
If you get up to speed (see Part 1) and employ these tactics you should be able to win a club championship.
第三部分是**关于竞赛技巧的介绍**。如果你能够掌握第一部分中的技能并且能够快速航行，你将有机会在俱乐部级别的比赛中取胜。

Part 4 is a **Masterclass** with Dave Cockerill, National Topper Coach. Follow his advice, get out on the water, practise hard, and the sky’s the limit…
And finally, we show you how to have fun in the Topper... even when you aren’t sailing!
第四部分是**大师级别的技能**。国家级Topper教练Dave Cockerill将带领你出海并刻苦训练，突破你的极限……
最后，我们将教你几招使用Topper的好玩儿游戏，即使你不是在航行……

THE STORY OF THE TOPPER
Topper的故事

The Topper was designed by Ian Proctor as a simple ‘beach boat’ and as an introduction to sailing. Originally made in GRP it was chosen by ICI to form the core of an experiment to see how big injection mouldings could be made. Clearly successful, it is said to be the biggest injection moulding product in the world some forty years later. Most boats are made in wood or GRP (Glassfibre Reinforced Plastic) and increasingly in Polythene by a rotary moulding technique. The Topper is unique in that it is made by injecting polypropylene between two huge moulds in a way that controls the thickness and allows strengthening to be placed only where required. The results is an extremely lightweight and durable boat (especially compared to the recent upsurge of plastic boats using rotary moulding techniques) and gives the Topper its spritely performance.

摄影：庄丽

Ian Proctor当初为了造一艘简单的入门级“沙滩型帆船”而设计了Topper。ICI（英国化学工业集团）选择了玻璃钢制造的Topper来试验用喷塑技术能制造多大的船体。结果是成功的，据说Topper是过去的四十年中世界上最大的注塑产品。现在大多数的船体都用木制或玻璃钢制造，同时随着滚塑技术的应用，聚乙烯塑料船体也越来越多。但Topper的独特性在于使用两个巨大的模具进行聚乙烯注塑，工艺中对于材料厚度进行控制，同时在必要之处进行强化处理。最终造就了轻盈而坚固耐用的船体（特别是与最近流行的滚塑制造的塑料船体相比），赋予Topper轻巧的性能。

They have all come out of the same mould and it is quite possible to find an old Topper in the corner of a boat park and bring it back to race spec. With the addition of some new controls and a reasonable amount of hard work good racing can be had at a very reasonable cost.

所有的Topper都使用同一款模具制造。即便是在船只仓库里的一只年代久远的Topper，依然可以用它进行比赛。通过一番努力和有限的预算，增加一些新式控制器具，它依然会有优异的比赛性能。

The great strengths of the Topper
Topper的伟大之处：

- Fundamentally they are all the same.
  船型基本是一样的。
- They are extremely durable.
  坚固耐用。
- Their lightweight construction makes them really lively and fun.
  船体轻盈，充满乐趣。
- They can be found everywhere and can be made into an effective race machine or excellent ‘beach boat’ for little cost.
  身影随处可见，竞赛性能优异，是物美价廉的沙滩型帆船。
- All spare parts are readily available.
  所有的配件都容易获取。

How the Topper has changed
Topper是如何改进的

It is amazing that a boat designed for recreation and training could adapt so well to the increased loads associated with racing. There have been a number of relatively minor changes over the years in response to this:

作为娱乐和训练之用的Topper依然可以对压力巨大的比赛应付自如，这一点令人惊叹。过去的几十年中，针对下面情况对船只进行了微调：

- The old 1 1/4″ (25mm) boom has been changed to one of 1.5″ (32.5mm) external diameter. The thinner boom is fine for a beach boat but will break in time if used with the modern controls for racing. Aim to replace yours as soon as possible (or when it breaks!).
  主帆横杆由老款的25毫米直径换成32.5毫米直径。老款的细横杆非常适合在沙滩上下水，但在使用现代索具比赛时易于损坏。如果你还在使用旧的横杆尽量早点更换。
- Originally aft sheeted, there is now the option to use a centre sheeting system. Aft sheeting is fine for a beach boat, if only because there is more room in the cockpit, but centre sheeting is far better for racing. (Please see Part 1, chapter 2 - The centre mainsheet).
  主缭滑轮组原来放置在船尾，现在可以选择放在船体中央部位。主缭后置很适合沙滩型帆船，好处仅在于给船舱留下更大的空间。而主缭中置则在比赛时有明显的好处（请参阅第一部分第二章：主缭中置）。
- The original tiller extension was limited, by class rules, to 712mm. This has been upgraded to 975mm and the use of a rubber universal joint is allowed.
  最初的副舵柄长度由于级别规则的限制是712毫米。现在升级为975毫米并且允许使用橡胶制万向节。
- The introduction of an alternative sail (Part 2 - The Topper 4.2) allows lighter sailors to join in the fun.
  小型帆的使用（请参阅第二部分：Topper 4.2）可以让体重轻的选手也能享受航行的乐趣。

- At one time the purchase ① on the downhaul was a maximum of 3:1. 6:1 is now allowed and is an essential upgrade for racing at anything beyond club level (photo 1).
  曾经帆前下角拉索的最大力矩比是3:1，现在达到6:1，比赛性能有本质性提升（图1）。
- All other purchases have remained unaltered but the quality of the kit has improved by the use of ball-bearing blocks and Dyneema rope.
  其他所有的设备都保持原样。但随着滚珠滑轮和迪尼玛纤维（超高相对分子质量聚乙烯）绳索的使用，设备质量有很大提升。
- The centre toestrap can be any length whereas previously it was controlled. This suits smaller sailors and can even be made to be adjustable, for length, on the water.
  中央压舷带由固定长度改为可变长度。这对身材小巧的选手非常适用，压舷带甚至长度可调。
- The halyard has been replaced with a short loop of rope (the halyard loop) which stretches very little. Subsequently sails have a webbing strap across the top which is easier to fit and cannot stretch at all. A new masthead fitting is used with a grove to prevent the sail unwrapping when reefed (photo 2).
  升帆索被一种拉伸度很小的短绳套代替（升帆套）。后来主帆拥有了横贯顶部的硬边使其易于装配并不可拉伸。新的桅杆顶设计了一个凹槽来防止主帆缩帆时无法折叠（图2）。
- Originally the outhaul cleat was a small 'v cleat' which prevented any meaningful adjustment on the water. A cam cleat can now be attached to the boom, originally with a specially designed plate and more recently using a dedicated plastic fitting. The later is fixed with one rivet on the top of the boom and has virtually eliminated booms breaking at that point (photo 1).
  最初的后拉索夹绳器是一种简单的V形夹绳器，防止任何有效的调整。现在变为固定在横杆上的凸轮夹绳器，材料曾经是特别设计的转盘，后来改为特制的塑料凸轮。这种夹绳器被一颗铆钉固定在横杆顶部，最终消除了横杆在此处折断的隐患。（图1）
- As increasing loads were transferred to the spars via the controls masts were breaking too often. The kicker take off points on mast and boom are now via rings attached by webbing straps. Another cause of breakages was eradicated.
  桅杆经常由于控制杆件负荷过重而损坏。Topper则采用硬制尼龙带固定斜拉索代替传统的铰接式斜拉器，排除了此类原因造成的桅杆损坏。
- The attachment of the rudder to the boat via the transom plate has changed from aluminium to stainless steel. Most recently a new top pintle fitting has been introduced which removes any unwanted movement and improves the strength in that area of the deck (photo 3).

1

2

注释：① **purchase** 指多个滑轮组成的缭绳装置，拉动时由于力矩原理比单根缭绳更省力。如果三个滑轮，则力矩比是3:1。

舵叶和船尾板的连接件从铝制变成了不锈钢。最近开始应用一种新的高级舵拴，可以避免任何不需要的移动并且改善周边船体区域的强度（图3）。

- Finally a new gooseneck system has replaced the original ‘rollock’ type to make it more reliable (photos 4 & 5).

  一种新型的帆杆插头系统代替了原来的环形锁方式并且更加可靠（图4和图5）。

So a great little boat has been made even better. It just needs to be enjoyed!

这样一只伟大的小船被造得越来越好，来享受它吧！

3

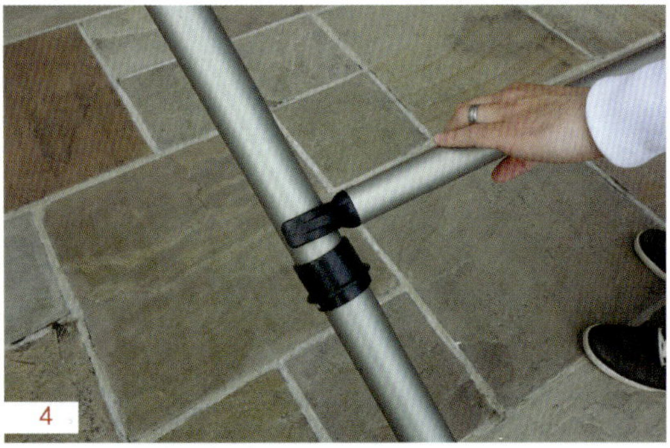
4

5

摄影：庄丽

CAR TOPPERING 车顶运载

The Topper got its name in the first place because of the ease with which it could be transported on the roof of a car and this great mobility has certainly played a considerable part in the boat’s worldwide success. The inverted boat presents a smooth, aerodynamic shape to the wind and neither speed nor fuel consumption is greatly affected during ‘car toppering’. In fact, many caravan owners claim an improvement in consumption when towing because the Topper’s shape guides the airflow around the bluff front of their vans.

Topper的名字来源于它非常容易放置在汽车顶上进行运输。这种超级机动性是其获得全球成功的主要原因之一。倒置过来的船体展示出流线型的空气动力学形状，因此车顶装载运输时的速度和油耗基本不受影响。实际上很多旅行车车主都表示装载Topper行驶时的油耗其实有节约，因为旅行车直钝的车头被船身形状导引了空气流动而减少阻力。

In spite of the simplicity of the operation there are some important guidelines to follow if – like us – you drive many thousands of miles each year beneath a Topper. Position the two roof bars as far apart as possible on the car roof up to about a 4-foot/1.2m maximum. It is quite acceptable for them to be much closer together than this as may be necessary if you drive a coupe or rigid-topped sports car. Load the Topper upside down, bow forward and ensure that the front bar supports the side decks immediately behind the aft end of the foredeck. Ideally, the rear bar should support the side deck immediately ahead of the stern deck. Quick-release straps are by far the simplest means of securing the Topper and the least likely to come undone. If the bars are wide enough, you can lay the spars alongside the hull and take the straps right around the whole lot, which will greatly reduce loading time. Always tie the boat down to the bumpers (fenders) fore and aft. The bow painter can be used forward – this will stop the wind from lifting the boat – and the horse (traveller) can be used aft, where it will check any tendency for the boat to run forward in an emergency stop. A trolley can also be carried on top of the upside-down hull.

虽然车载运输的操作很简单，依然有一些重要的规矩要遵守—如果你像我们一样每年要装载Topper行驶数千英里的话。把车顶横杆架安装得尽量远，最大间距是4英尺或1.2米。当然如果你驾驶一辆轿跑车或者硬顶跑车时，车顶横杆架也可以距离很近。将Topper底朝上放置，船头向前并确保汽车前支柱支撑在船只前甲板与中仓交汇处。理想情况下，汽车后柱要支撑在船只后甲板与中仓交汇处。快速包装带可以很方便地固定Topper并且不易松脱。如果车身宽度足够，就可以把桅杆及横杆捆在船身侧面，充分节省包装时间。一定要把船体和汽车前后保险杠相连，前面用船头缆绳固定，防止气流把船体举起。后面用主帆滑车与后保险杠相连，防止紧急刹车时船体前移。船车也可以放在反扣的船体上面。

It is quite feasible to carry two Toppers on the roof of most cars but remember that the all-up weight will be 190lb/85kg. The lower hull should be loaded right way up, bows forward. You will find that two Toppers fit together very snugly in this way – but do make sure that they are very well strapped down.

对于大多数汽车来说，车顶装载两条Topper也是可行的。但请注意两条船的总重量为190磅或85公斤。放在下面的船体必须甲板朝上，船头向前。你会发现两条船叠放在一起非常妥贴——但一定要确保捆绑结实。

Part 1 第一部分
Sailing the boat 航行

摄影：黄乙能

1 Parts and rigging
组件和装船

The Topper is exceptionally simple and is supplied complete and ready to sail. The diagram opposite shows all the standard parts in place.
Earlier boats had a halyard to pull up the sail: rigging this is shown in Sleeving the sail: halyard method, page 20.
Topper船体格外简单而且是完整供货，随时可以航行。下页的图示展示了全部标准组件。早期的Topper装备了主帆升帆索，装配方法将在第20页介绍。
Race boats tend to have a centre mainsheet and chapter 2 shows how to fit this. They also have advanced control lines and these are detailed in Masterclass 3.
竞赛型Topper是中置式主缭，装配方法将在第二部分介绍。这种船也装配了高级索具，将在大师级别3中介绍。

OK, let's put the boat together.
OK,让我们把船装配起来。

Sail numbers 帆号

Before you sail your new boat for the first time, it is most important to apply the self-adhesive numbers to the sail. The sail number is exclusive to the boat and corresponds to the serial number/sail number plate. These are inside the boat attached to the toestrap.
新船首次使用之前有件重要的事，就是把自粘式帆号粘在帆面上。帆号是帆船专用的并且和系列号/帆号铭牌相一致。铭牌缝制在船用压舷带上。

Follow the instructions carefully.
要细心地按照说明书进行操作。

摄影：张琦

Standard Topper 标准型Topper

Sail numbers and national lettering

帆号和国籍字母

- **Sail numbers** 帆号
  （请注意所有都是最小尺寸）
- 帆的两面都应该粘贴帆号，右舷的帆号要高于左舷帆号。
- 必须位于礼帽标志下面的第二格（如右图）。
- 帆号的高度为230毫米。
- 应该使用Digital Eights字体。
- 数字上下左右之间的距离为45毫米。
- 帆号必须使用白色帆面的对比色。

Starboard side 右舷帆面

- 帆号的上缘应该距上一格的缝制线45毫米。
- 从距帆后缘45毫米处开始。

Port side 左舷帆面

- 帆号的上缘应该低于右舷帆号底部45毫米。
- 必须在距后缘45毫米处结束。

National letters 国籍字母标识

- 帆的两面都应该粘贴字母标识，右舷的字母要高于左舷字母。
- 位于礼帽标志下面的一格。
- 字母的高度为230毫米。
- 使用Helvetica字体。
- 每个字母之间的距离为45毫米。
- 字母与帆号颜色相同。

Starboard side右舷帆面

- 字母的上缘应该距上一格的缝制线45毫米。
- 从距帆后缘45毫米处开始。

Port side 左舷帆面

- 字母的上缘应该低于右舷字母底部45毫米。
- 必须在距后缘45毫米处结束。

Topper 4.2

Topper 4.2 帆号和国籍字母排列方式和标准型相同，但国际字母要贴在帆号下面的位置。

Attaching numbers and letters

黏贴帆号和字母

最佳的方式为把数字的边角处撕开衬纸，先粘贴边角，慢慢撕下衬纸并把帆号压实。

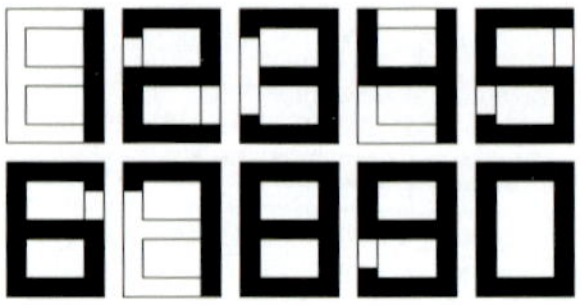

1 Hull 船身
2 Daggerboard (prevents sideways drift)
稳向板（防止横向侧移）

Ropes 索具

3 Halyard (if fitted – keeps sail up) 升帆索（固定帆上部）
4 Kicking strap or vang (prevents boom rising) 斜拉器（防止横杆抬起）
5 Downhaul (tightens front edge of sail) 下拉索（拉紧帆前缘）
6 Mainsheet (trims sail) Centre mainsheet also available 主帆缭绳（调节帆角度）
7 Outhaul (tightens foot of sail) 后拉索（拉紧下帆脚）
8 Clew tie-down (attaches corner of sail to boom)
后帆角固定索 （把后帆角固定在横杆上）
9 Horse (traveller) 主帆滑车
10 Painter (for tying up or towing)船头绳（拖船或固定船头）

Spars 杆件

11 Two-part mast 两段式桅杆
12 Boom 横杆

For steering 舵

13 Rudder 舵叶
14 Rudder stock 舵栓
15 Tiller 舵柄
16Tiller extension
(lets you steer when sitting out) 副舵柄
（向外压舷时使用）

Sail 帆具

17 Sail 帆
18 Sail numbers 帆号
19 Topper insignia 礼帽标志

Other fittings 其它

20 Toestraps
(hiking straps) 压舷带
21 Self bailer
(to remove water) 排水筏
22 Masthead crane 桅顶扣盖
23 Mast gate 桅杆插槽

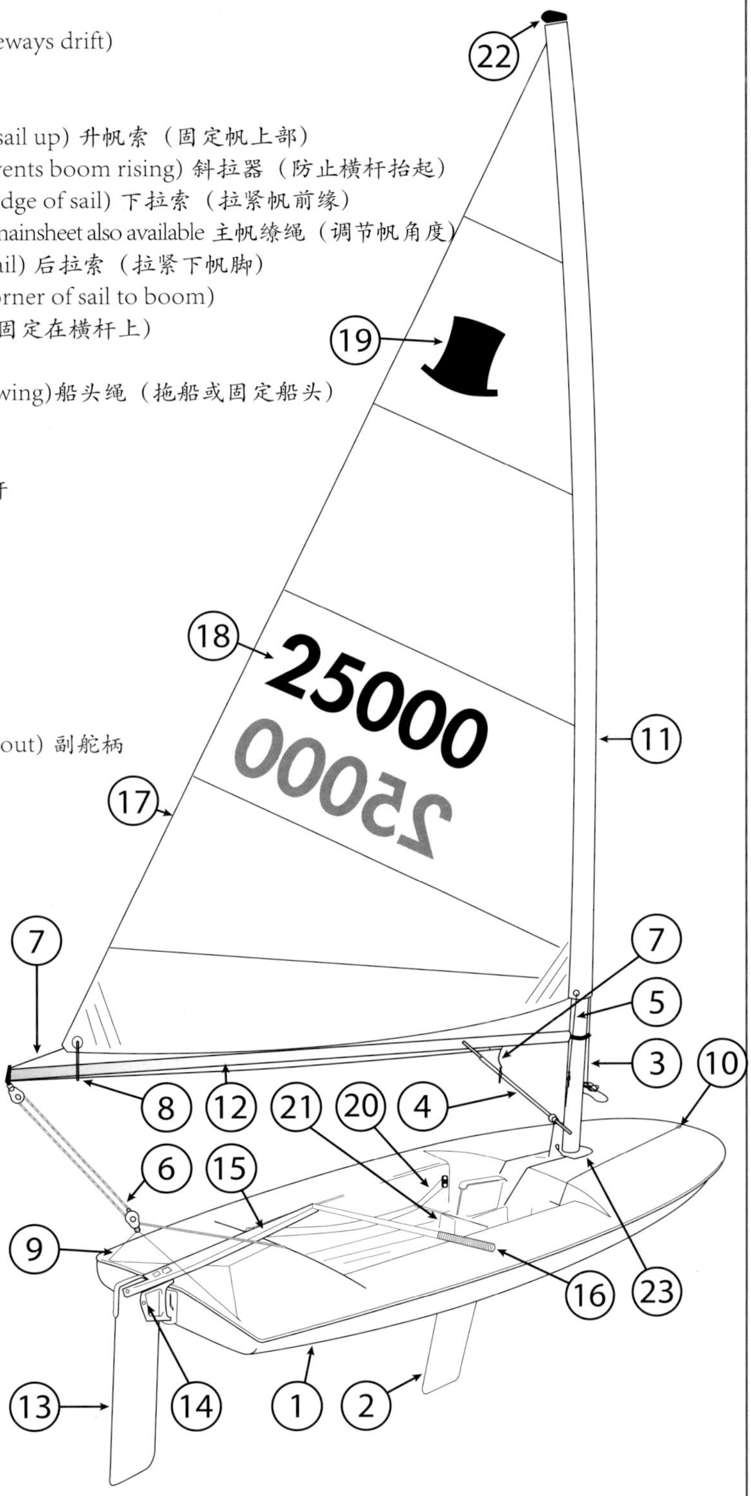

When you have unpacked everything, lay out the various control lines on the foredeck and identify them:
当你把所有包装打开后，把各类索具放置在前甲板上一一识别：

A Halyard loop 升帆绳套
B Kicking strap (vang) 斜拉索
C Downhaul 前下角拉帆索(简称下拉索)
D Mainsheet system 主帆索
E Bow painter 船头绳
F Outhaul 后下角拉帆索(简称后拉索)
G Rope horse (traveller) 滑车索
H Daggerboard elastic (shockcord) 稳向板弹力绳
I Toestrap elastic (shockcord) 压舷带弹力绳

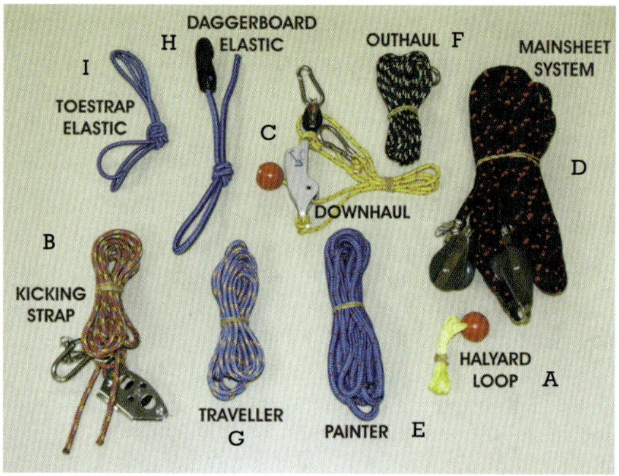

1. Slot the two mast sections together 将两段桅杆对接

making sure that the slots in the upper section have engaged properly with the rivets in the lower section (photo A).
注意把上段桅杆的插槽与下段桅杆的铆钉相扣（图A）。

2. Sleeving the sail: halyard loop method
装配主帆：使用升帆套索

1. Unfold the sail and lay it on the ground with the bottom edge of the luff sleeve near the top of the mast.
   打开主帆并铺在地上，把帆前缘圈套的底部对准桅杆头。

Halyard Loop 升帆套索

Please note that the upper mast has been turned so the crane faces forward.
请注意转动桅杆上段，使桅顶扣盖向前。

1. Feed the halyard loop up through the front hole in the mast crane.
   把做好的升帆套索穿进桅杆顶部扣盖。
2. Down the back hole. 从扣盖后部的孔中穿出。
3. Through the eyelets of the sail and back up the back hole (which might need enlarging slightly with a drill).
   穿过帆面顶部的吊孔，再从扣盖孔中穿回（可能需要用螺丝刀帮忙）
4. Loop the end over the bobble at the front.
   把套索绕到橡胶球上。
5. So that it tucks under the bobble.
   橡胶球把套索卡住固定。

6 & 7. Pull the rope both sides of the crane and up into the groove on top of the mast-crane. This will tension the rope and so lift the sail.
从杆顶扣盖两边拉紧套索，并嵌入扣盖顶部的卡槽，这样会将套索拉紧并提起主帆。

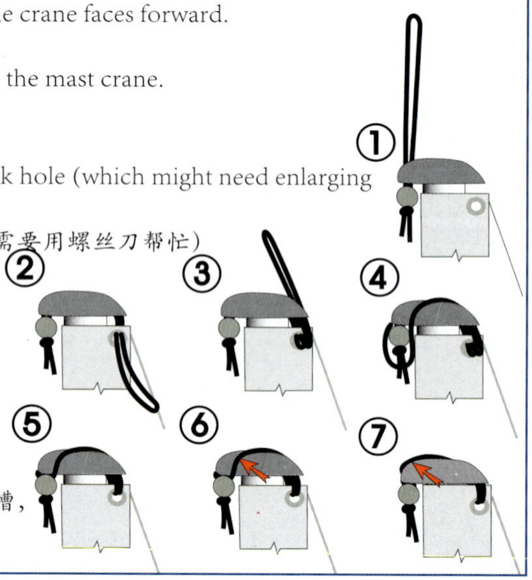

2. Insert the mast into the luff sleeve (photo B) and pull the sail down the mast (photo C). If it is at all windy, keep your back to the wind!
把桅杆装入圈套（图B）然后把帆面向下拉（图C）。大风时切记要后背朝风!
3. Continue until the whole sail is sleeved and the masthead has appeared through the top of the sail.
继续下拉，直到整个帆面头套在桅杆中，桅杆头从帆顶露出。

B

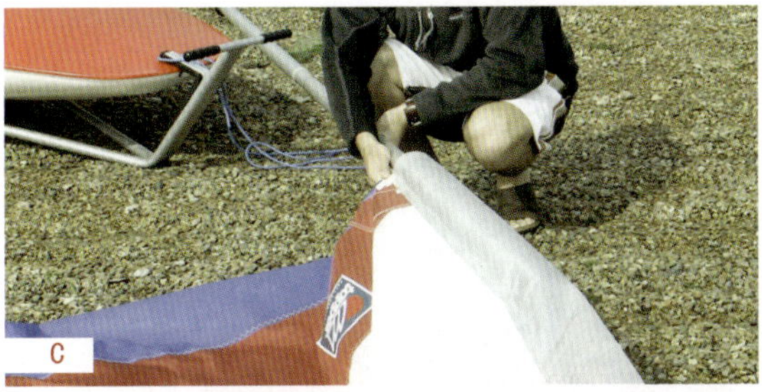
C

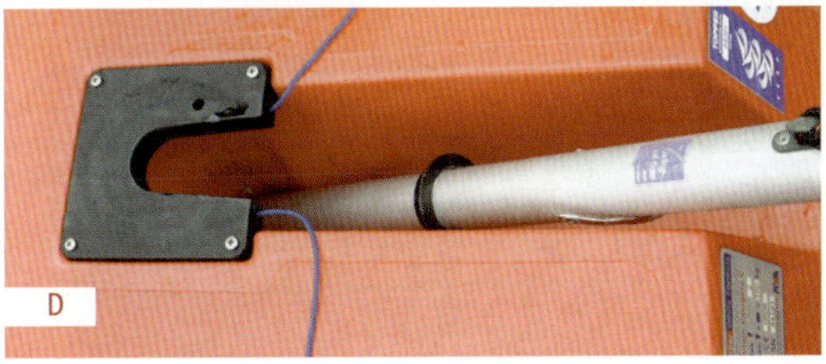
D

4. Use the halyard loop to attach the sail to the top of the mast as shown, left.
按（左图）方法把升帆索套固定在桅杆头。

3. Stepping the mast 装配桅杆

Point the boat into the wind. Support the mast at a 45 degree angle and engage the base of the mast in the cup under the mast gate (D).
把船头向风，扶起桅杆呈45度，把桅杆底部插进桅杆锁扣下面的插槽中（图D）。

Walk the mast forward into an upright position, ensuring that the collar is underneath the mast gate (E).
推动桅杆上部向前，使桅杆完全直立，确保桅杆套环在锁扣下面（图E）。

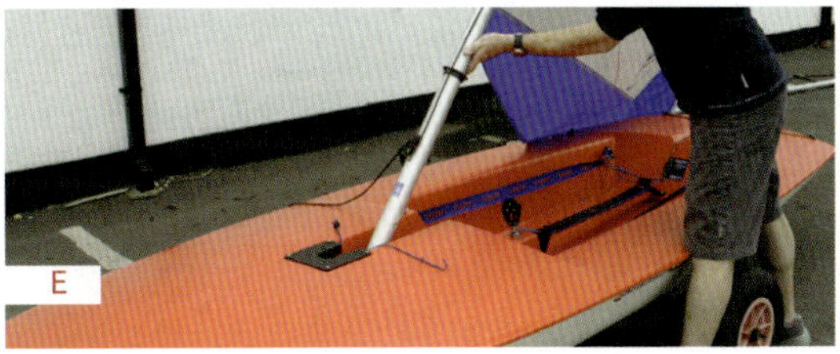
E

Pull the cord to close the gate (F).
拉紧引绳扣住桅杆锁扣（图F）。

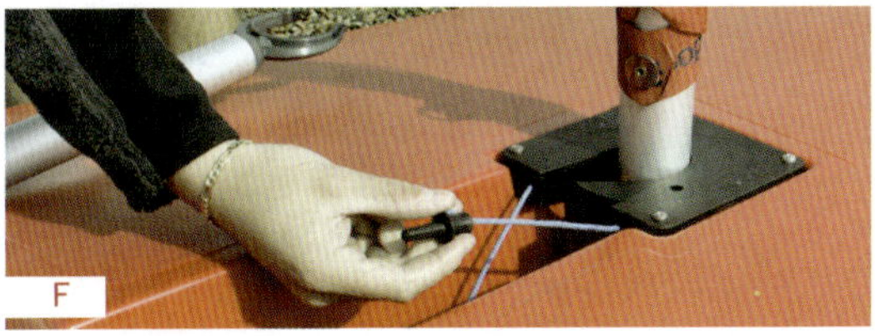
F

Tie a loop in the rope as a backup in case the toggle comes out (G).
系一个绳套防止桅杆锁扣松脱（图G）。

G

Push the toggle in firmly to lock the gate (H).
插入扣拴，锁住桅杆锁扣（图H）。

H

Sleeving the sail: halyard method
装配套筒式主帆：使用升帆索

- Pass one end of the main halyard through the masthead crane and tie a knot.
  把升帆索的一端穿过桅杆顶部扣盖并打结。
- Pull the halyard tight and cleat off on the halyard cleat. This will hold the mast together while you pull the sail onto it.
  把升帆索拉紧，在升帆索羊角上固定。这样可以在你拉升主帆时让桅杆的上下两段收紧。
- Thread the mast through the sleeve of the sail (photo A).
  把桅杆插入主帆套筒（图A）。
- When the mast appears through at the top, undo both ends and tie the halyard to the top of the sail (photo B). If you’ re using a burgee, fit it into the top of the mast now.
  当桅杆头露出来时暂停插入，把升帆索与帆顶打结固定（图B）。如果你要使用桅顶风向标，现在就要固定在桅杆头。
- Go back to the foot of the mast, pull the halyard very tight and re-fasten it to the cleat at the front of the mast.
  回到桅杆尾部，用力拉紧升帆索并卡入桅杆前部的羊角。
- Coil the rope and tuck it under itself, above the cleat.
  把剩余的绳索打成卷，在羊角上方塞在自身后面。
- Attach the downhaul to the tack cringle (photo C).
  把下拉索钩住前下角锁孔（图C）。
- Make off on the cleat (photo D).
  在羊角上拴好（图D）。
- If it is at all windy it is advisable to roll up the sail around the mast before stepping (overleaf).
  如果风一直很大，建议在立起桅杆前把帆面卷起。

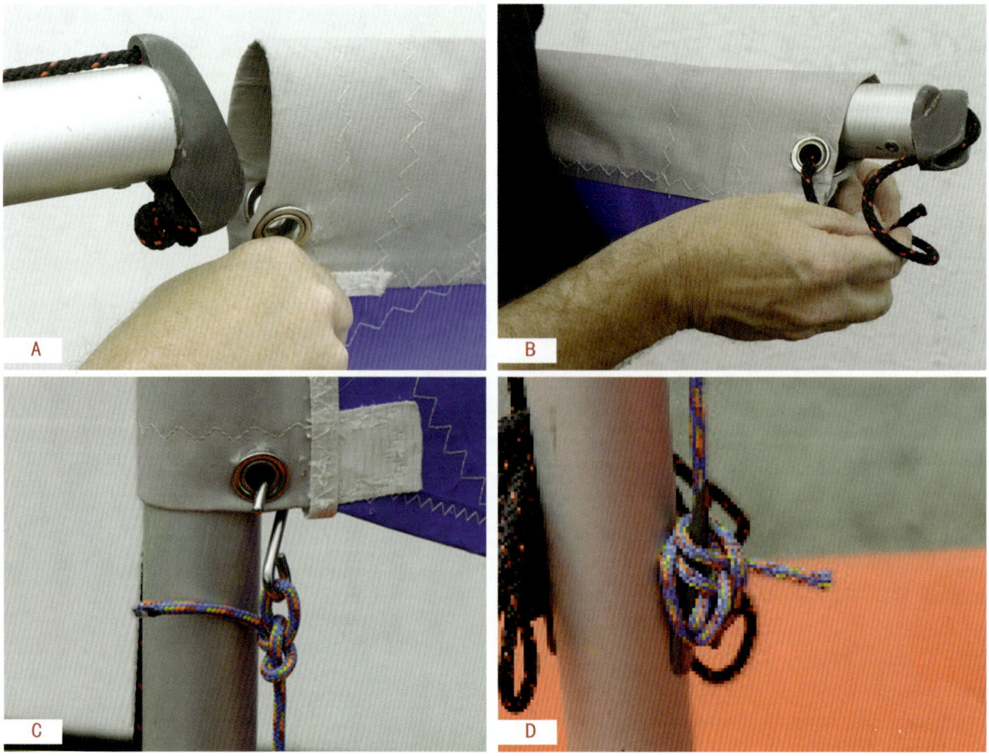

4. Rigging the outhaul
装配帆后下角索（后拉索）

Take the outhaul line through the boom-end fitting and outhaul hook and back through the boom-end eye. Finish with a figure of eight knot (A-F).

把后拉索从横杆尾部的堵头下部孔穿出，从上部孔穿回，套住后下角钩之后再穿回上部孔，索尾打个八字结（图A-图F）。

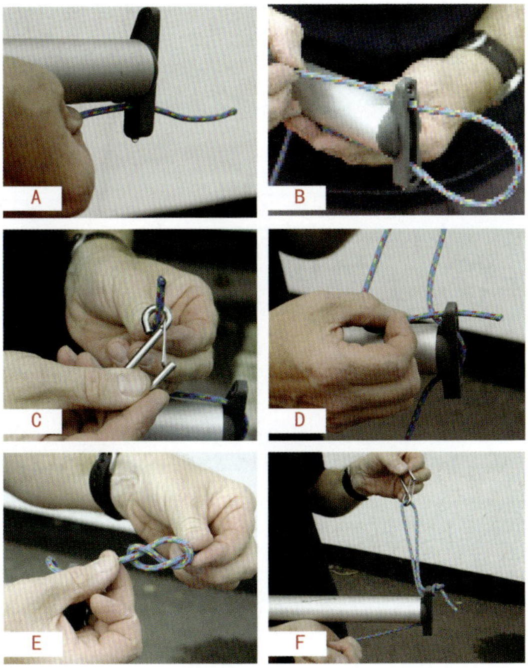

Take the other end of the outhaul line through the kicker fitting and cleat, and tie a loop (G-H). Note: the outhaul is long, to allow for reefing (see chapter 4).

把后拉索的另一端穿过斜拉器套环和夹绳器，尾部打一个套环（图G-H）。请注意：后拉索比较长，以便缩帆时使用（见第四部分）。

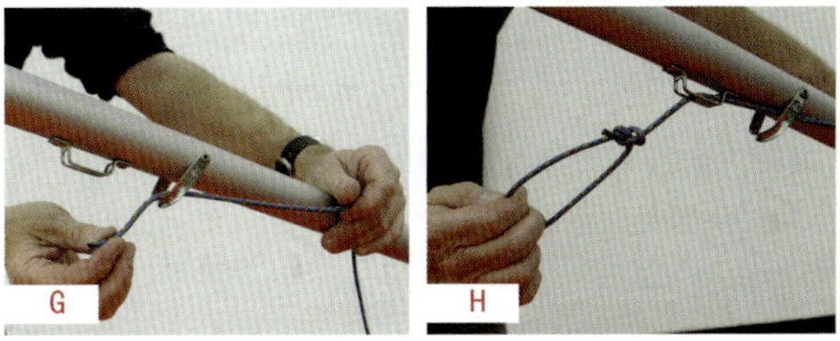

Finally, push the boom onto the mast above the collar, making sure that the down-haul is outside the crutch (I).

最后推动横杆挂在桅杆套环之上，确保后拉索保持在横杆插架外面（I）。

Setting the outhau
调节后拉索

Tension the outhaul initially to give a slight curve in the foot of the sail. The maximum draft should not exceed 75-100mm between sail and boom at the midpoint.

拉紧后拉索使帆下缘微微弯曲。帆和横杆中点之间的距离不要超过75~100毫米。

5. Rigging the sheet horse (traveller) and mainsheet
装配主缭及滑车索

Tie a bowline (20mm) in one end of the rope that will become the sheet horse (traveller). Thread the tail through the two fairleads, back through the bowline loop and down through the horse Clamcleat. Tie a figure of eight knot in the end of the sheet horse (A).

在主帆滑车索的一端打个水手结（20毫米）。把绳尾穿过船尾的两个对称导缆孔，再导回并穿过水手结套环，固定在夹绳器上，绳尾系八字结（图A）。

Shackle the lower mainsheet block to the sheet horse (traveller) (B) and shackle the upper mainsheet block to the boom (C).
把主缭的下滑轮用快挂与滑车索连接（图B），把主缭上滑轮用快挂与横杆连接（图C）。

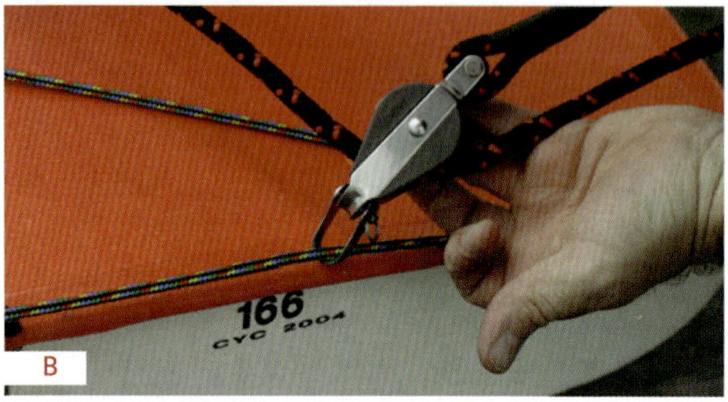

B

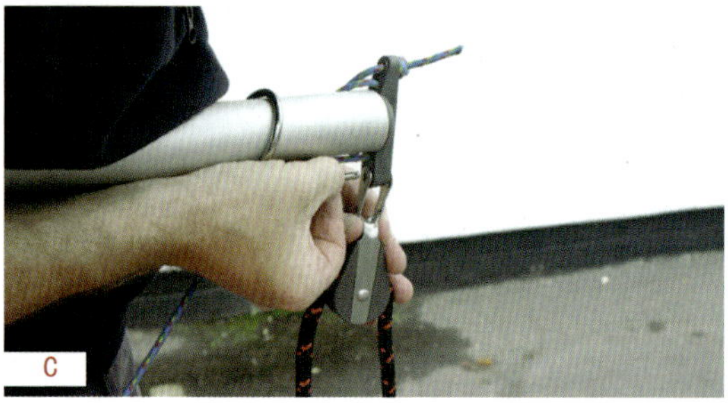
C

Tie a knot in the free end of the mainsheet (D).
在主缭的自由端打个八字结（图D）。

D

Photo E shows the complete system.
图E展示了整个系统。
If the sail was rolled, unroll it.
Attach the clew to the outhaul clip and to the clew ring (F, G and H).
如果帆还是卷着的，打开帆面。把帆后下角与后拉索和后下角环连接（图F，图G，图H）。

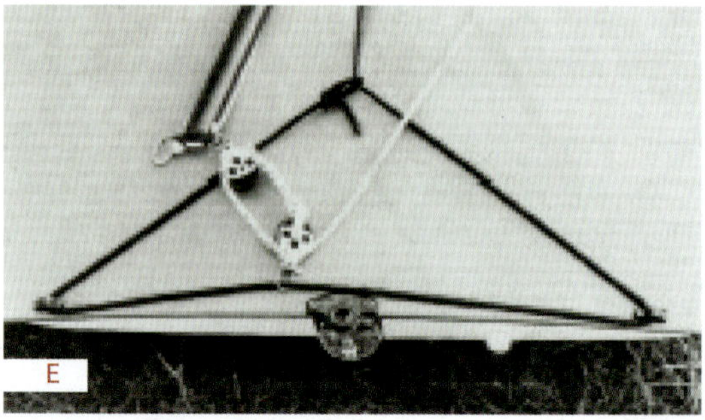
E

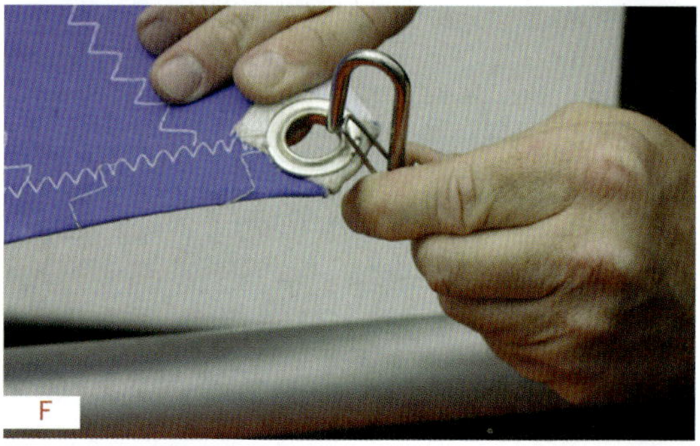
F

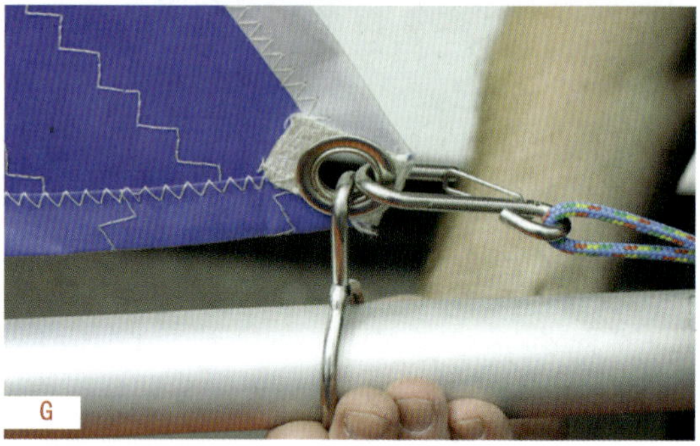
G

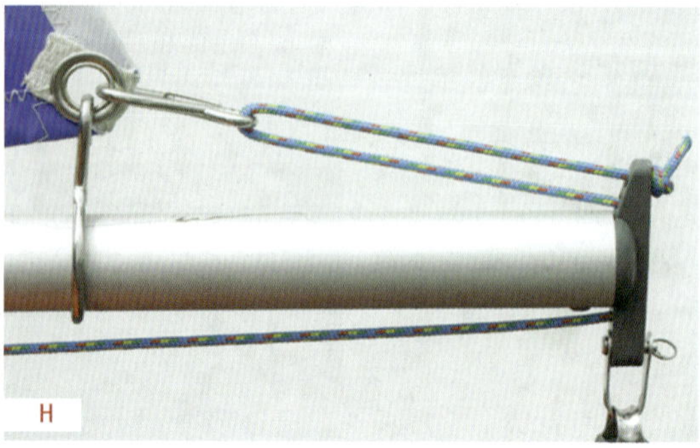
H

6. Rigging the kicking strap (vang) and downhaul
装配斜拉索和帆前下角索（下拉索）

Attach the kicking strap (vang) to the mast with the clevis pin and split ring. Attach the other end by clipping the hook onto the metal ring beneath the boom (A).

用U型扣拴和尼龙搭扣带把斜拉索的一端固定在桅杆上。用U型钩把另一端固定在横杆下面的金属环上（图A）。

A

Clip the downhaul hook through both tack cringles on the sail. Clip the other end to the ring on the aft face of the mast (B).

把帆前下角索的一端用钩子挂住两个帆前下角孔，另一端挂在桅杆后面的圆环上（图B）。

B

On older boats the kicker looks like these two photos (below).

在旧款船上的斜拉索固定方式如下面两图所示（下图）。

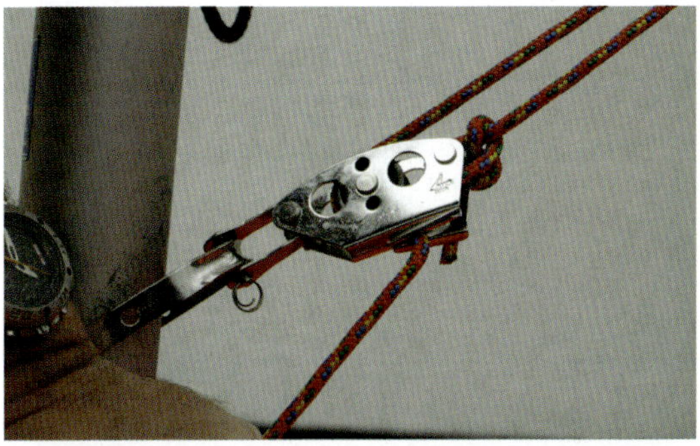

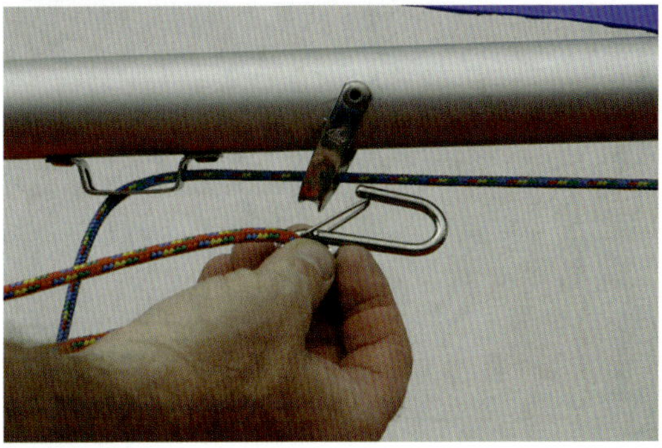

Setting the kicking strap (vang)
调节斜拉索

The ‘normal’ tension is achieved by first tightening the mainsheet and then taking up the slack on the kicking strap so it is just tight. This will give the correct tension on the boom when reaching or running. Since the mainsheet’s tension will be varied for different wind conditions the kicking strap should be varied accordingly. It is not easy to adjust the standard kicking strap while actually reaching or running except in very light winds. The race kicking strap is easily adjusted anytime.

通过拉紧主帆缭绳和斜拉索可以让主帆张紧，在横风或顺风航行时让横杆适当受力。由于在不同的风力条件下主帆承受的压力不同，需要斜拉索也进行相应的调整。但是旧款的斜拉索在横风或顺风时很难做出调整（除非风力很小），而竞赛型斜拉索可以在任何条件下进行调整。

7. Rudder, toestrap and daggerboard
船舵、压舷带和中插板

1. Attach the tiller to the rudder blade with the bolt provided.
   用配送的螺栓将舵杆和舵叶相连接。
2. With the blade in the raised position, pass the tiller under the rope traveller and lower the rudder onto the transom fitting (A). Ensure that it is completely home and that the spring retaining clip has engaged to prevent the rudder becoming detached in a capsize (B). The blade is lowered by lifting and pushing back on the tiller. Lower the tiller again when the blade is down (i.e. vertical).
   保持舵叶与地面平行，把舵杆伸进滑车索下面，把舵叶向下插入船尾的固定拴（图A）确保舵叶完全就位并且弹力固定夹已拉紧（避免翻船时舵叶与舵杆脱离）（图B）。向上抬舵叶的同时向船尾方向推舵杆，使舵叶向下。当舵叶垂直时把舵杆放平。

A

B

3. With the shockcord provided, tie the toestraps tightly towards each other at the aft end – you can stow the daggerboard behind one of the outer toestraps when it' s not in use (C).
   用配送的弹力绳将两条压舷带在船尾处套在一起方便压舷时用脚钩住，同时在紧急情况下可以用手抓住压舷带。在稳向板不使用时可以插在外侧压舷带与船舱空隙处（图C）。

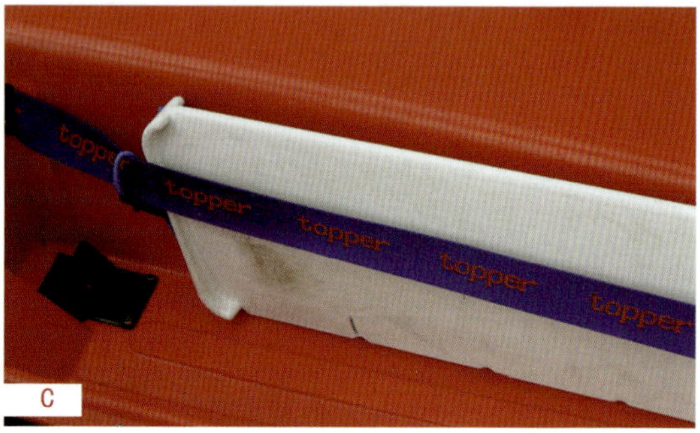

C

4. The daggerboard is kept in the desired position by the tension in the shockcord, which creates a forward wedging action in the daggerboard housing. Loop the shock-cord round the mast between the webbing strap and mastgate and clip it onto itself with the hook (D). Pass the free end of the shockcord through the top of the hole in the daggerboard rim (E). Adjust the tension to suit, then tie a retaining knot (F).
   稳向板放置在需要的位置，弹力绳产生的拉力在稳向板就位时使其保持稳定。弹力绳应该在下拉索固定带和锁扣之间绕过桅杆，并且用钩子夹住（图D）。弹力绳的另一端穿过稳向板顶部的圆孔（图E），调整弹力，打一个防脱结（图F）。

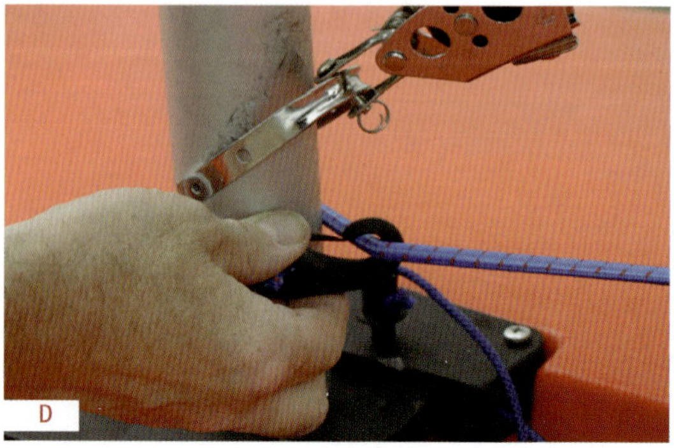
D

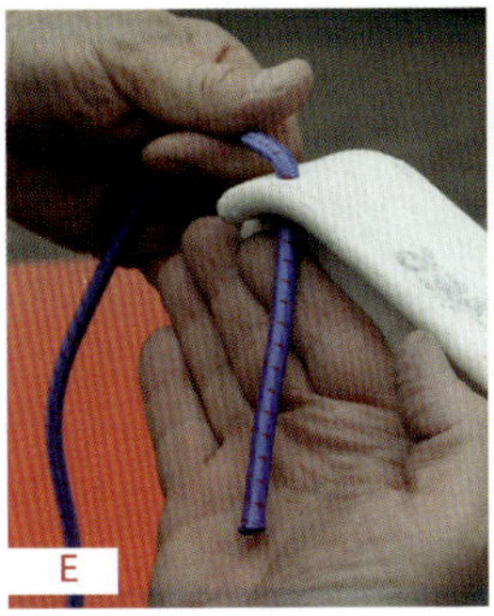

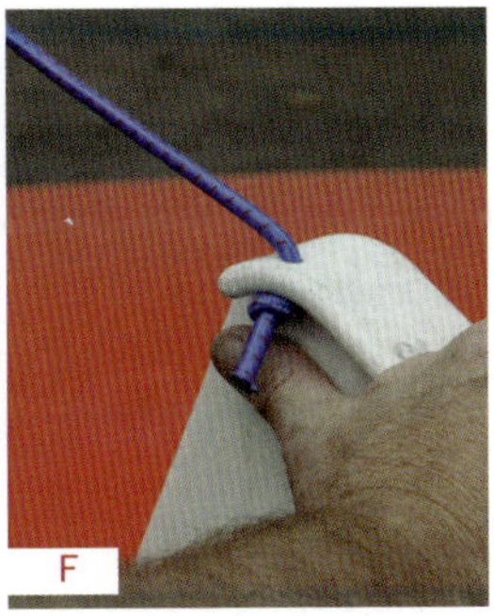

You may be surprised to discover that the daggerboard floats. But the rudder assembly – due to its cast-alloy stock – does not! So be careful when shipping or unshipping the rudder when afloat.
你可能会吃惊地发现稳向板可以浮于水面，但是船舵组合却由于含有合金不能浮起来！所以在水上装卸船舵时一定要十分小心。

Going further 进阶

The Topper is easier to sail with better control lines and certainly if you want to race, the standard boat should be upgraded. It is fine as a beach boat but if you want to get into the top 90% of the fleet you need race controls and you will need to know how to use them properly.
如果你想把Topper用来竞赛，那么换上高级索具后依然可以轻便地操控。应该把标准型船进行升级，虽然作为一条沙滩型帆船已经很不错了，但如果你想进入船队成绩的前10%就要更换成竞赛型索具并运用自如。
The standard traveller rope is replaced by non-stretch rope, with a better cleat. The kicking strap, outhaul and downhaul have increased purchases. Details are in Masterclass 3. The centre mainsheet is discussed in chapter 2, overleaf.
非弹力型索具代替了标准型的主缭滑车索，并装配了更好的羊角。斜拉索、后拉索和下拉索的机械效率都增加了。细节将在大师级别3介绍，中置主缭将在第2章介绍。

2 The centre mainsheet 中置主缭

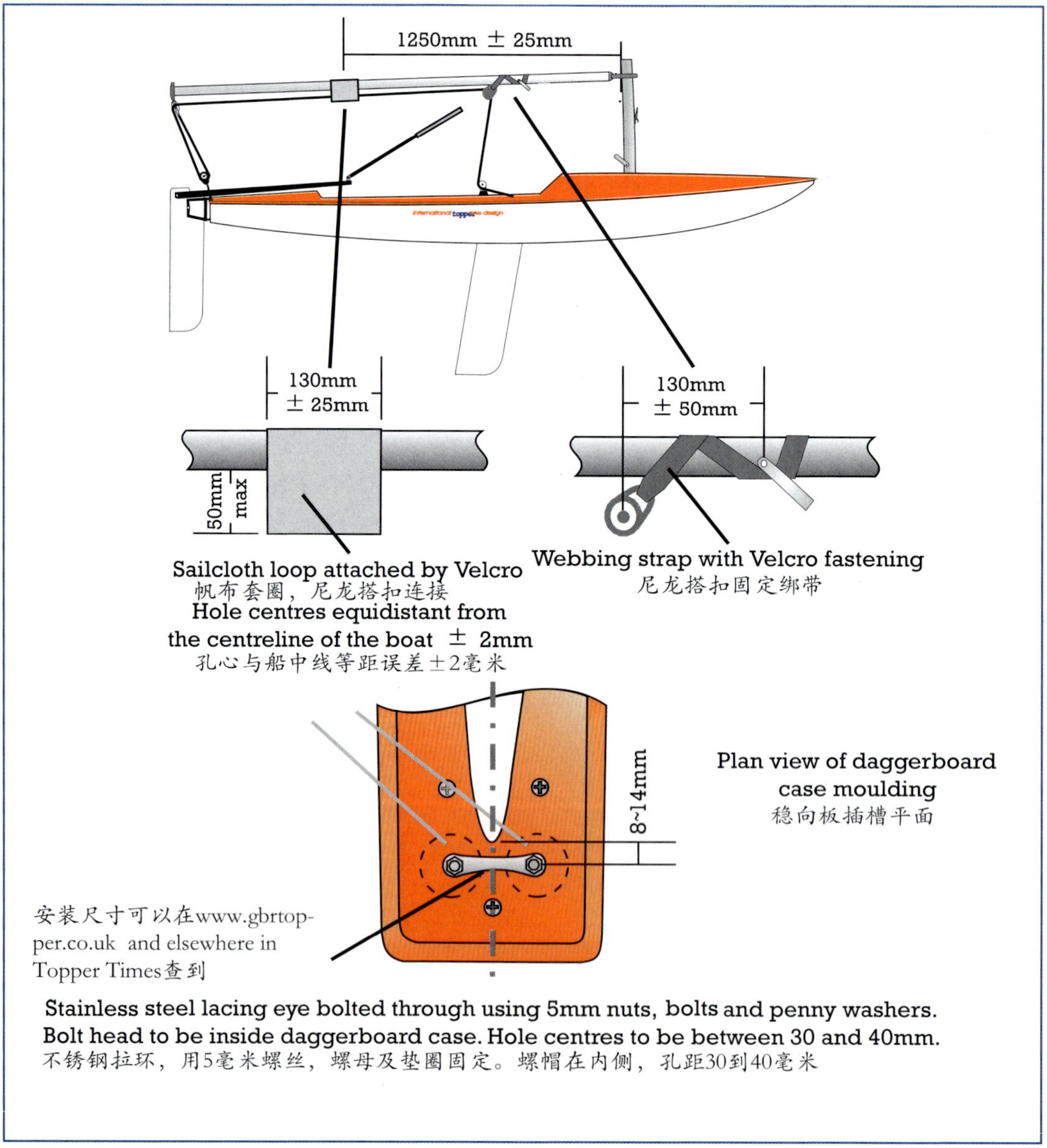

For years the aft sheeting system was the only one allowed. Now we can lead the mainsheet forward to the top of the daggerboard case. This has proved a great success and the photos in this book show the centre mainsheet.
相当长的时间里，主缭只被允许设置在船体后部。现在我们可以把主缭前移到稳向板卡槽的上面。这被证明是一个巨大的成功，本书的照片中全部是中置主缭。
The aft sheeting system, with a traveller across the transom, was retained with the rope being led along the boom and down to a ratchet block on the top of the dagger-board case moulding. The attachment at this point is by bolting through from the inside of the moulding, a straightforward job. A sailcloth loop is added on the boom to prevent the rope dangling, when slack, and lassoing the poor sailor!
后置主缭通过船尾的滑车索连接横杆，并沿横杆经过一个逆止滑轮连接到稳向板卡槽的顶部，在此处依靠在卡槽内侧的铆钉连接。这是一种直截了当的办法。在横杆上必须加装一个帆布制作的套圈防止主缭松弛时下垂套住可怜的水手的脖子！
Webbing straps and Velcro are used to attach the additional block to the boom, as there seemed no point in weakening the boom by drilling extra holes.
还需要用绑带和尼龙搭扣把额外的滑轮固定在横杆上，而不需要在横杆上额外打孔而削弱其刚度。

Why has the centre mainsheet become the preferred arrangement for racing?
为什么中置主缭成为竞赛船的优选方式呢?

- Transferring to and from other boats is less challenging.
  这是一个逐渐演化的必然结果。
- In strong winds the aft sheeting pulled you to the back of the boat. The way to prevent this was to twist forward, which was both uncomfortable and tiring. Sailors can now hike straight out.
  后置主缭在大风时会把你拖到船的后部，而你又要拼命顾及前面的操作而疲惫不堪。中置主缭可以让你尽情地向外压舷。
- By the same token, sailors can pivot backwards more effectively when beating through waves.
  同理，在大浪时迎风航行的选手可以自如地向后转身移动，破浪前行。
- Pulling in the mainsheet across your body was less efficient than pulling towards you. The sheet loads on a Topper were a challenge for younger sailors. Less strength is required with the centre sheeting.
  如果想收紧主缭，中置主缭需要向内拉，而后置主缭需要向外推，前者更有效。以前，年轻的选手要应付主缭的力量一直是个挑战，而中置主缭需要的力量要小些。
- Gybing and tacking facing forward allow the sailor to see where they are going. After all we don’t corner a car while looking out of the back window!
  中置主缭可以让选手在迎风转向和顺风转向时面向前方，观察航向。你开车转弯时总不能向后看吧!

HOW IS IT DONE? 如何调整的?

The boom 横杆

The boom end block
横杆端部滑轮

This is hung in the same way as the original. The present block needs changing for a becket version and a shorter rigging link needs to be used between the boom end fitting and the block. This keeps the mainsheet closer to the boom.
悬挂方式没有变化。新的吊桶式滑轮与横杆后端的连接处距离缩短，让主缭更接近横杆。

The forward boom block
横杆前部滑轮

This is attached to the boom with a webbing strap (or rope) by weaving it through the kicker take off point. The ends of the webbing are joined with Velcro or the rope is tied with a reef knot.
滑轮用绑带或绳索固定，并且要穿过斜拉索固定环。绑带的端部有尼龙搭扣，如果是绳索就要打一个缩帆结。

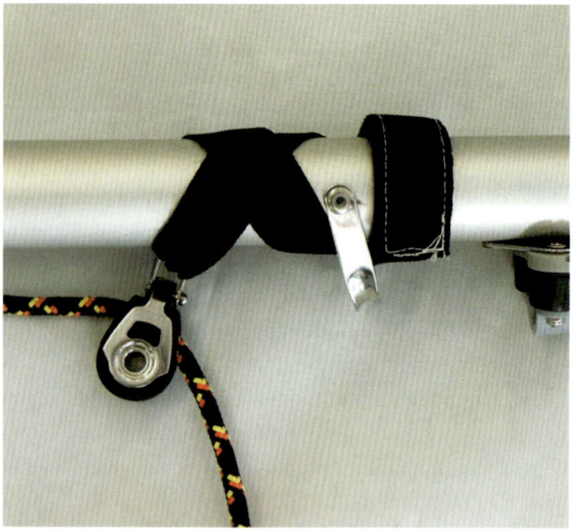

Strapping the forward block to the boom.
把前滑轮绑在横杆上

The boom loop. 横杆拉环

The traveller block 滑车滑轮

The current ratchet block is changed for a non-becket block. Use a rounded (forged) shackle so the traveller rope doesn’t get worn.

棘齿滑轮换成了非吊桶式滑轮。圆形挂钩可以避免滑车索磨损。

The boom loop 横杆圈带

The loop, to prevent the sailor being lassoed, is attached to the boom with self-adhesive Velcro. Most dealers will supply the material with Velcro sewn on.

圈带是用尼龙搭扣固定在横杆上，以防止选手的脖子被绳索套住。大部分的供应商都会提供端部缝制了尼龙搭扣的圈带。

The hull fittings 船体装置

Two holes need drilling in the hull. Your dealer should include a template with the kit. The process is:

船体上需要钻两个孔。供应商应该提供一个定位模板，方法如下：

- Unscrew the hull plate (A).
  卸下船身板(图A)。
- Remove the bladders (B).
  卸下稳向板(图B)。
- Mark out and drill the two holes right through the hull from above (C)。
  标记两个孔的位置并从上部钻孔(图C)
- Put penny washers on the bolts and push the bolts through from the inside (D)。
  螺丝套好垫圈，从内侧把螺丝穿出(图D)
- Bolt on the deck eye. It is best to use nyloc nuts (E).
  用尼龙锁紧螺帽固定(图E)。
- Shackle on the ratchet block, and away you go!
  用挂钩固定棘齿滑轮，搞定！

A

B

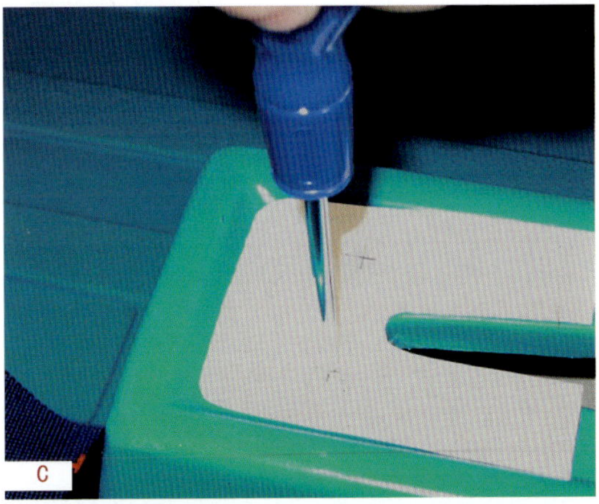
C

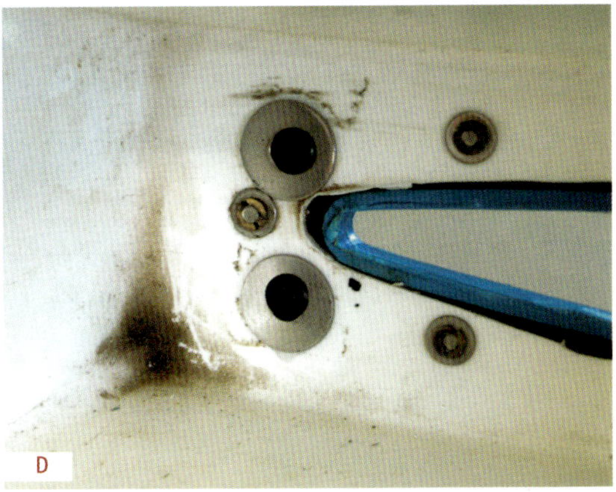
D

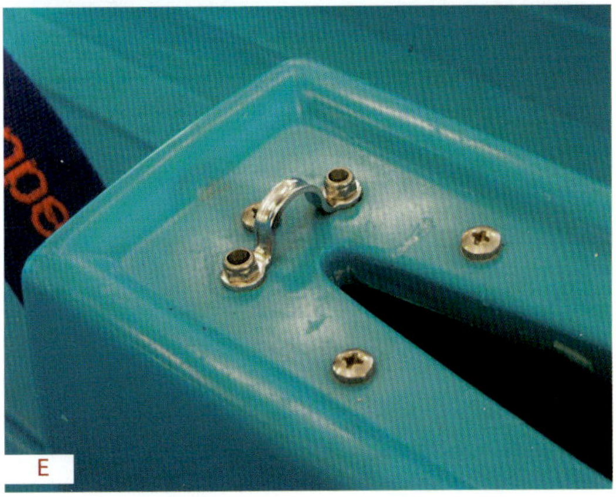
E

3 Sailing theory 航行原理

Take a careful look at these photographs. You will see that:

仔细看一下这些图片，你可以发现：

- The helmsman sits on the windward side of the boat (to balance the wind pushing on the sail).
  舵手坐在上风一侧（来平衡帆的受力）。
- The helmsman always holds the tiller in his aft (back) hand. He steers with the tiller.
  舵手时刻用后面的手握住舵柄，用其控制方向。

- The helmsman always holds the mainsheet in his forward (front) hand. The mainsheet adjusts the angle of the sail to the centreline of the boat.
  舵手时刻用前面的手握住主缭，以调整主帆与船中心线的角度。

How does the boat sail?
帆船如何航行？

Wind is the Topper’s driving force. The wind flows over the windward side of the sail (causing pressure) and round the leeward side (causing suction). The resulting force on the sail is in the direction of arrow A (Figure 1), i.e. it is at right angles to the sail.

The force pushes the boat forwards and sideways. The forwards push is welcome! The sideways push is counteracted by water pressure on the daggerboard (Figure 2).

The helmsman’s weight counteracts the heeling (capsizing) effect. The further he leans out, the more leverage he gets.

风是Topper前进的动力。风吹过帆的上风一侧产生压力，绕过下风一侧产生吸力。帆受力的方向是箭头A（图1），也就是与帆面呈直角。这力量推动帆船前行和侧移。向前的推力多多益善！横向的推力被作用在稳向板上的水推力抵消（图2）。舵手的体重抵消了船侧翻的倾向力。他越向外压舷，力矩越大。

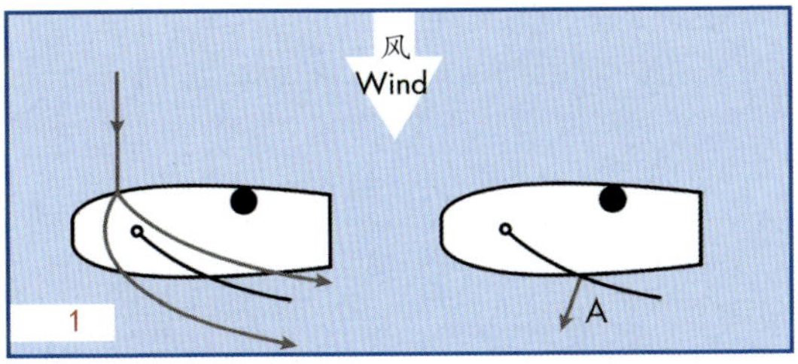

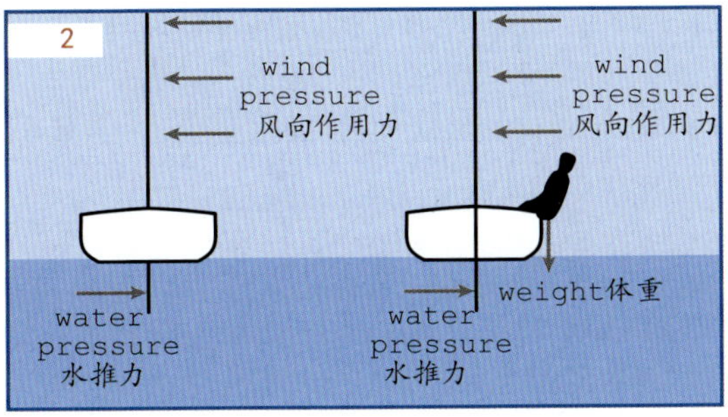

If the sail is pulled in, force A will be almost at right angles to the boat: the sideways force is maximum, and the daggerboard needs to be pushed right down to counteract it. If the sail is let out, force A points forwards: there is no sideways force, so the daggerboard can be pulled up (Figure 3).

如果把帆收紧，推力方向基本垂直于船体，侧移的力量达到最大值，因此要把稳向板完全放下以抵消侧移。如果把帆放出，推力会指向前方：侧移力基本消失，要把稳向板完全拉起（图3）。

How can I steer?
如何控制方向？

When a boat is sailing straight, the water flows past the rudder undisturbed. When the rudder is turned, the water is deflected. The water hitting the rudder pushes it, and the back of the boat, in direction B (Figure 4). The bow turns to the left. In short, pulling the tiller towards you turns the bow away from you, and vice versa.

如果帆船直线航行，水流不受干扰地穿过舵叶。如果转动舵叶则水流也被偏转，水流会推动舵叶和船的后部转向方向B（图4），船头就左转。简而言之，拉舵让船头向外转，推舵让船头向内转。

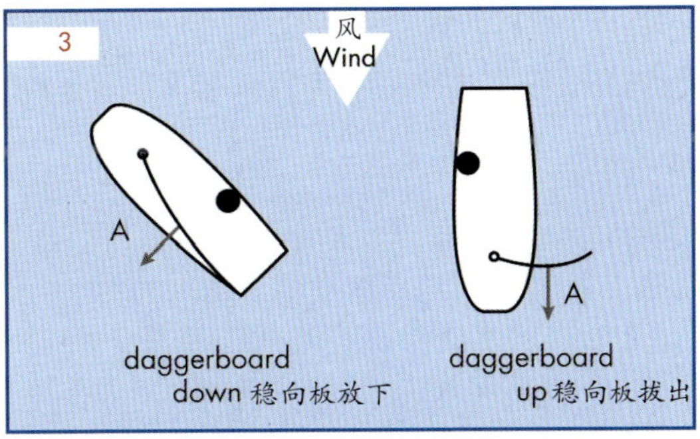

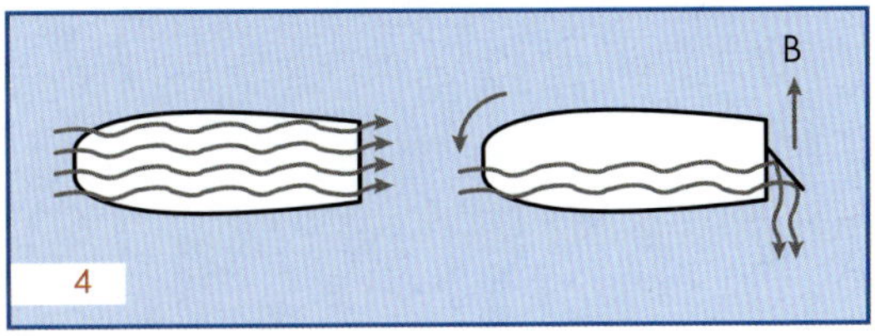

How can I stop?
如何让船停住？

It is the wind in the sail that makes a boat go forward. To stop it, take the wind out of the sail either by letting go of the mainsheet, or by altering course towards the wind (Figure 5).

风作用在帆面上使船前进。如果想把船停下来可以把帆放出或让船头指向风，使帆不受力继而让船停住（图5）。

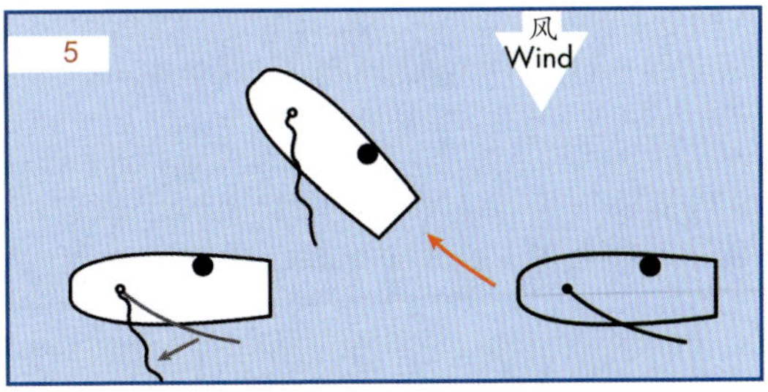

How can I tell which way the wind is blowing?
如何辨认风向？

Everything in sailing is related to the wind direction. You can tell which way it’s blowing by the feel of it on your cheek, by the wave direction or by using a burgee or wind indicator.

帆船航行的一切都和风向有关。你可以通过脸颊感受、浪的方向以及风向标来感知风向。

POINTS OF SAILING 航向

Look at Figure 7 (opposite).
There are three points of sailing:
请看图7，有三种航向：

1 Reaching – the boat sails across the wind (photo A).
横风航行：船从风中穿过（图A）。
2 Beating – the boat sails towards the wind (photo B).
迎风航行：迎向风航行（图B）。
3 Running – the boat sails with the wind from behind (photo C).
顺风航行：船顺着风的方向航行（图C）。

Reaching 横风航行

The boat in photo A is reaching. It is sailing at right angles to the wind, which is blowing from behind the helmsman's back. The sail is about halfway out and the daggerboard halfway up.
图A的船在横风行驶，船身与风向呈90度，也就是说风从舵手的背后吹来。主帆松开一半，稳向板拔起一半。

Beating 迎风航行

If you want to change course towards the wind, you must push the daggerboard down and pull in the sail as you turn. You can go on turning towards the wind until the sail is pulled right in. Then you are beating (photo B).
如果你想改变航线向上风航行，必须把稳向板完全放下然后边转向边收紧主帆。你可以继续上风直到主帆完全收紧，这样就是迎风航行了（图B）。

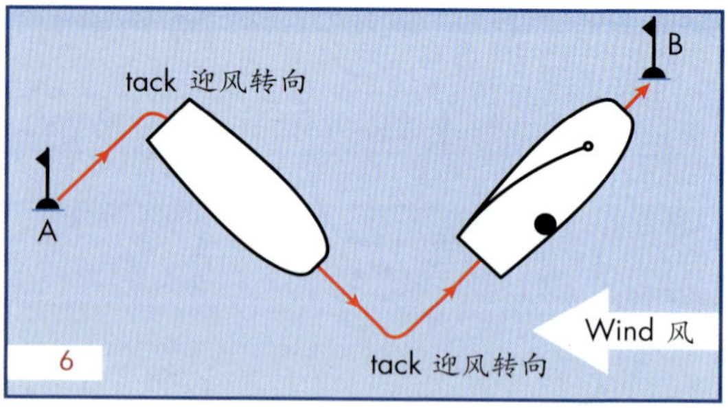

6

If you try to turn further towards the wind, you enter the 'no go area'. The sail flaps and the boat stops. To get from A to B (Figure 6), the only way is to beat in a zigzag fashion. At the end of each 'zig' the boat turns through an angle of 90°. This is called a tack. The boat turns 'through' the wind – the sail blows across to the other side and the helmsman must shift his weight across the boat to balance it.
如果你继续靠近风，就会进入“顶风区”（或叫不可航行区）。船帆飘摆并停止前进。在图6中如果你要从A点到达B点，唯一的办法是做之字形迎风航行。在之字的每一段末尾船要做90度的转向，这就是迎风转向。船在转向时穿过正迎风，船帆被吹向另一边，舵手必须移动到船的另一边以保持平衡。

Running 顺风航行

From a reach, you may want to change course away from the wind. Pull up the daggerboard (not more than three-quarters up) and let out the sail as you turn. You can go on turning until the wind is coming from behind the boat. Then you are running (photo C). If you turn more the boat will

A

B

C

摄影：张琦

gybe. That is, you will find the wind is suddenly blowing from the opposite side of the sail which then flies across to the other side of the boat very quickly. Be on your guard against this happening inadvertently.

当你横风航行时，如果你想改变航线向下风航行，要把稳向板拔起（不超过3/4）并且把帆放出去。继续转向直到风从船体后部吹来，这样就是顺风航行了（图C）。如果再继续转向，船就会顺风过帆，你会发现风从帆的另一面吹来，把帆突然吹到船的另一边，这一刻你一定要提高警觉。

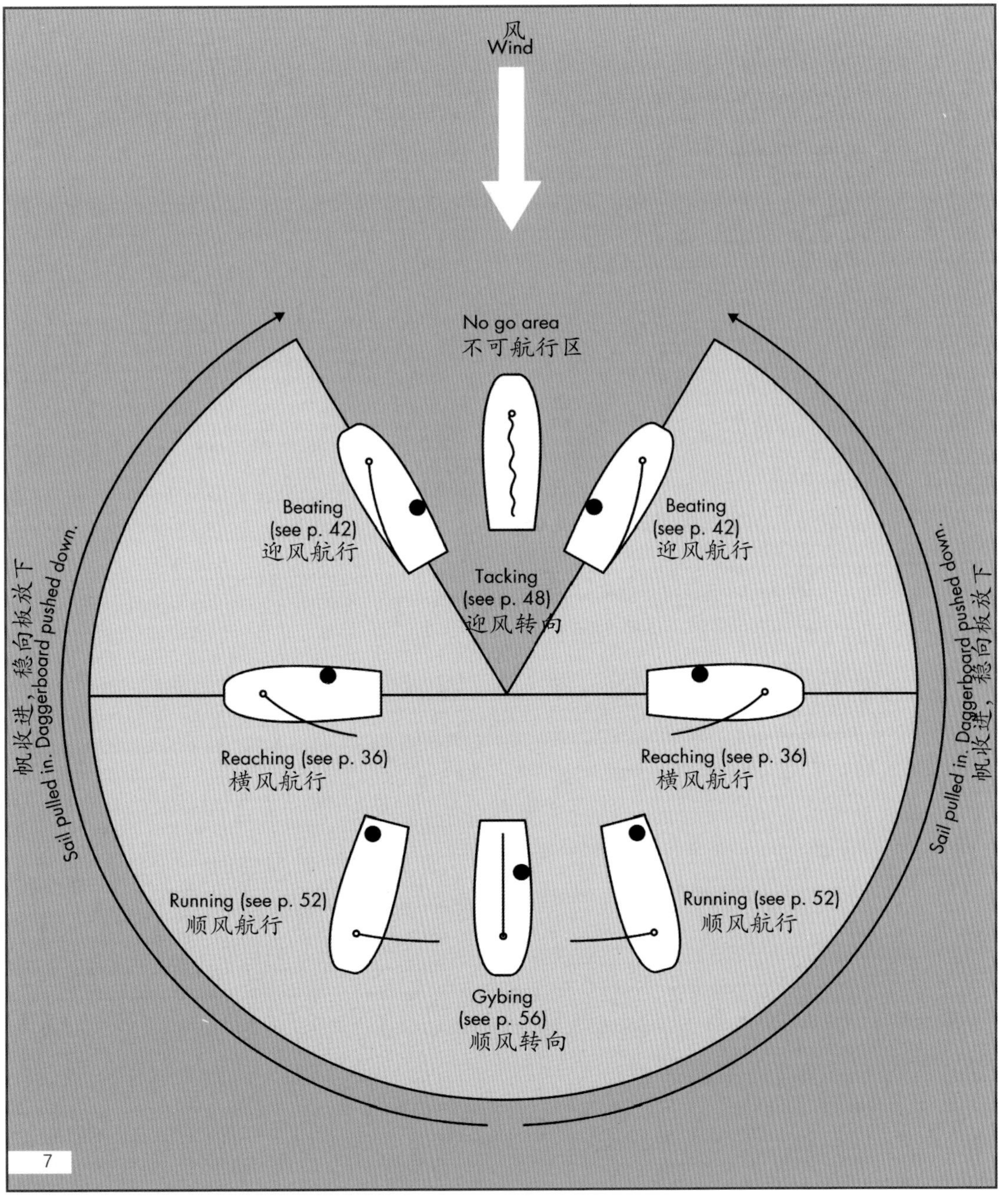

4 Reefing 缩帆

You need to reef (reduce sail) when the wind is strong. If you think you will have difficulty in holding the boat up on the beat, or will capsize on the run, then reef. (Alternatively, invest in a 4.2m sail - see Part 2, from p83.)

当风力强时，你需要把帆缩小。如果你觉得迎风航行时压不住船或者顺风航行时有可能翻船，就要选择缩帆。（或者换成面积小的4.2米帆，详见第83页第二部分。）

The Topper has been carefully designed so that you can reef on the water. However, for the first few times you will find it easier to work on land or at the jetty. Here are the steps you take:

Topper的设计很精细，可以让你在海上完成缩帆。不过最初的几次你最好在陆地或码头上进行操作比较容易，以下是基本步骤：

1 Start with the sail rigged normally.
开始时，帆处于正常状态。
2 Take off the kicker at the mast end only (A).
把斜拉索在桅杆的一侧松开（图A）。

3 Pul l on lots of downhaul, to prevent the sail twisting when you have rolled it up (B).
尽量拉紧前下角索，防止卷动时帆面折叠（图B）。

4 Ease out the outhaul. Rotate the mast at least twice, making sure the halyard (if fitted) moves properly outside the gooseneck. If the downhaul is on the port side, rotate the mast anticlockwise, viewed from above (C). The pull of the downhall will prevent it un-furling.
松开后下角拉索，旋转桅杆至少两圈并确保升帆索在横杆插头外面可自由移动。如果前下角索在左舷一侧，就把桅杆逆时针旋转（图C）。拉紧前下角索有助于卷帆。
5 Tighten the outhaul (D) and re-rig the kicking strap (vang) (E).
拉紧后下角索（图D）然后把斜拉索重新装好拉紧（图E）。

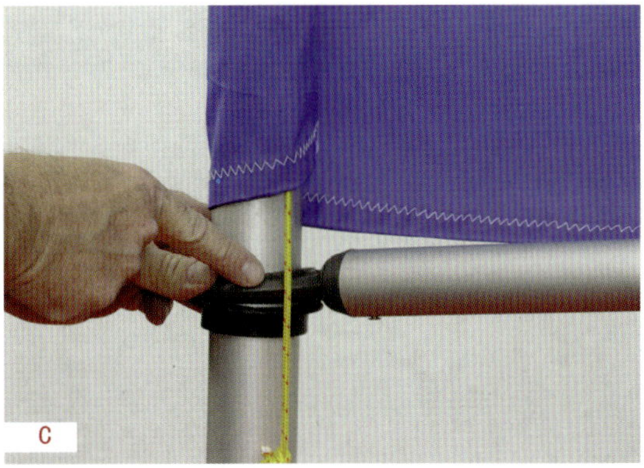

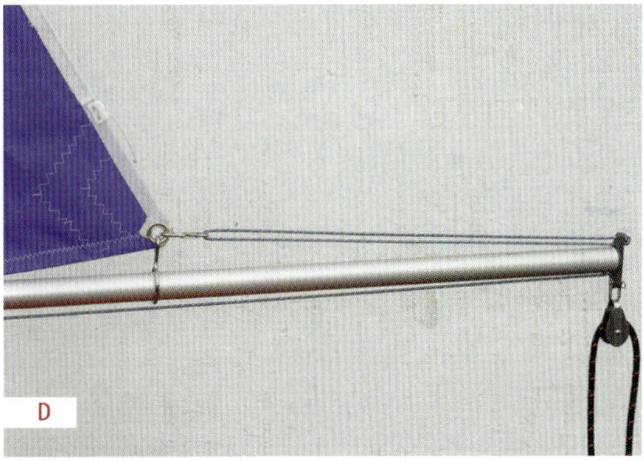

6 If the wind drops, take out the reefs: let the sail flap, unclip the kicking strap, unroll the sail and tighten the outhaul. Re-rig the kicking strap, pull in the mainsheet and you’re away again!
如果风力减弱，就要中止缩帆：让帆飘动，松开斜拉索，拉紧后下角索把帆恢复原状。装好斜拉索并收紧主帆，然后继续航行！

5 Launching 下水

A

Always rig the boat before launching; if you are sailing from a jetty the sail can be rolled up completely around the mast and unfurled just before you set off.

Put the rudder on but pull it right up. Launch the boat on its trolley, keeping it pointing into the wind all the time. Once the boat is floating you can slide out the trolley and pass it to a friend (photo A).

Always use the trolley to launch and retrieve your Topper – without it you are very likely to scratch the bottom of the boat.

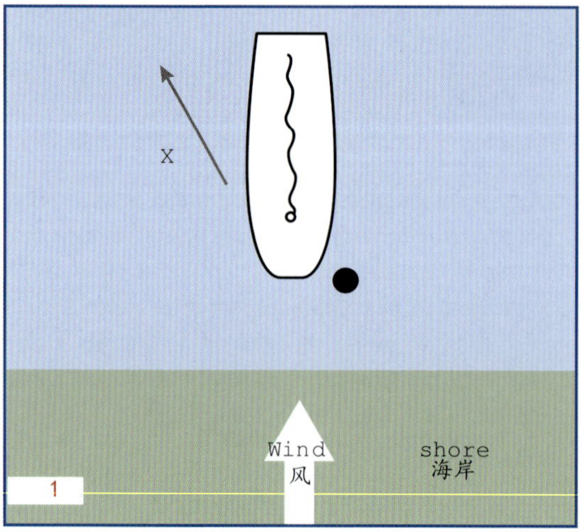

1

下水前把船装好；如果是从码头下水，先把主帆完全绕桅杆卷起，下水前再打开。装好舵但保持舵叶升起，用船车推船下水时要一直保持船头向风。一旦船浮起来就可以驶离船车并把它交给别人（图A）。一定要用船车放船和收船，否则船底很容易刮擦。

Launching from a beach with an offshore wind
离岸风时从沙滩下水

This is the easiest wind direction to launch in (Figure 1). Push a little rudder and dagger-board down (photo B). Turn the boat slightly away from the wind, jump in, pull in the mainsheet slightly and sail slowly into deeper water (direction X) (photos C and D), where you can put the rudder and board right down. Don’t try to sail hard or allow the boat to heel excessively with the rudder up or you may damage the rudder or it’s fastenings.

离岸风时下水是最容易的（图1）。把舵和稳向板都稍微放下一些（图B）。把船头转向下风并跳进船，轻拉主帆，慢慢沿X方向驶入深水区（图C和D），水深足够时把舵叶和稳向板完全放下。注意不要快速航行或在舵叶向上时让船身过度倾斜，以免损坏舵叶和控制绳。

Launching with an onshore wind
近岸风时下水

This is more difficult since you will need to beat in shallow water to get away from the shore. Launch with the rudder up and the boat pointing into the wind. Choose the tack which takes you away from the shore at the greatest angle; push off, getting as much daggerboard down as the depth will allow as early as possible (Figure 2).

近岸风下水要困难一些，因为你需要在浅水中顶风驶离岸边。下水时舵叶抬起，船头向风，选择与风角度最大的一侧把船推出，在水深允许的情况下尽早放下稳向板（图2）。

B 摄影：田野

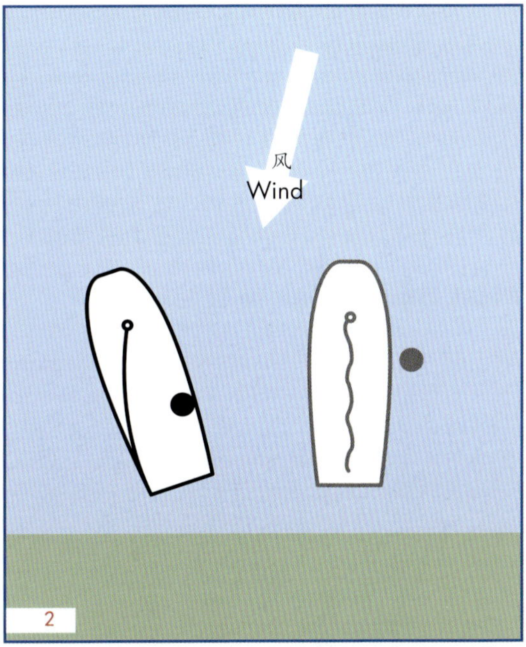

2

C 摄影：张琦

D 摄影：张琦

6 A first sail 首次航行

A dry run ashore 岸上模拟练习

Before setting sail for the first time it is a very good idea to rig the boat completely, place it on a soft surface such as grass, and practise steering (with rudder and daggerboard up, of course!), adjusting the mainsheet, tacking, etc. This will give you much more confidence when you finally go afloat.

在第一次下水航行之前，把装好的船放在岸上练习操作是一个好主意（当然稳向板和舵叶要收起）。可以调整主帆、迎风转向什么的，这样你在实际下水航行时会更有自信。

First time afloat 首次下水

Try to choose a day with a gentle breeze for your first sail. Wind is measured either on the Beaufort scale or in knots. Force 4 (11 knots) or above would be unsuitable.

首次下水航行最好选一个小风天。风力的级别是按蒲福氏风级或者节来表示的。超过蒲福氏四级或者11节的风力就不适合了。

A reservoir, river or estuary is a good place to learn to sail. If you are learning on the open sea try to avoid an offshore wind (wind blowing from shore to sea) – you may get blown a long way from the shore. Always wear a lifejacket, and stay with the boat whatever happens.

水库、河流或者河口都是学习航行的好地方。如果你在开放海面上学习，尽量避免离岸风（风向从陆地吹向海面），否则你有可能被风吹离海岸。随时穿着救生衣，在任何情况下都不要和船分开。

Rig the boat as described in chapter 1. Reef (chapter 4) or use a smaller sail if there's much wind. Get a friend to help you launch (chapter 5); they should hold the boat for you while you lower the rudder and put in the daggerboard – then one good push and you're away.

按照第一章的要求把船装好，在风大时缩帆（第四章）或者选择小号帆。请一个朋友帮助你下水（第五章），他可以在你放下舵叶和稳向板时帮你稳定住船，然后适当地一推，你就可以航行了。

As soon as you can, get sailing on a reach (photo A) with the wind blowing at right angles to the boat. The daggerboard should be about half up and the sail about half out. Sit on the side opposite the sail. Practise adjusting the mainsheet and steering. Try to get the 'feel' of the boat, particularly using your weight to balance the wind in the sail. (Reaching is discussed in chapter 7.)

你要尽早地横风航行（图A），也就是让风向与船身呈90度角。稳向板放下一半，帆也放出一半，坐在帆的对面一侧。练习调整主帆和方向。尝试找到“船感”，特别是用身体重量来平衡作用在帆面上的风力。（横风航行在第七章介绍）

Eventually you will need to tack (turn round) and reach back again (photos B and C). Tacking is described in chapter 9. Try to tack smoothly, changing sides and swapping hands on the tiller and mainsheet as you do so.

最后你还是需要迎风转向，然后重新横风航行（图B和图C）。迎风转向在第九章介绍。推舵时注意要平滑，反复练习转向时的换舷移动，舵柄和主缭在两手之间交换。

If the boat stops during a tack, keep the tiller central and wait until the boat starts to drift backwards. Eventually it will turn to one side and you'll be able to get sailing again (photos D, E and F).

如果迎风转向时船停了下来，注意把舵摆正，等待船向后漂流。等帆面受风后就可以继续航行了（图D，图E，图F）。

Reach back and forth until you feel confident. Try picking an object and sailing straight towards it, adjusting the mainsheet so the sail is as far out as possible without flapping. If a gust comes, let out the mainsheet (photos G and H). Try to keep the boat moving.

来回地横风航行直到你感觉自信了。尝试瞄准一个固定目标航行，调整主缭尽可能放出主帆，避免飘帆。有阵风时把主帆放出（图G和图H），尽可能让船保持前进。

D, E & F If you get stuck halfway through a tack, wait until the boat drifts backwards (you can help it by pushing out the boom). Eventually it will turn. Then pull in the mainsheet and sail off again.

如果你在迎风转向时不慎正迎风停船，可以等待船被水流向后推（可以推出帆杆来帮助后退），船最终会转向，赶快收进主帆继续航行。

G In a gust, let out the mainsheet.

在阵风情况下，放松主缭。

H The boat will stop heeling immediately!

船会马上停止倾斜！

Lots of fun can be had with two in a Topper, no matter the age gap!
两人同乘一条Topper会别有乐趣，不管年龄差距多大！

Next try picking objects slightly closer to or slightly further away from the wind. Try sailing towards them, adjusting the mainsheet.
下一步选择一个稍微上风或者下风的目标，调整主帆对准航行。
When you have had enough, head for the shore, taking care to pull up the daggerboard and rudder in good time. Just before stepping out of the boat ease the sheet right out and head into the wind – making sure the water is shallow! Landing is discussed in more detail in chapter 14.
充分练习之后，航向岸边。在恰当的时候收起稳向板和舵叶，确保处于浅滩时在离船之前把船头向风并且松开主缭。我们在第十四章会仔细介绍上岸技术。

Sailing two up 双人航行

Although the class rules, at the time of writing, do not permit more than one person in the boat when racing, two people can have great fun in a Topper.
虽然撰写本书时级别规则不允许比赛时每条船超过一个人，其实两个人也可以共同驾驶一条Topper享受乐趣。
To stop the stern dragging in the water and slowing the boat down, it is important that both helm and crew sit as far forward as possible. This also helps when tacking – so long as the crew at the front is careful to duck under the kicking strap (vang) when crossing the boat. When running or reaching in light winds, the boat is easily balanced by one person sitting on each sidedeck.

为了避免船尾下沉导致阻力过大，舵手和缭手要尽可能坐在靠前的位置。位置靠前对迎风转向也有帮助：前面的缭手要小心地低头从斜拉索下面穿过换弦。微风条件下的横风或顺风航行时，甲板两侧各坐一人可以轻易的平衡船身。

The next steps 下一步

When you feel happy reaching and tacking, you are ready to try the other points of sailing (see pages 32 and33). You should still reef if there is much wind (more than Force 3).

One good way to practise is to sail round a square ‘course’ (Figure 1).

当你可以自如地横风航行并转向后，你已经为其他方向的行驶做好了准备（见32和33页）。如果风力大于3级就继续保持缩帆。

沿着方形线路练习航行是个好办法（图1）。

From a reach, gradually turn away from the wind, letting out the sail and pulling the daggerboard three-quarters up. You are now running. After a while, pull the tiller towards you, and gybe. Now reach the other way, with the daggerboard half down and the mainsheet half out. Next, push the daggerboard right down and turn towards the wind, pulling in your sail. You are beating. Tack, and beat the other way. When you are far enough into the wind turn off onto a reach, letting the sail out and pulling the daggerboard half up. Try several laps.

在横风航行时，逐渐向下风走，放出主帆并且把稳向板收起3/4，你就在顺风航行了。过一会儿，拉舵转向进入另一侧顺风航行，保持稳向板一半放下，主帆放出一半。下一步，把稳向板完全放下，转向上风并收帆，你就在迎风航行了。转向进入另一侧迎风航行。当你足够迎风后，转向横风，放出主帆并把稳向板拉起一半。如此反复几次。

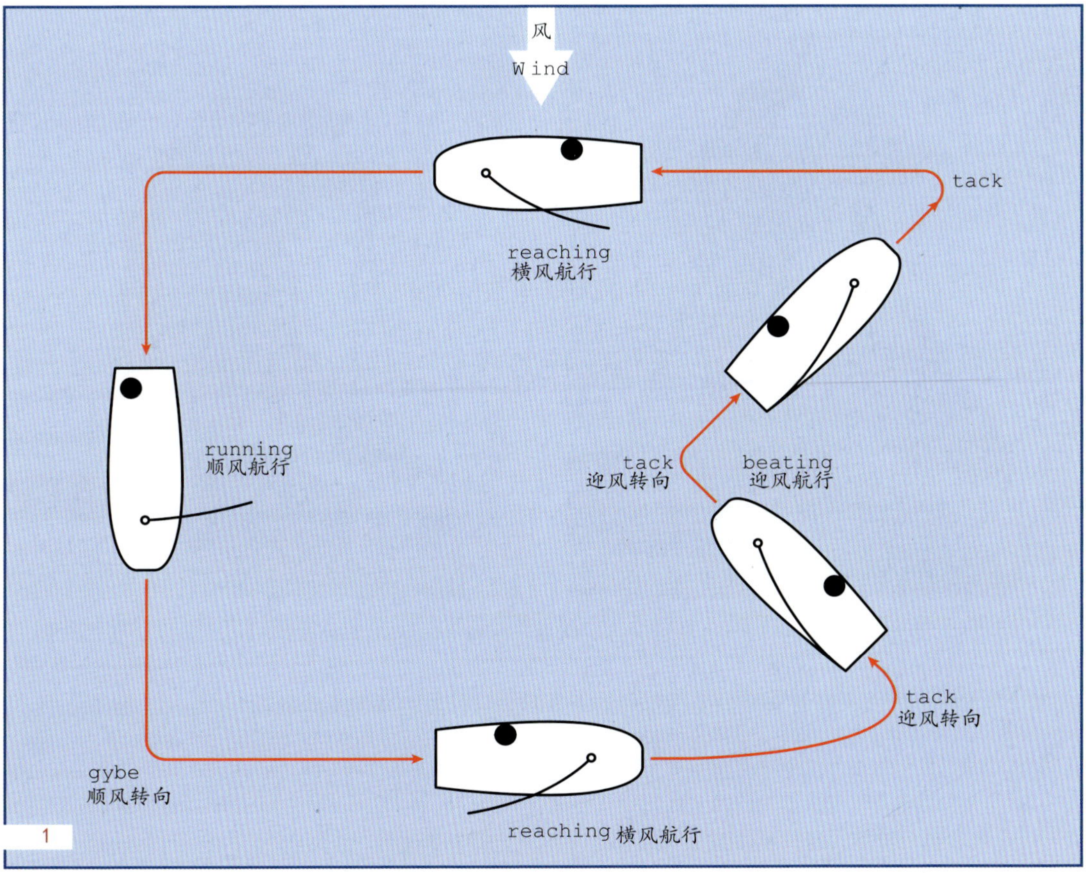

1

Remember:记住

- Sit on the windward side.
  坐在迎风一侧船舷。
- Keep the mainsheet in your front hand, the tiller in your back hand
  前手拿主缭，后手拿舵柄。
- If you get out of control, let go of the mainsheet.
  如果无法控制船，放出主缭。

I, J & K If you need to pull in lots of mainsheet...
如果你需要把主缭收紧...

...use your sheet hand, then your tiller hand (still holding the tiller extension).
Repeat as often as is necessary.
先用拿缭绳的手，然后用持舵柄的手（副舵柄不能松开），如此按需要反复。

7 Reaching 横风航行

Reaching is the easiest point of sailing and in a breeze the fastest and most exciting.
横风航行是微风时最容易的航行角度，也是最快和最刺激的。

What is reaching? 什么是横风航行

The Toppers in Figure 1 are reaching. Their courses are roughly at right angles to the wind.
图1中的船就是横风航行。航线与风向的角度基本垂直。

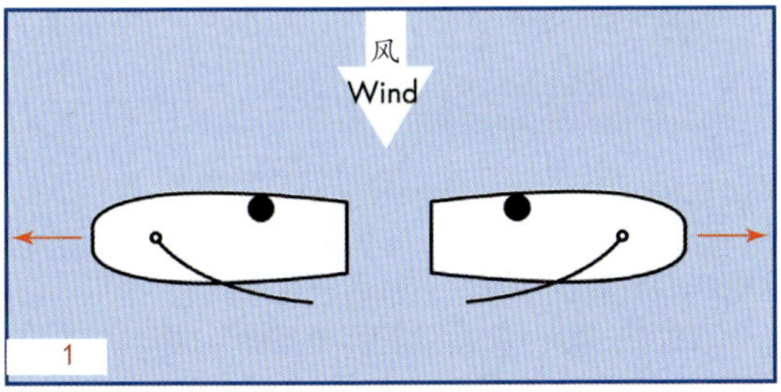

Adjusting the sail 调整主帆

The secret of reaching is sail trim. Always try to let the sail out as far as it will go without flapping. Although the wind may vary in direction from moment to moment it is always possible when reaching to continue to steer in the direction that you wish to go. However, to maintain the fastest speed you must continually adjust the position of the boom, and hence the sail, via the mainsheet. Every few seconds, ease the mainsheet out until the front edge of the sail (luff) begins to lift and then pull it in until this flapping stops (Figure 2).
横风航行的秘诀在于主帆的调整。不断地尝试把主帆尽可能放出，而又避免飘帆。虽然风向会随时变化，但你可以在横风时根据你的目标调整航向。当然，为了保持最快的速度你必须随时通过主缭来调整横杆和主帆。每几秒钟你就要松主缭直到主帆前缘卷起，然后稍拉紧让飘动停止（图2）。

When you alter course you will have to adjust the sail angle accordingly. As you luff up (point your boat nearer the wind direction) pull the sail in, and as you bear away (point your boat away from the wind direction) ease the sail out.
当你调整航线时也必须同时调整帆的角度。当你向上风时（让船头接近风）收进主帆；当你向下风时（让船头远离风）则把主帆放出。

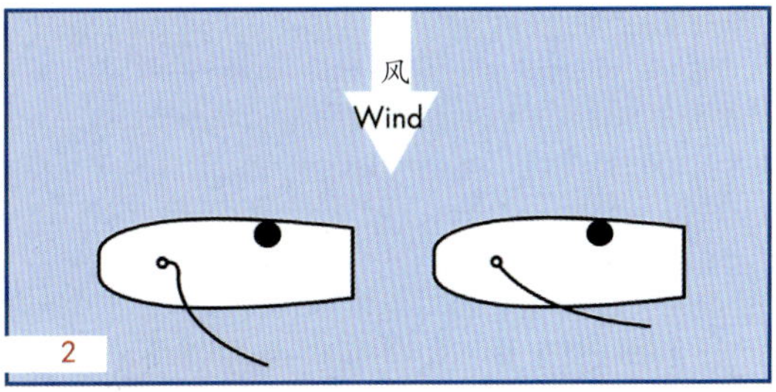

Steering 操舵

Try to keep a reasonably straight course. Everything being equal the shortest distance between two points is a straight line! Remember, every time you move the rudder you slow the boat very slightly.
尽力保持直线航行，因为两点间直线最短。记住每次你转动船舵都会微微降低船速。

Trim 船体平衡

The trim of the boat (the angle at which the hull sits in the water) is affected by the wind strength, the boat's speed and, above all, the location of your body weight. Sit forward in light winds to reduce the amount of hull skin in the water (and so reduce skin friction). Move aft in strong winds to lift the bow and help the boat skim over the water – this is planing. Do not allow the boat to heel excessively since this will encourage it to turn into the wind. You will have to take corrective action with the rudder (with associated braking) to maintain a straight course – this is called 'weather helm' ①.

注释：①**weather helm** 上风舵 迎风航行时由于船体倾斜，帆的受力中心与稳向板不在一条垂直线上，形成的力矩作用会使船头转向上风，需要拉舵以保持直线航行，因此称为“上风舵”（见62页图片）。

Bear away each time a wave picks up the boat, and try to surf on the wave.
船体平衡（船体处在水中的角度）的因素有风力、船速，最重要的是你所坐的位置。微风时要向前坐以减少船体和水接触的面积（降低摩擦力）。大风时要向后坐以保持船头抬起，让船体掠过水面——这叫作滑浪。不要让船体过度倾斜，因为这样会很容易使船头顶风。为了保持直线航向，你必须不断调整船舵（当然会降低船速）——这叫作“上风舵”。转向下风时最好选择船被浪举起时，可以尝试滑浪。

Daggerboard 稳向板

The daggerboard should not be fully down when reaching. The less you have down the less will be the drag resistance, and therefore the faster you will go. Half board is a good starting point, more being needed as you luff closer to the wind, to stop you slipping sideways.
横风航行时稳向板不能全部放下。放下得越少拖拉阻力越小，你就可以航行得更快。开始时可以放下一半，如果向上风航行就要放下更多，以减少横向位移。

Sail controls 调帆

The sail should be set with a good curve or belly in it. A maximum of 100mm between the foot of the sail and the boom at its mid-point is desirable. The kicking strap (vang) should be normal but the outhaul and down-haul should both be eased considerably.
帆面应该保持良好的弧线或饱满度。帆下缘与横杆中点的距离保持最大100毫米为宜。斜拉索保持中度收紧，下拉索和后拉索保持明显松弛。

Gusts 阵风

When overpowered (i.e. when the wind is too strong for you to hold the boat flat without letting the sail flap) ease the mainsheet and bear away from the wind. Sheet in again and luff back to your normal course when the gust has passed.
当阵风太大令你无法控制船体平衡（除非飘帆）时，松开主缭驶入下风。当阵风过去后收紧主缭重新驶回正常航线。

摄影：张琦

Going faster 快速航行

Fast reaching helps win races. Here are some important points:
快速地横风航行可以帮助你赢得比赛，以下是一些重要事项：

- Adjust the mainsheet all the time.
  不断地调节主缭。
- Continually let out the sail until it flaps at the front, then pull it in until it just stops.
  持续地放出主帆直到前缘飘动，然后收紧直到停止飘动。
- Keep the boat upright all the time; sit out hard rather than ease the mainsheet to spill wind. Move back in the gusts and forward again as the wind drops.
  永远保持船体正直；尽可能向外压舷而不要松帆泄力。阵风时向后坐，风力减弱时向前坐。
- Steer a straight course (except during gusts).
  保持直线航行（阵风时除外）。
- Look over your shoulder to see if a gust is coming – the water looks darker where a gust is travelling across it. When the gust hits bear away and sit out harder and ease the mainsheet a little. As the gust passes, luff up, sit inboard and pull the mainsheet in again.
  随时观察是否有阵风到来——阵风掠过水面时水的颜色变深。风到时转向下风，向

Look at the telltales on the sail to help you trim it (A). Excellent reaching technique (B & C). 摄影：张琦
调帆时注意风向线（A）。优秀的横风技术（B和C）

外压舷并略微松主缭。阵风结束后转向上风，坐进船舱并收紧主缭。

- Pull up the daggerboard one notch (on the back of the board). Sit with your knees against the daggerboard case.
  把稳向板拔起一个刻度（在板的背后），用脚抵住稳向板插槽。
- Set the downhaul completely slack. Set the outhaul so there is a hand-width between the foot of the sail and the boom. Set the kicker so that the leech just opens when a gust comes through.
  完全放松下拉索调节后拉索让帆下缘与横杆中点距离保持一个手掌宽度。调节斜拉索让帆后缘在阵风来时可以打开。

The photos above show good reaching style. The sailors are using their weight to keep the boat absolutely level. Their attention is on the front part of the sail (as well as where they’re going!) and they continually adjust the mainsheet. Because the boat is level, they can steer gently and easily. The kicking strap (vang) is tight, but the other controls are loose. The sail has a good curve in it for maximum power.
上面的图片表现了很好的横风航行姿态，船员借助体重保持船体完全水平，他们的注意力在帆的前部和航行的方向，不断地调节主缭。由于船体保持水平，很容易进行微调航向。斜拉索是收紧的，其他的控制索则保持松弛。帆面的弧度很好，受力最优。

REACHING IN LIGHT WINDS
微风时的横风航行

Reaching in light winds, like all light wind sailing, needs patience. Keep very still so you don’t shake the shape out of the sail. If you need to move, do so slowly.
在微风时横风航行，和其他的航行一样，需要耐心。尽可能保持身体静止以避免影响帆面受力。如果必须移动身体，要尽可能慢。

Trim 船体平衡

Sit forward to lift the stern out of the water and reduce the wetted area of the hull, and hence skin friction.
Heel the boat to windward if there is sufficient wind to fill the sail, holding the boom out with your forward hand. This reduces the wetted area still further and neutralises the weather helm normally created by the sail effort turning the boat into the wind.
In extremely light airs sit to leeward on the foredeck just behind the mast. This reduces the wetted area to a minimum and helps hold some shape in the sail.
向前坐以保持船尾离开水面，减少船体和水接触的面积以降低阻力。如果风力足够时让船体向上风一侧倾斜让帆面吃风，并用前臂推出横杆。这样可以减少船体与水接触的面积并平衡船体以免驶入顶风。在极端微风时，坐在下风一侧的甲板前部也就是桅杆后

*Good light wind technique.*微风时的技术

面。这样也可减少船体与水接触面积并帮助帆面保持一定的形状。

Gusts 阵风

When a puff arrives, bear away to try and stay with it as long as possible. Above all this will take you below the direct line to the next mark and enable you to luff up in the lulls, thereby increasing your speed by up to 50 per cent in certain conditions.
当轻微阵风到来时，转向下风尽可能一直利用这个风。这样会让你沿着低于指向下一标航线的线路前进并在风小时转向上风，令你的速度最多提高50%。

Sail controls 调帆

The downhaul and outhaul should be loose. The kicking strap (vang) should be slightly looser than normal. Aim for a lot of curve in the sail (see photos).
下拉索和后拉索保持松弛，斜拉索要比正常时略松，目的是让帆面弧度尽量大（见照片）。

Steering 操舵

Move the tiller as infrequently and slowly as possible.
尽可能少而慢地调整船舵。

Going faster on a light reach 微风时横风快速航行

Use the rudder as little as possible. Set the kicking strap so the leach opens occasionally. Sit as far forward as you can without hitting the foredeck. The outhaul is loose to give a fairly deep sail. The downhaul is right off, but if the wind dies more, pull the outhaul out to flatten the sail. Then also put on a bit more kicker to take the slack out of the sail. Notice the boat is heeled slightly to windward to balance the rudder.
尽可能少用船舵。调节斜拉索让帆后缘保持不松不紧。尽可能向前坐当然不要碰到前甲板。后拉索放松尽可能让帆面凹进。下拉索完全打开，但如果风持续减小，则拉紧后拉索让帆面平直。然后轻轻收进斜拉索让帆面略为收紧。注意让船身向上风侧略微倾斜以平衡舵效。

REACHING IN STRONG WINDS 大风时横风航行

Reaching in a Topper is extremely exhilarating in a blow. You are close to the water so the sensation of speed is remarkable.
使用Topper在大风时横风航行是令人愉悦的。由于你贴近水面，那种速度的感觉令你难忘。

Trim 船体平衡

Sit back enough to bring the bow up and promote a good planing angle. You will be at the back of

摄影：Simon McIlwaine

the daggerboard case. In very strong winds hike from the middle of the side deck (this is the widest part of the boat so your weight gives the maximum righting effect here).
尽可能向后坐以使船头翘起，形成最佳的滑浪角度。你应该坐在稳向板插槽的后面。在强风中你要在船侧甲板的中部压舷（这里是船身最宽的部分，你的体重可以获得最大的平衡效果）。

Gusts 阵风

When overpowered (i.e. when the wind is too strong for you to hold the boat flat without letting the sail flap) bear away from the wind, luffing back above the direct course only when the gust passes. Never let the sail flap more than is necessary to keep the boat flat and always sit out as far as possible. In this way you will keep the maximum power on.
当阵风太大令你无法控制船体平衡（除非飘帆）时，松开主缭驶入下风。当阵风过去后收紧主缭重新驶回正常航线。让帆面飘动仅限于为了保持船身水平，绝不能过度，并永远尽可能向外坐。这样你就可以保持帆面最大受力。

Sail controls 调帆

In strong winds the kicking strap (vang), outhaul and downhaul should be set up quite tightly and not touched (in any case you would find it difficult to make adjust-ments in these conditions, unless you have race controls).
强风时斜拉索、下拉索和后拉索都应该拉紧，不去碰它们（强风时无论如何都很难。调整这些控制索，除非你装备了竞赛型索具）。

Daggerboard 稳向板

With the daggerboard half up there will be adequate board in the water to offset the sideways forces, yet not enough to create excessive drag.
稳向板收起一半就足可抵消水中的横向推力，并且不产生额外阻力。

REACHING – SOME COMMON MISTAKES 横风航行——常见错误

A

The kicking strap is too tight.
斜拉索过紧。

B

It is now too loose (note the boom goes up in the air and power is lost).
斜拉索太松（注意横杆抬起，受力减弱）

C

Correct!
正确！

The sail is too far out. Pull in the mainsheet until the front edge of the sail just stops flapping.
帆放出太多。收进主缭直到帆的前缘停止飘动。

The sail is too far in, which is heeling the boat.
帆收进太多，令船身过度倾斜。

Don’t let the boat heel. Note the tiller pulled to windward to keep the boat straight.
不要让船身倾斜。注意选手在拉舵以保持直线航向。

That’s better! Use your weight to bring the boat level. Note the straight rudder.
这样好多了！用你的身体来平衡船身，注意舵叶是直的。

8 Beating 迎风航行

Beating to windward in a Topper is particularly satisfying. The boat is so lively and responsive that it' s a joy to sail in virtually all conditions.
使用Topper进行迎风航行的感觉格外舒服。它活力十足并且反应敏捷，在任何条件下进行航行都是一种享受。

What is beating? 什么是迎风航行？

A boat cannot sail straight from X to Y (Figure 1). The sail will flap, and the boat will be blown backwards. The only way is to beat – to sail a zigzag course at an angle of about 45° to the wind.
在图1中，船是不能从X点直接航行到Y点的，否则帆会飘打，船会被风吹动倒退。唯一的方法是用大约45度的迎风角度走之字形路线。

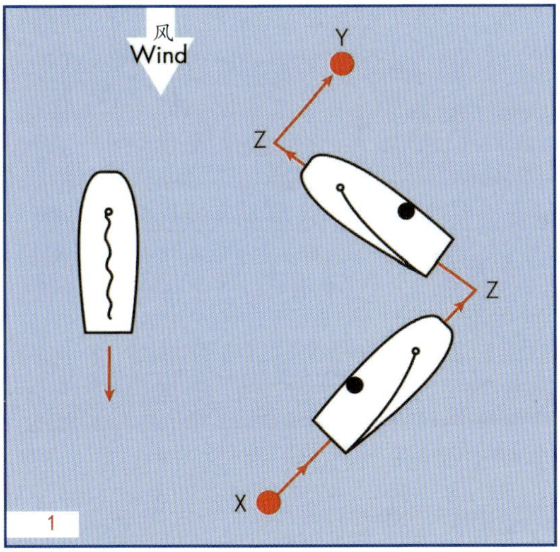

1

Steering 操舵

To beat, pull in the mainsheet pretty much as hard as you can until the mainsheet block and boom end block nearly touch; sit out, and steer as close to the wind as you can. The course is a compromise: if you steer too close to the wind you slow down, even though you are pointing closer to Y. If you steer too far from the wind, you go faster, but are pointing well away from Y (Figure 2).

迎风航行时，尽力收紧主缭直到主缭滑轮和横杆尾部滑轮几乎碰到一起。向外坐，操舵让船尽可能靠近风。航线是妥协的结果：如果过于靠近风则速度会减慢，即使航向离目标更近；如果过于下风则速度会快，但航向会离目标更远（图2）。

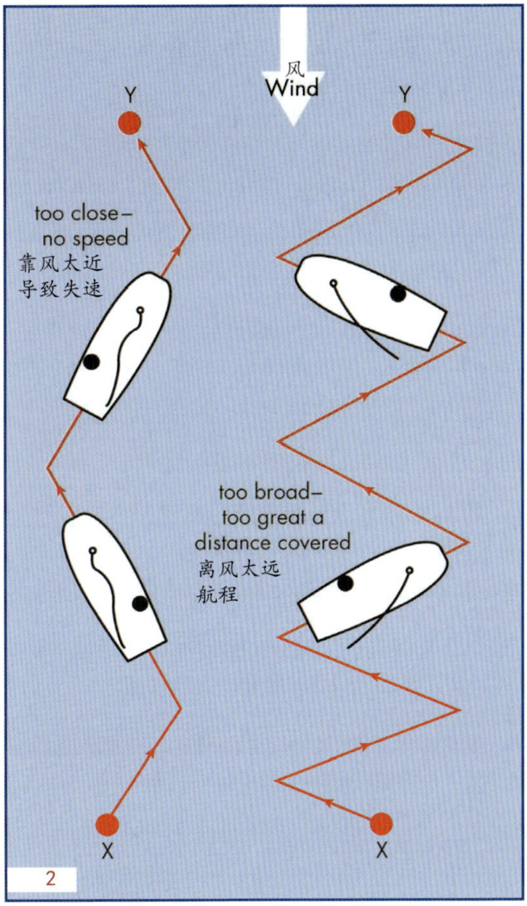

2

The simplest check on your course is to watch the front of the sail. Turn towards the wind until the sail begins to flap, then turn back until it just stops flapping. You are now on course. Repeat this every few seconds – both to check your course, and because the wind constantly changes its direction. At points Z the boat tacks through about 90°. Tacking is discussed in chapter 9.

摄影：Simon Mcllwaine

最简单的检查航线的办法是注意帆的前缘。向上风航行直到帆面开始飘动，然后向下风调整直到停止飘动，这时你的航向正确。每过几秒钟重复一下这个过程，一方面检查航向，另一方面也是防止风向变化（风摆）。在Z点船进行90度迎风转向。我们在第9章会讨论迎风转向。

Adjusting the horse (traveller) 调整主帆滑车索

Normally the horse should be pulled i n tight – very tight in strong winds and only eased very slightly in light winds.
正常情况下，滑车索应该拉紧——强风时非常紧，仅在微风时略微松开。

Adjusting the sail 调帆

When beating in medium or light winds there is no need to adjust the mainsheet. Keep it pulled in, and concentrate on using the tiller to keep the boat at the proper angle to the wind.
The tension on the mainsheet is important. In medium winds, pull it in until the main-sheet and boom end blocks are nearly touching. In light and in very strong winds, you will need to let the mainsheet out a little.
中等风力和微风时不需要调整主缭，保持主帆收紧，集中精力控制舵柄保持最佳迎风角。主缭的拉力非常重要。中等风力时，尽力收紧主缭直到主缭滑轮和横杆尾部滑轮几乎碰到一起。微风和强风时，你需要略微放松主缭。

Trim 船体平衡

Sit forward, right up against the bulkhead, then either sit out or slide down to leeward with knees bent depending on the wind strength – you should aim for a constant 5° heel to leeward. Don’t allow the boat to heel further than this in strong winds.
尽量向前坐在前舱壁位置，然后根据风的强度或向外压舷或屈膝滑到下风一侧——你的目标是保持船身向下风侧倾斜5度。大风时不要超过这个角度。

Daggerboard 稳向板

The daggerboard should be right down when beating, except in strong winds.
迎风航行时稳向板完全放下，除非有强风。

Gusts 阵风

You should learn to spot a gust approaching by the dark pattern (tiny wavelets) that it creates on the water. As it arrives luff up slightly and sit out hard – it is much easier to prevent the boat from heeling than to recover when it does!
你应该学会通过水面上的深色波纹来发现阵风的走向。阵风来时略微迎风并且向外压舷。提前动作防止船体倾斜比倾斜后再恢复正常要容易。

Windshifts 风摆

The wind constantly alters in direction. However, some changes are larger and/or last longer. These are windshifts, and it is vital you spot them and react to them when racing. Windshifts are discussed in Part 3.

风向是随时变化的。并且有的变化很大而且持续很长，这就是风摆。比赛时识别风摆并做出反应是很重要的，我们会在第三部分讨论。

Sail controls 调帆

The sail should be flattened off when beating to reduce heeling forces and drag. The stronger the wind the flatter it needs to be.

The downhaul (Cunningham) should be set just to remove the horizontal creases in light winds, and tightened progressively as the wind gets stronger. This tension affects the whole of the sail and pulls the draft (maximum curve) of the sail forward, reducing drag.

The outhaul should normally be set to give 50-100mm of draft in the middle of the foot in light and medium winds. It needs to be tensioned

Pull in the mainsheet to correct beating position (about 10cm between the blocks). Then tighten the kicking strap (vang) – and pull it a bit more!

收紧主缭以保持正确的迎风位置（横杆端部与滑车滑轮的距离大约10厘米）。然后拉紧斜拉索-尽量紧。

Then, when you ease the mainsheet in a gust, the boom goes out, not up.

阵风出现时放松主缭，横杆会向外移动而不是向上。

When sailing in waves it is virtually impossible to stop water coming into the cockpit. If you get a chance, kick the water out of the back of the cockpit. It will be quicker than relying on the self bailer, but remember it is illegal in a race.

在浪中航行切记不要让水涌入船仓。如果可能的话，用脚把水踢出去，这样比用排水筏更有效。但在比赛中这样做是非法的。

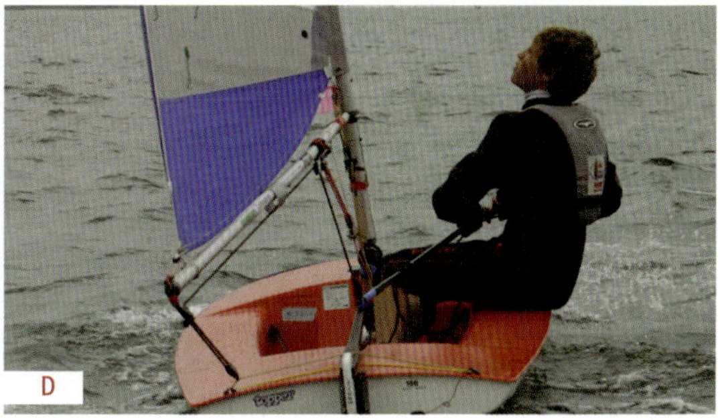

Good beating. The daggerboard is right down, the downhaul is pulled to remove most (but not all) of the creases. The outhaul is off so that the gap between the sail and the boom is from your fingertips to half way up your wrist.

漂亮的迎风航行：稳向板全部放下，下拉索足够紧保证帆面基本没有皱褶，后拉索适当松弛，保证帆与横杆的距离为半个手掌。

If you have the race control lines, this is how you tension the kicking strap (vang) and downhaul while beating. 如果你装配了竞赛型索具，可以按图在迎风段拉紧斜拉索和下拉索。

as the wind increases until it is curling the foot upwards in over-powering conditions. This control affects the draft in the lower part of the sail only.
迎风航行时要保持帆面平直以减少横向受力和船体阻力。风越大帆面就要越平。微风时调整下拉索减少帆面的褶皱，并在风力变强时逐次拉紧下拉索。这种拉力对帆效影响很大，加大了帆面凹度，减少阻力。在微风和中等风力时调整后拉索，让帆下缘与横杆中点的距离保持在50~100毫米。当风力加强时拉紧后拉索，直到帆下缘因过分受力而向上卷起。
The kicking strap (vang) tension is quite critical when beating. It needs to be slightly less tight when sailing over waves in light weather but quite tight in smooth water, particularly in strong winds (i.e. tighter than just taking up the slack after the mainsheet is pulled block to block).
In certain conditions such as beating in heavy weather or sailing in a choppy sea the mast bend can be retained with the kicking strap while the mainsheet (and boom) is eased out to reduce the hook-back of the leech.
迎风航行时斜拉索的拉力非常关键。风小有浪时斜拉索不能太紧，但是无浪时就要收紧，大风时尤其要更紧（让主缭的两个滑轮几乎靠在一起）。在大风或涌浪较大时迎风航行时需要拉紧斜拉索保持桅杆和横杆弯曲度，同时略松开主缭让帆后缘展开。

Going faster 快速航行

Fast beating is essential for racing since the majority of races start on a beat. Here are some points to watch and ideas to try:
快速地迎风航行对于比赛很关键，因为大部分的比赛都是迎风起航。这里有一些注意事项和可尝试的的办法：

- Never allow the boat to heel excessively.
  保持船身不要过度倾斜
- Sit out hard in strong winds. Ease the mainsheet as needed to keep boat level.

Good light wind technique. 小风技术

摄影：Simon Mcllwaine

大风时向外压舷，如有必要放松主缭以保持船身平衡。
- Keep the mainsheet pulled in tight except in light or very strong winds.
  除微风和强风情况外，均收紧主缭。
- Watch the front of the sail like a hawk. Keep trying to luff① up, yet bear away every time the sail starts to flap.
  像鹰隼一样盯着帆的前部，不断尝试上风，当帆面飘动时再略向下风。
- Keep a good look-out for other boats.
  注意观察其他的船
- Watch for windshifts.
  注意观察风摆

BEATING IN LIGHT WINDS 微风时迎风航行

Patience and stealth are the order of the day. Move around the boat as little as possible; when you must, move slowly taking care not to shake the shape out of the sail.
耐心和小心翼翼是主旋律。尽可能减少在船上的移动。如果必须移动也要缓慢小心，减少对帆形的影响。

Setting the traveller/horse and mainsheet 调节滑车索和主缭

Ease the traveller a tiny amount in very light winds (only). With the mainsheet now eased a little the boom will still stay approximately over the corner of the transom (using a fair bit of tension on the kicker will encourage the boom to stay there). Always remember that maximum speed through the water is more important than good pointing in these conditions since a well-sailed boat can quite easily go twice as fast as a badly-sailed one.
仅在风很小时把滑车索略微放松。主缭些许放松，让横杆处在后船角的位置（适当拉紧斜拉索可以帮助横杆固定在那个位置）。永远记住船速比航向重要得多，因为帆形调校好的船的速度可以很轻松地超过没有调校好的船两倍。

Steering 操舵

Continuously watch the luff of the sail, bearing away immediately if it begins to lift.
持续盯着帆的前部，不断尝试上风，当帆面飘动时再略向下风。

Trim 船身平衡

Sit over the well between the daggerboard and the leeward deck with your knees bent double and your legs along the leeward sidedeck (see photos, left). This heels the boat which helps fill the sail (by gravity) and reduce hull-to-water skin friction. Heel the boat until the leeward gunwale is nearly under water. The lighter you are, the further to leeward you need to move.
坐在稳向板和下风侧甲板之间的空当处，双腿屈膝，贴在侧甲板边（见左侧照片）。这样可以帮助船身倾斜让帆靠重力鼓起，并减少船身与水的摩擦力。压舷直到甲板边沿几乎入水。你体重越轻就要更向下风处移动。

Sail controls 调帆

The downhaul (Cunningham) should be loose. The outhaul should be normal (i.e. 50mm of draft in the middle of the foot) and tightened in extremely light winds to help keep what wind there is moving over the sail.
下拉索应该放松。后拉索处在正常拉力以保证帆下缘与横杆中点距离为50毫米。风力特别小时拉紧后拉索以保证风吹过帆面。

BEATING IN STRONG WINDS 大风时迎风航行

Even with the easy-to-handle Topper this can be

注释：① luff 上风

hard work, yet very rewarding. Sit out hard and aim for speed rather than close sailing to the wind – especially in waves which tend to stop the boat.
在大风中迎风航行也是个苦活，但也非常刺激。向外压舷追求速度而不要太靠近风——特别是有涌浪阻挡船前进时。

Setting the traveller/horse and mainsheet 调节滑车索和主缭

The traveller must be pulled as tight as possible so that when the mainsail is sheeted in hard (bending the mast and flattening the sail) the boom will not come too close to the centreline of the boat and cause excessive heeling forces and drag. Ease the sail to spill wind only when the boat heels beyond 5°.
滑车索要尽可能拉紧，这样当主缭也收紧时（使桅杆弯曲拉平帆面）横杆不会靠船中线太近而导致过度侧倾力和阻力。只有在船身侧倾超过5度时再放松主缭。

Steering over waves 破浪航行

Try to steer so that the boat has an easy passage over the waves, luffing as you go up the wave and bearing away as you dip back down.
尝试让船在涌浪之间找到一条轻松的路径，上浪时向上风走（因为浪峰会令你偏向下风），下浪时向下风走（以提高船速，应对下一个浪）。

Daggerboard 稳向板

When it is difficult to hold the boat upright, or if it luffs of its own accord, you will find it helps to raise the board so the top is level with the foredeck. This reduces heeling.
当你很难保持船身平衡，或者自行上风，你会发现把稳向板顶部升起到前甲板的高度会很有用，会减少侧倾。

Trim 船身平衡

Sit out as hard as possible keeping reasonably far forward – waves permitting. This reduces weather helm by tilting the sail's centre of effort forward of the daggerboard. Be ready to move aft or pivot backwards at the waist quickly if the bow begins to bury itself.
尽可能向外压舷并在涌浪条件下适当向前坐。可以减少由于帆面的受力中心处在稳向板之前引起的上风舵。随时准备向后移动身体或躯干后倾以防止船头插入水中（你要尽一切努力让船身尽可能水平）。

Gusts 阵风

Watch for gusts approaching. Sit out and be prepared to spill wind from the sail.
观察阵风来向，向外坐准备随时减少帆面受力。

Sail controls 调帆

Pull the downhaul very tight and the outhaul tight. The kicking strap (vang) should be tight enough to bend the boom and eased a little off wind.
收紧下拉索和后拉索。斜拉索也要拉紧，促使横杆弯曲，并略微放出主帆。

SORTING OUT PROBLEMS WHEN BEATING IN STRONG WINDS 强风时迎风航行的问题处理

The main problem is the boat luffing up (turning into the wind). Try:
主要的问题是船会驶入顶风，可以做以下尝试:

- Pulling up the centreboard to at least the first notch.
  升起稳向板，至少到第一个刻度。
- Pulling on loads of downhaul (pull as hard as you can so the front of the sail touches the boom).
  用力拉下拉索，让帆前缘碰到横杆。
- To prevent the daggerboard floating up, put progrip on the bladders inside the daggerboard case.
  为防止稳向板滑出，在插槽里用专用绷带把稳向板的边刃包住。
- To stop the boat filling up with water lean back as you approach a wave.
  为防止船体充水，在上浪之前向船后靠
- If you get into irons (pointing into the wind) pull up the daggerboard and sit at the back. Keep the rudder straight and the boat will pivot about the rudder. You may need to push out the boom a bit, too. (See photos A-F, opposite.)
  如果你已经驶入顶风，拉起稳向板并坐在船的后部。保持舵叶垂直，船身会以舵叶为轴转动。你可能需要推一推横杆（见55页图A~图F）。

BEATING - COMMON MISTAKES
迎风航行时的常见错误

G. The foot of the sail is too loose and will prevent you sailing close to the wind.
帆下缘太松，导致你无法足够迎风行驶。

H. Mainsheet too far out. Again, this will prevent you pointing close to the wind.
主缭放出过多，也会阻止你充分迎风。

I. Sitting too far back. Sitting further forward will stop the stern (back) of the boat dragging through the water.
坐的位置过于靠后。应该尽量向前坐以防止船尾产生拖弋阻力。

J. This boat is heeled too much. The sailor will have to pull too hard on the tiller to keep the boat from luffing up (turning in to the wind). Hike out!
船身过度倾斜。这样你必须使出全身的力气控制船舵以防止船驶入顶风。向外压舷！

K. "Pinching" (sailing too close to the wind.) It looks good to start with because you point closer to your goal, but the boat will slow far too much.
生切（过于迎风）。这样看上去很好，因为你的方向离目标更近，但是船速会大大降低。

9 Tacking 迎风转向

What is tacking? 什么是迎风转向？

The boat in Figure 1 is beating with the sail on the starboard side (a). The boat turns into the wind (b) and keeps turning until it is beating with the sail on the port side (c). This turn is called a tack.

图1中的船正在迎风航行，帆在右舷(a)。船驶进顶风(b)，继续转向直到帆摆到左舷继续迎风行驶(c)。这样的转向称作“迎风转向”。

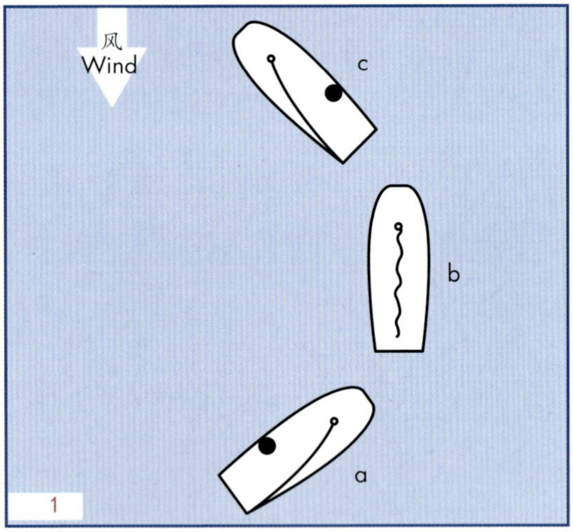

Tacking in light to moderate winds 微风和中等风力时的迎风转向

Never tack unless you are travelling at or near the maximum speed for the conditions. If the boat has insufficient momentum you will come to a stop and blow backwards (‘get into irons’) before you can point the boat onto the new tack.

迎风转向时一定要确保你在当时条件下已经达到或接近最高速度，否则就不要转向。如果船体不具备足够的动能，在你完成转向之前船就可能停下来然后向后退（完全顶风）。

Tacking with a centre mainsheet - shot from above.
中置式主缭的迎风转向

Tacking with the centre mainsheet - step by step 主缭中置的迎风转向——顺序步骤

Both photo sequences (1-9 & A-H) show the manoeuvre with the centre mainsheet.

两组图（1~9和A~H）演示了主缭中置的船如何迎风转向。

Look for these steps:

注意以下步骤：

1. Sail straight and pick up speed.
   直线航行，尽量加速。

2. Push the tiller away firmly, lean back and begin to turn.
果断推舵，身体后仰准备转向。
3. Stay on the old side and keep on turning.
保持在原来的一侧，继续转向。
4. Keep turning through the wind. The sail will begin to fill on the new side.
继续转向穿过正迎风，帆会摆到新的一侧船舷。
5. As the boat begins to heel in the new direction, cross the boat facing forwards and land on the "new" sidedeck. Straighten up (don't let the boat spin round too far onto a reach, you are trying to get to windward).
当船进入新的航线并且倾斜，头朝前跨过船舱坐到新的一侧边甲板上。保持直行（不要让船转向过度而成为横风航行，你要坐在上风舷）。
6. Use your weight to bring the boat flat, still steering with your hand behind your back.
用你的体重保持船身水平，依然用背后的手操控船舵。
7. Only when you are steering the boat properly on the new course should you change hands on the tiller extension and mainsheet. Do this by bringing the mainsheet hand (still holding the mainsheet) to the tiller extension.
只有当你控制船只在新航线上正常航行时，才可以把手中的舵柄和主缭交换。拿住主缭的手伸向拿住副舵柄的手。
8. Transfer your old tiller hand around your body to the mainsheet.
原来持舵的手拿住主缭绕回身前。
9. Hike (sit out), and pull in the mainsheet. Take a bow!
压舷，收紧主缭。你做得很棒！

Tacking with a centre mainsheet - shot from the foredeck.
中置式主缭的迎风转向

Tacking with the stern mainsheet - step by step
主缭后置的迎风转向——顺序步骤

(photo sequences below)（照片顺序如下）

1. Push the tiller gently but firmly away from you and at the same time sit out on the windward side.
   果断而柔和地推舵，同时向上风压舷。
2. Ease the mainsheet slightly and place it under the thumb of the hand that is holding the tiller extension. Let go with the other hand.
   轻轻地松开主缭并把主缭放在持舵柄的手的拇指下。另一只手松开。
3. As the boat begins to roll on top of you, start to move to the opposite side.
   Face the stern of the boat as you move, pushing the tiller extension in front of your body. As you reach the halfway point take the tiller in your 'new' steering hand and grasp the mainsheet in your 'new' sheet hand.
   当船身转动到你头上时，开始移动到对面一侧。移动时面朝后并推舵。当你移动到一半时把舵柄换到另一只手上，同时交换主缭。
4. As the boat turns through the eye of the wind and begins to heel in the new direction, 'land' on the other deck.
   当船头转过正迎风后，船身开始倾斜，坐到新的一侧甲板上。
5. Sit on the new side, steer straight ahead and pull in the mainsheet once again. Check that you are on a good close-hauled course by observing the luff of the sail (and wind indicator).
   坐在新的一侧船舷，直线行驶并再次收紧主缭。观察帆前缘和风向标，确认你处在正确的迎风角度。

Tacking in strong winds
大风时迎风转向

It is very easy to stall the boat in heavy weather. Here are some precautions to help avoid this:
大风天气时很容易失速，下面的措施可以防止这种情况出现:

Tacking with a stern mainsheet, shot from above.
后置式主缭的船迎风转向

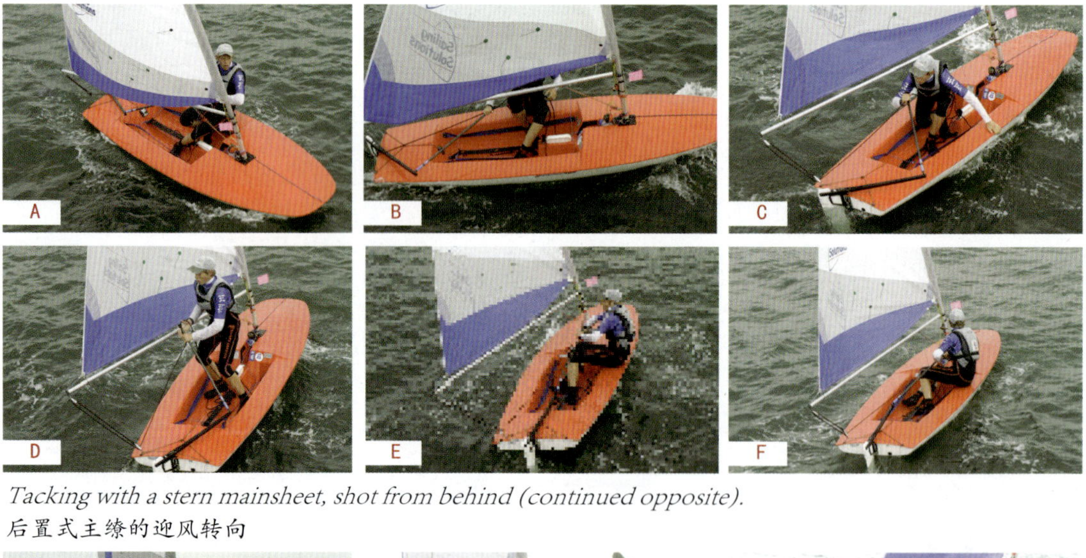

Tacking with a stern mainsheet, shot from behind (continued opposite).
后置式主缭的迎风转向

D

E

F

G

- Always tack when travelling at maximum speed.
  永远在达到最高船速时转向。
- Raise the daggerboard to the first or second notch to reduce weather helm.
  把稳向板升起到第一或第二刻度，减少上风舵。
- Push the tiller over hard.
  果断有力地推舵。
- As the sail comes over dive across the boat as quickly as possible, easing the mainsheet 150mm.
  当迎风过帆时快速俯身移动到另一侧，把主缭松开150毫米。
- Sit out hard with your body weight well forward to counter the weather helm, and sheet in again.
  利用体重向外压舷，抵消上风舵。再次收紧主缭。

TACKING – SOME COMMON MISTAKES
迎风转向的常见错误(A-D, 右图)

A. Wait until the boat is head to wind before you cross to the ‘new’ side.
直到船头顶风时，你还没有换舷。

B. If you straighten up too soon the boat will stop, pointing into the wind. Keep turning, “through” the wind.
如果你太早进入直线航行，船会停下来。当船头顶风时要继续转向，“通过”风。

C. But don’t turn too far. Here the boat has swung round onto a reach after the tack, and may capsize.
也不要转向过度。这样船会进入横风航行，容易翻覆。

D. With a centre mainsheet tack facing forwards!
主缭中置迎风转向时要面朝前方。

A

B

C

D

10 Running 顺风航行

What is running? 什么是顺风航行？

Both boats in Figure 1 are running – i.e. they are sailing with the wind directly behind.
图1中的两条船是在顺风航行，也就是说航行时风从船的后面吹来。

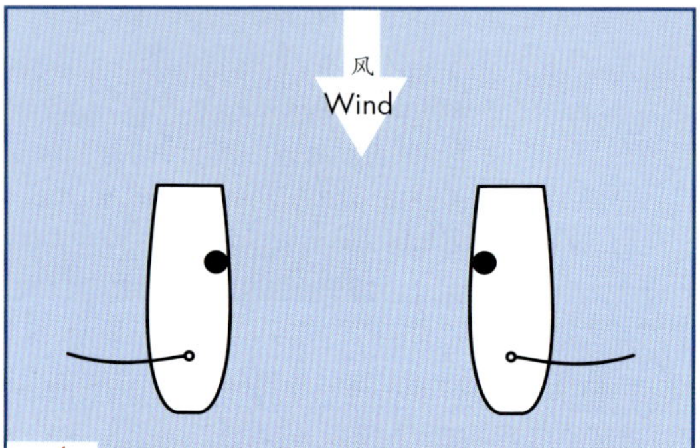

1

Adjusting the sail 调帆

In medium and light winds the mainsheet should be out so that the boom is at 90° to the boat. In strong winds, when the boat tends to roll, pull the mainsheet in a little – but remember that the boat goes fastest with the sail right out. Don't forget to tie a knot in the end of the mainsheet!
中等风力和微风时，主缭放出，横杆与船体呈90度。大风时，如果船即将发生偏转，把主缭收回一些。但你要记住主缭完全放出时船速最快，别忘记在主缭的尾部打个结。

Trim 船身平衡

Except in heavy winds or big waves sit forward in the cockpit and lean out to heel the boat to windward. In this way you will be able to steer a straight course with very little use of the rudder and also have the minimum wetted area.
坐在船舱前部，向外压舷以保持船身有一定的倾斜（强风和大浪时除外）。这样你可以很少操舵就可以保持直线航线，同时船体和水的接触面最少。

Steering 操舵

It is vital to avoid an unexpected gybe (gybing is discussed in chapter 11). Watch the burgee carefully and avoid turning so that the wind is blowing from the same side as the boom (Figure 2). This is 'running by the lee'① – the wind is able to get behind the boom and flip it across. If you find yourself in this position, quickly push the tiller away from you for a moment, then straighten up.
一定要避免无准备的顺风转向（第11章会讨论顺风转向）。小心观察风向标避免横杆转动，保持风总是从横杆的同一侧吹来（图2）。这叫作"running by the lee"，风可以从横杆后面吹来并使它翻转到另一侧。如果你发现这种情况，立即推舵，然后直线航行。

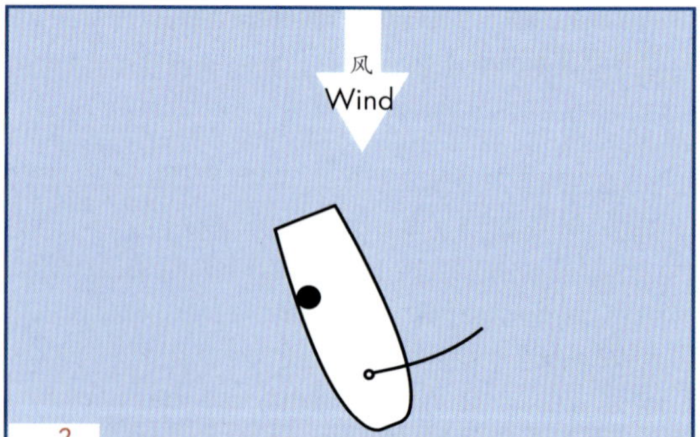

2

注释：① **running by the lee** is when the wind is blowing from the same side of the boat as the sail. Imagine sailing on a broad reach course and then bearing away onto a run. You are now sailing directly downwind. If you continue to bear away, but not enough to gybe, you are sailing 'by the lee'. Often the sail is beyond 90 degrees to the boat so other people are correct but you could have the sail beyond 90 degrees but not sailing 'by the lee'.
后顺风航行时继续走向下风，通过正顺风，帆保持不换舷而继续下风，放出主缭让横杆与船身的角度超过90度，此时风和帆位于船的同一侧（而通常帆处于下风一侧），这就是running by the lee。比如你在绕下风标时，你不愿意因为做顺风转向而降低船速，就可以选择running by the lee, 直接到达并绕标。

摄影：Simon Mcllwaine

Daggerboard 稳向板

Pull the daggerboard up about half way. The Topper has a flat bottom and needs the daggerboard for directional stability.
稳向板升起一半。Topper的船底很平，因此需要稳向板保持稳定的航向。

Gusts 阵风

As a gust arrives the boat will tend to roll so pull in the mainsheet and put down a little more daggerboard. Counter the boat's tendency to tip on top of you by luffing slightly. If the boat heels to leeward bear away a little.
阵风到来时船身会趋向翻转，所以要收紧主缭并把稳向板放下一部分。略微上风航行以制衡船身翻覆的趋势。如果船向下风倾斜过度则略微转向下风航行。

Sail controls 调帆

The kicking strap (vang) should be 'normal' (page 23). Ease the outhaul a little to give more curve to the bottom third of the sail.
斜拉索应该处于正常张力（第23页）。略微松开后拉索让帆下缘保持更大弧度。

Going faster 快速航行

This is one point of sailing where it is an advantage to be behind another boat, since you can blanket the boat in front of you and catch it up.
这是一个秘诀：在另一条船后面航行，因为这样可以把风挡住并超过它。

Here are some points to watch and ideas to try:
下面是一些要点和可尝试的办法：

- Let the mainsheet out so the boom is at right angles to the boat or even further out.
  放出主缭，让横杆和船身垂直或角度更大。
- Make sure you have the daggerboard up about half way.
  确定稳向板升起一半。
- Heel the boat to windward until the 'pull' on the tiller stops.
  保持船体向上风侧倾斜，直到舵柄上的拉力消失。
- When a gust comes, run straight downwind with it. Try to stay with the gust as long as possible. If you see a gust to one side of the course, sail over to it and then ride it.

摄影：张琦

阵风到来时，保持正顺风航行。尽可能保持利用阵风。如果你看到航线的一侧有阵风，要紧贴过去乘风航行。

- Try to surf on waves as much as you can. Pull the mainsheet in as the boat accelerates down each wave and keep it there until the extra speed disappears (because the wind direction comes forward as you speed up).

尽可能利用涌浪滑行。每次从浪峰加速下行时要收紧主帆，直到加速停止（因为当你加速时，风从前方而来）。

For once you don’t want to sail the boat flat! If you do sail flat, the centre of effort of the sail is to the side of the boat so makes it luff up (turn into the wind).

Far better to heel the boat towindward, bringing the centre of effort more directly above the axis of the boat. This removes the turning effect. You can even steer the boat by altering the heel, keeping the rudder straight. (If the boat heels towards you it will turn away from you, and vice-versa.)

有一种情况你会故意不让船身水平！因为船身水平时帆面的受力中心位于船的一侧，会让船偏向上风（转向迎风，也就是上风舵）。更好的方式是让船身向上风一侧倾斜，保持帆面受力中心在船身的正上方。这样可以避免航向偏移。你甚至可以不使用舵，仅仅通过调整船身倾斜度就可以控制方向（如果船身向你倾斜，船就会向下风偏转，反之亦然）。

Centre of effort 帆面受力中心

Centre of effort 帆面受力中心

Sit forward and heel to windward. Try not to hold the daggerboard with your mainsheet hand to top you falling out. You need that hand to adjust the mainsheet.
向前坐并让船身向上风侧倾斜。尽量不要用拿主缭的手抓住稳向板，因为你需要不断调整主缭。

RUNNING IN LIGHT WINDS 微风时顺风航行

Trim 船身平衡

Sit well forward. Heel the boat to windward holding the boom right out with your hand. If the wind is so light that the sail falls out of shape it may be better to heel the boat to leeward, but watch the mainsheet doesn’t drag in the water! Alternatively, let the sail out more than 90 degrees and heel to windward. The sail will “fall” forward to windward and will hold its shape.
尽可能向前坐，保持船体向上风侧倾斜，用手拉住横杆向外推。如果风实在太小导致失去帆形，最好让船体向下风侧倾斜。但要注意不要让主缭落到水里！或者让横杆放出超过90度，船身向上风侧倾斜。这样帆面会向上风侧下垂来保持帆形。

Steering 操舵

Use the tiller as little as possible.
尽可能少用舵。

Sail controls 调帆

All sail controls should be looser to give a slightly fuller sail.
所有的控制索具都应该放松，让帆尽可能受满风。

摄影：Simon Mcllwaine

RUNNING IN STRONG WINDS 强风时顺风航行

Steering 操舵

Don’t be in a hurry to get on a run when the wind is really blowing. Steer round gradually from a reach, letting the sail out slowly as you do so. Move back in the boat to help the bow lift.
If the boat starts to roll as you come onto the run, quickly pull the mainsheet back in a little. Keep a firm hand on the tiller, and don’t let the boat turn back onto a reach.
风力强劲时进行顺风航行不必慌张。在横风状态下逐渐转入顺风，同时慢慢把帆放出去。尽可能向后坐以使船头抬起。如果进入顺风时船开始偏，马上把帆收回一些。握牢舵柄，不要让船走回横风。
Running by the lee is a little risky for the unwary and can result in an unexpected gybe, but it can be a very effective way to avoid nosediving into a wave. The technique is to luff a little to catch a wave as it comes up behind you, then bear off quickly down the face of it. If, as you shoot down, the bow looks as though it’s going to bury itself in the wave ahead, sheet in and bear away further. The act of bearing off just before an imminent nosedive reduces the pressure in the sail (as does sheeting in) and greatly reduces the tendency for the bow to go under. But do watch the accidental gybe! The trick here is to sail waves at an angle and look for the gaps.
running by the lee是略有风险的，可能发生意外的顺风转向。但也可以有效地避免船头扎入浪中。技巧是当后面的浪上来时略微上风，然后转下风，沿着浪峰滑下去。如果滑浪时你发现船头可能扎入浪中，收紧主缭再向下风走。在扎头之前向下风走可以减少帆面受力（收紧主缭有同样效果），有力地避免船头入水。但一定要小心意外的顺风转向！诀窍是航行时与浪保持一定角度，并且小心地在浪峰之间穿行（如同你在停车场从车辆之间穿过，找到合适的停车位）。

Adjusting the sail 调帆

Rolling is caused particularly by the top of the sail twisting forward in a gust and pushing the boat over to windward. If this is likely to happen, pull on more kicking strap (vang) before the run starts. If the boat does roll, pull in the mainsheet. In any case, beware of letting the mainsheet out too far on a hairy run. Keep the dagger-board at least half down to dampen rolling.

船只翻转的发生，是由于阵风时帆的顶部前压，推动船体向横杆的另一侧翻覆。如果即将发生翻转，在开始顺风航行时要拉紧斜拉索。如果翻转已经发生，拉紧主缭。在任何情况下都不要把主缭放出太多，否则很容易翻转。 至少把稳向板放下一半来控制翻转的程度。

Sail controls 控帆

If it is really blowing it is not worth easing the sail controls except the downhaul (which must be right off) and the kicker a little – you won’t gain much and time will be lost resetting on the next leg of the course.

风确实很大时，放松控制索具就不太值得了（但下拉索必须完全打开，斜拉索略为放松），因为你也获得不了太多好处而且在下一个航段时你又要浪费时间来调整回位。

Trim 船身平衡

Sit halfway between the daggerboard and the back of the cockpit.

坐在稳向板与船舱后部的中间位置。

RUNNING – SOME COMMON MISTAKES 顺风航行的常见错误

Sit back in strong winds! Sheet in and bear away if the boat begins to nosedive. You should have put on more kicking strap (vang) for these conditions.

在强风中要坐在船身后部！如果船头扎水就要收进主缭并航向下风。这种条件下一般要把斜拉索拉紧些。

Spot the deliberate mistake! (Don’t let the sail out too far.)

记住这个故意的失误！（不要把帆放出太多）

Kicking strap (vang) too loose. The sail is losing drive and may force the boat to heel to windward.

斜拉索太松导致主帆动力减弱，船被迫向上风侧倾斜。

11 Gybing 顺风转向

What is gybing?
什么是顺风转向？

In Figure 1, boat (a) is running with the sail on the starboard side. The helmsman turns through a small angle (b) and the wind forces the sail out to the port side of the boat (c). This turn is called a gybe.

图1中的船(a)正在顺风航行，帆在右舷。舵手让船偏转一个较小的角度(b)，风会推动帆转到左舷(c)，这就是顺风转向。

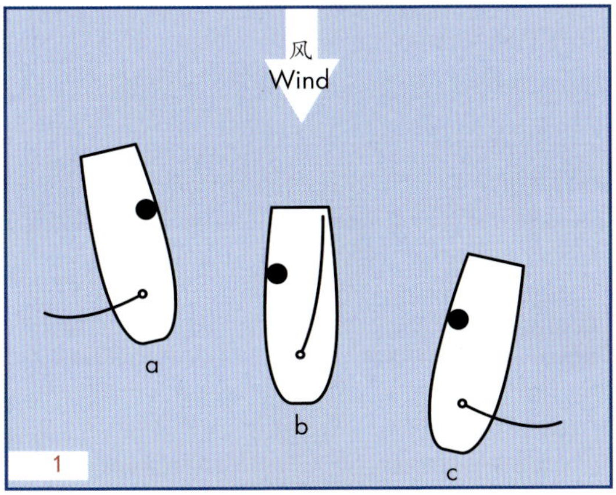

Get ready. 准备好

Turn. 转向

Keep the boat flat.
保持船身水平

Look at the flag.
观察风向标

Pull the mainsheet.
收进主缭

Cross the boat.
过帆

Land on the new deck.
换舷

Straighten up (tiller behind back).
直线航行（舵柄在身后）

Change hands.
换手

Why is gybing difficult?
为什么顺风转向比较难？

Gybing is the hardest sailing manoeuvre. Unlike tacking, the wind pushes on the sail throughout the turn. The boat is moving at high speed, so is very sensitive to tiller movements. A miscalculation results in the boat rolling – with the sail ‘edge on’ there’s not much to dampen the roll and the helmsman tends to take an involuntary dip.

顺风转向是航行机动动作中最难的。和迎风转向不同，顺风转向时风一直在推动帆面。船速很快，因此对舵的动作很敏感。如果计算失误船只就会翻转——当风向和帆面平行时你很难控制翻转，直至完全翻覆。

Decide when you want to gybe, and then do it! The best moment is when the boat is moving fast down a wave – since you're travelling away from the wind, the pressure on the sail is lessened.

考虑好何时顺风转向，然后果断地做！最好的时机是当船从波峰下滑时——因为你在加速，风作用在帆面的力量会减小。

Eight steps to a good gybe – centre mainsheet
顺风转向的八个步骤——中置主缭

1. **Get ready** Push the daggerboard half down (never gybe with the board right up or right down).
   准备好 稳向板放下一半(千万不要在稳向板全部收起或全部放下时转向)。
2. **Trim** Make sure the boat is flat or heeling slightly to windward.
   船身平衡 确保船身水平或者略微向上风侧倾斜。
3. **Turn** Turn slowly away from the wind until it

How to change hands on the tiller extension and mainsheet
如何把主缭和舵柄在两手间交换

Ready to gybe. 准备顺风转向

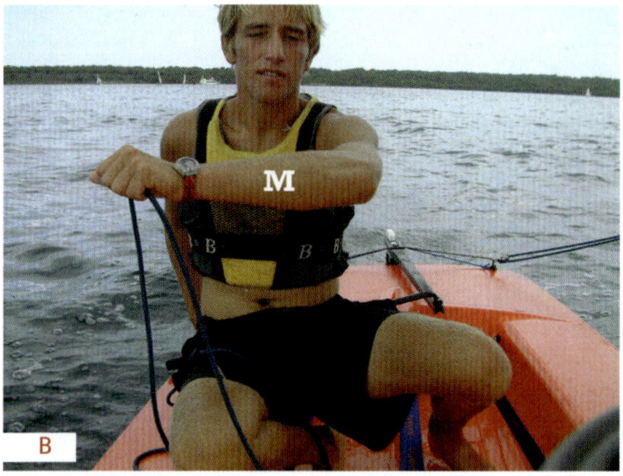

Land on the new side. The tiller extension is behind your back.
坐到新的一侧船舷，副舵柄在背后。

Take the mainsheet hand (M) across your body and grab the tiller, still holding the mainsheet.
拿主缭的手绕到身后抓住副舵柄，主缭不松手

Let go with your old tiller hand (T) and grab the mainsheet.
松开原来持舵柄的手，从身前绕过去抓住主缭

is directly behind you. By now the boat will be heeling to windward.

转向慢慢 向下风转向，直到正顺风。这时船会向上风侧倾斜。

4. **Mainsheet** Pump the mainsheet to start the boom moving.

   主缭 猛力拉动主缭让横杆开始移动。

5. **Duck** and cross the boat, facing forwards, as the boom comes across.

   低头 跨过船舱，面向前。同时横杆转动。

6. **Land** As you land on the new side, straighten the tiller. This stops the boat turning through too large an angle. You should find yourself sitting with the tiller behind your back and the mainsheet held across your body.

   落座 当你坐到另一侧船舷后把舵摆直，防止转向过度。这时舵柄在你身后，主缭在你身前穿过。

7. **Steer** Pull the tiller towards you to get back on course.

   操舵 拉舵让船保持正确航线。

8. **Smile** You made it! If the boat rolls, pull in the mainsheet: otherwise let it out to the normal running position. Finally, when the boat is under control, change hands on the tiller and the mainsheet and bring the tiller extension across your body.

   微笑 你做到啦! 如果船开始翻转，收紧主缭；否则就放出主缭，正常顺风航行。最后，你控制住了船，两手交换主缭和舵柄，把副舵柄放在身前。

摄影：张琦

Six steps to a good gybe - stern mainsheet
顺风转向的六个步骤——后置主缭

1. **Get ready** Push the daggerboard half down (never gybe with the board right up or right down). Bear away until the wind is almost directly behind the boat.

   准备 稳向板放下一半(千万不要在稳向板全部收起或全部放下时顺风转向)。转向下风直到正顺风。

2. **Pull in the mainsheet** Pull in an arm’s length of mainsheet, face aft, and heel the boat to windward (if you let it heel away from you, you can’t turn).

   收紧主缭 把主缭收紧一个臂长，面向后，让船向上风侧倾斜（如果向下风侧倾斜，你将不能转向）。

3. **Change hands** Clamp the mainsheet under the thumb of the hand holding the tiller extension. Let go with the other hand.

   换手 把主缭卡在握舵柄的手的拇指下，另一只手松开。

4. **Turn** Bear away further until the boom comes across (don’t forget to duck!) At the same time grip the leeward gunwale with your free hand.

   转向 继续向下风转向直到横杆转过去（别忘了低头！）。同时用另一只手抓住下风侧的船边缘。

5. **Cross the boat** As the boom comes over, cross the boat facing aft. Reach under the mainsheet and grasp the tiller extension with your free hand. Lift the mainsheet with your other hand, giving a short pull to prevent the sheet fouling up on the rudder stock.

   跨过船舱 当横杆转过头顶，跨过船舱并脸朝后。握住主缭并用另一只手握住副舵柄。举起主缭并拉一下，防止主缭缠绕在舵杆。

6. **Straighten up** ‘Reverse’ the tiller hard to bring the boat back on course.

   直行 快速回正舵杆让船正常航行。

Gybing - stern mainsheet 顺风转向——后置式主缭

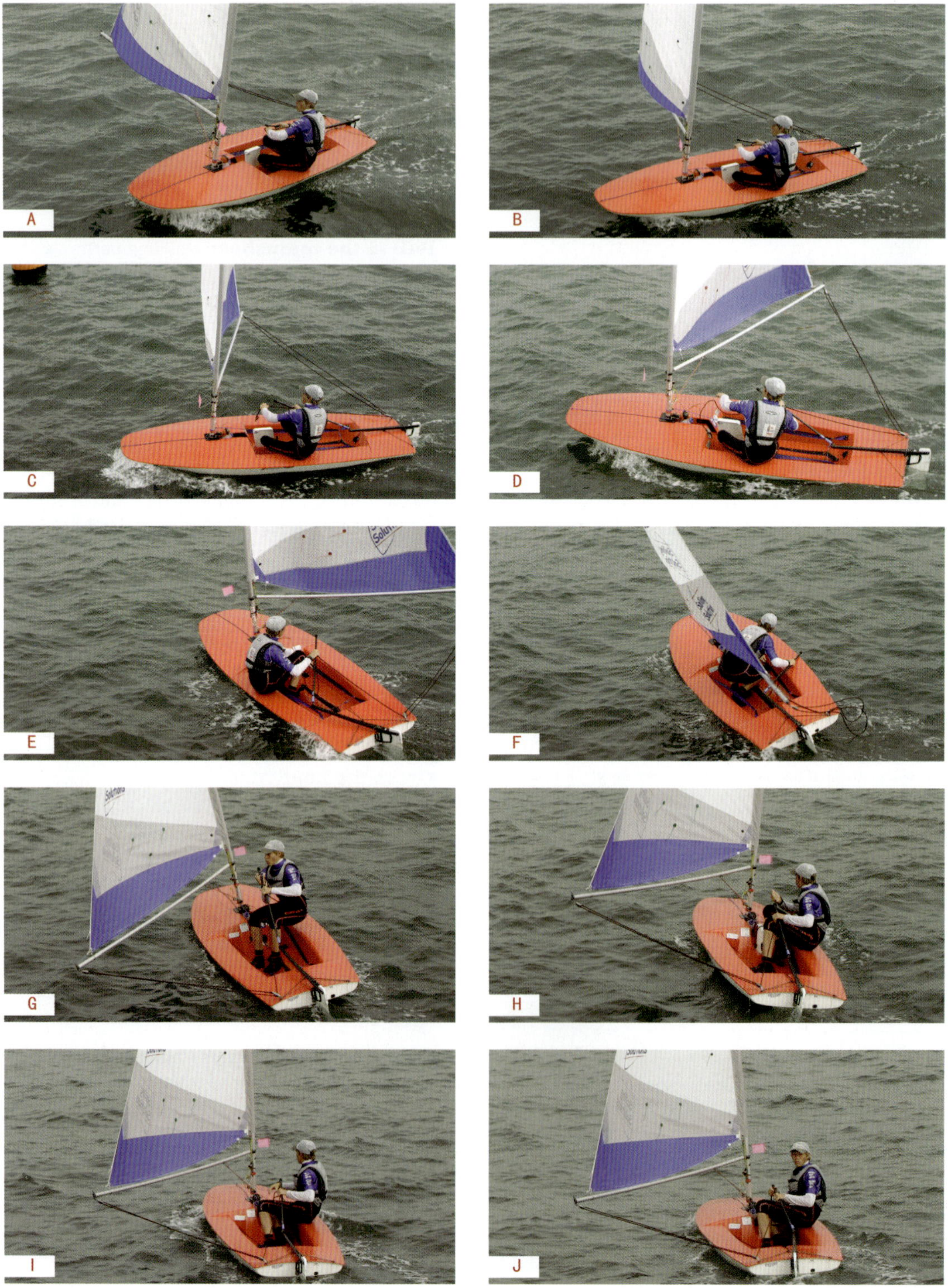

Changing hands on the tiller extension and mainsheet, facing aft. 面向后换手

Gybing in strong winds
强风时顺风转向

When the wind is very strong it is safer (though slower) to gybe without pulling in any mainsheet before the gybe. You will need to bear away a lot further before the sail comes over but when it does it will just fly harmlessly out on the other side like a flag. As you bear away again onto the new run be careful that the boat doesn' t roll on top of you!
如果风力很强，那么在转向前不要收紧主缭会让转向更加安全。在过帆之前需要多向下风走，帆会像旗子一样飞到另一侧船舷，不会造成伤害。当你再次向下风走进入新的顺风航行时要小心避免船体翻转！

If you consider that a capsize is almost inevitable you may prefer to wear round. This involves turning through almost 360° as shown in Figure 2. Do this with the daggerboard half up; pull in the mainsheet and spin the boat around fast.
如果你感觉几乎要翻船时，宁可原地转一圈。要像图2所示转动360度。要保持稳向板收起一半，收紧主缭，让船快速旋转。

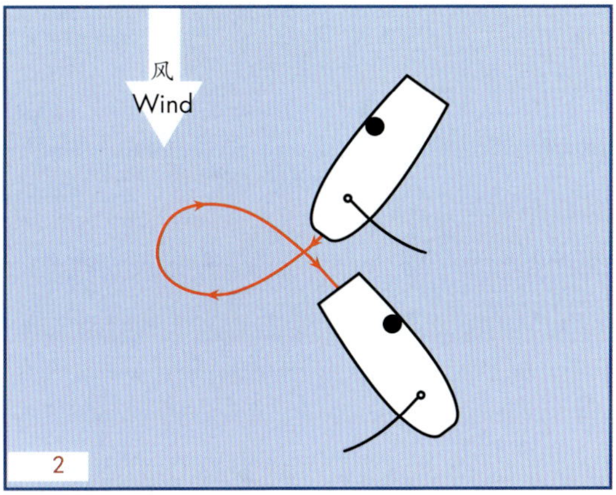

摄影：Simon McIlwaine

GYBING – SOME COMMON MISTAKES 顺风转向的常见错误

It is useless to go into a gybe heeling to leeward. The heeled boat tries to turn the wrong way. Before these skippers can gybe they will need to let out some mainsheet, bear away and heel the boat towards them as they turn.

如果船身向下风侧倾斜就无法完成顺风转向，因为倾斜的船身会导致船向错误的方向偏转。选手们必须放出主缭，航向下风并保持船身向他们倾斜，才能转向。

If you gybed like this in a breeze, you could get rather damp! You should centralise the tiller as the boom comes over and keep your weight low and aft. Be prepared to prevent the boat luffing up (slewing around into the wind).

如果像上图这样顺风转向，很容易停滞不前！过帆时要保持舵叶居中，保持身体重心降低并后移。小心避免船头转向上风。

12 Taking a penalty
受罚

The two turns penalty
两圈判罚

If you have a collision with someone in a race and are in the wrong you have to do two circles,

A

B

known in the trade as the Two Turns Penalty. You have to include two tacks and two gybes.

If you hit a buoy, you have to do one turn, including a tack and a gybe.

You are going to do plenty of these as you learn to race, so now that you can tack and gybe why not practise sailing in circles? The photo sequence shows a one turn penalty.

如果在比赛中由于你的错误而撞到别的船，你必须原地转动两圈，在规则里叫作“两圈判罚”，你要做两次迎风转向和两次顺风转向。如果你碰到浮标，则需要转动一圈，包括一次迎风转向和一次顺风转向。你在练习比赛时会多次被判罚，所以应该练习通过迎风转向和顺风转向来进行绕圈航行。这组照片说明了一圈判罚。

C

D

E

13 Capsizing 翻覆

Everyone capsizes. Indeed, if you don't capsize sometimes, you're probably not really trying! When the inevitable happens, try to stay on top of the boat. In most other classes, the crew needs to swim to right the boat! In the Topper this is unnecessary.

每个人都会翻船。如果不翻船，说明你可能没有努力尝试！当翻船不可避免要发生时，尽量待在船体的高处。如果是别的船型，船员需要在水中游动把船扶正，但如果是Topper就没这个必要。

Even if the boat turns upside-down, this is no problem in a Topper (see photo sequences, pages 74-75). Climb on the hull, stand with your back to the wind and lever the boat onto its side. Try to stay on the daggerboard; you can then right the boat as described below. If you do fall off then pulling the dagger-board towards the water will improve your chances of climbing back on.

即使Topper已经船底朝天也没有问题（见74~75页的组图）。爬到船身上部，后背朝风，让船身侧面朝上。尝试站在稳向板上，你就可以让船身回正。如果你不慎落水，就抓住稳向板向下拉这样可以帮助你爬回去。

Never leave the boat (to swim for the shore, for example). The hull will support you almost indefinitely – it has reserve buoyancy inside and will float even if the skin is punctured and it is more easily spotted than a swimmer. The boat will tip one of two ways: to leeward (which is more pleasant) or to windward.

永远不要弃船（比如游回岸上）。船体绝对可以支撑你的重量——即使表面破损，船身依然保存有多余的浮力。而且在海面上船体比游泳的人更容易被找到定位。船身翻覆会有两个可能：向下风向（比较舒适），向上风向。

Capsizing to leeward 向下风翻覆

As the boat capsizes climb over the side and onto the daggerboard, then lean back and slowly pull the boat upright. The boat automatically turns into the wind. At the last moment, straddle the deck and scramble into the cockpit. (See photo sequence, below.)

船身翻覆后爬过船舷站到稳向板上，向后仰慢慢地把船拉回正位。船会自动转入上风，在最后一刻穿过甲板爬回船舱。（见下面的组图）

Avoiding a capsize to leeward 避免向下风侧翻覆

- Watch for gusts. 注意阵风。
- Keep the mainsheet in your hand at all times. 保持主缭总在手中。
- Sit out hard in strong winds. 强风时向外压舷。
- On a reach or run, avoid letting the boat turn into the wind. 横风或顺风航行时，避免驶入上风。

Recovering from a capsize to leeward 把翻覆的船向下风侧回正

A

B

C

D

E

F

Capsizing to windward
向上风侧翻覆

Try to stay on top of the boat. However, you may well fall out as the boat capsizes to windward. If this happens on a reach or run, hang on to the mainsheet at all costs – the boat is travelling fast and might finish up some distance away. The mainsheet is your lifeline. Do not hang on to the tiller extension which might snap as you go over the side.Pull yourself back to the boat along the mainsheet. In these circumstances the Topper will almost certainly have inverted.

尽量待在船的顶部。当然船向上风翻覆时你可能会落水，如果在横风或顺风时落水，要不惜一切代价抓住主缭——因为船速很快并且可能航行一段之后才会停下。主缭就是你的生命线。不要挂在副舵柄上，因为你翻到一侧时可能会使副舵柄折断。抓住主缭把自己拉回船上，在这种情况下Topper很可能已经回正了。

1. Climb onto the upturned boat with your back to the wind. This is important.
   爬到船上，后背朝风，这个很重要。
2. Pull the daggerboard right out. If the elastic is tight enough it won't fall out and this is also important.
   把稳向板完全拔出。如果弹力绳过紧，可能拔不出来，这个也很重要。
3. Stand on the gunwale (lip) with your back to the wind.
   后背朝风，站在船侧帮上。
4. With your hands around the board, lever the boat upright until you can scramble onto the daggerboard.
   双手抱住稳向板，把船逐渐压过来，直到可以爬到稳向板上。
5. Right the boat!(See photo sequence, page 74.)
   完全扶正！(见74页的组图)

In shallow water, don't let the boat turn upside down or the mast may snap. If the mast gets stuck in mud, stand on the daggerboard close to the hull and gently bounce up and down to free it.

在浅水区域，不要让船底朝上，否则桅杆会触地。如果桅杆插入泥中，站在稳向板靠近船身的地方，小心地上下跳动，让桅杆拔出。

Recovering from a capsize to windward 把翻覆的船向上风一侧扶正

I

Avoiding a capsize to windward 避免向上风侧翻覆

- Be ready to move your weight inboard in lulls.
  随时准备向船内移动身体以防止风力突然减小。
- Pull in the mainsheet rapidly if the boat rolls to windward.
  如果船向上风偏转，迅速收回主缭。
- On a reach or run, avoid turning fast away from the wind.
  横风或顺风航行时，避免向下风转向过快。

Getting going again 重新航行

After righting, the boat will normally be head-to-wind. To get moving, lift the daggerboard, push out the boom and wait for the boat to swing away from the wind.Then push down the daggerboard, sheet in and away we go! (See pages 54-55.)

船回正后一般都是船头向风。这时要拔起稳向板，推出横杆，等待船身向下风转动。然后放下稳向板，收紧主缭继续前进！（见54和55页）

Recovering from turning turtle 把完全翻覆的船扶正

A

B

C

D

E

F

14 Landing 上岸

Think ahead before landing since a great deal of damage can result if you don't take care. Always try to land on a windward shore (wind blowing from shore to sea) if you can because this makes it easier to stop!
上岸之前一定要想清楚，如果你粗心大意，很可能造成很大损失。尽可能在离岸风时上岸（风从陆地吹向海面），这样比较容易让船停下来。

Landing on a windward shore 离岸风时上岸

1. Sail slowly towards the shore. Control the boat's speed by letting out the mainsheet. Ease the horse (traveller) so the tiller can be raised to pull up the rudder later.
   慢速向岸边航行，放出主缭控制船速。放松滑车索让舵柄可以抬起，随后可以把舵叶拉起来。
2. At the last minute, turn into the wind and quickly lift out the daggerboard and raise the rudder as you stop (Figure 1).
   在最后一刻，驶入正迎风，当船停止时迅速拉起稳向板，抬起舵叶（图 1）。

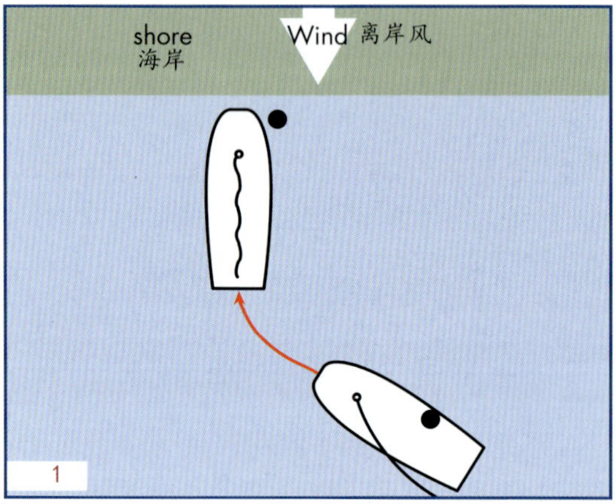

3. Step into the water on the shore side of the boat, holding it as near the bow as you can.
   在靠近岸边的一侧跳入水中，尽可能抓住船头。

Landing on a lee shore 近岸风时上岸

There may be times when landing on a lee shore is unavoidable. In this case approach the shore on the reach which is closest to the wind direction (Figure 2). Raise the dagger-board and rudder as far as possible while still keeping control. Let the sail out so that it is half flapping and not causing the boat to heel or go particularly fast. Sail in as close to the shore as the depth of water will allow before luffing head to wind, jumping out and holding the boat by the bow. Ask someone on the shore to bring you your launching trolley.
有时候你不得不在近岸风情况下上岸。这时你要尽量靠近风，横风行驶（图2）。在船只可控情况下尽量在远处抬起稳向板和船舵。把帆放出处于半飘帆状态，避免船速过快或倾斜过度。在水深允许情况下尽量靠近岸边并且收帆，然后让船头向风，跳进水中并抓住船头。请在岸上的人帮助把船车推过来。

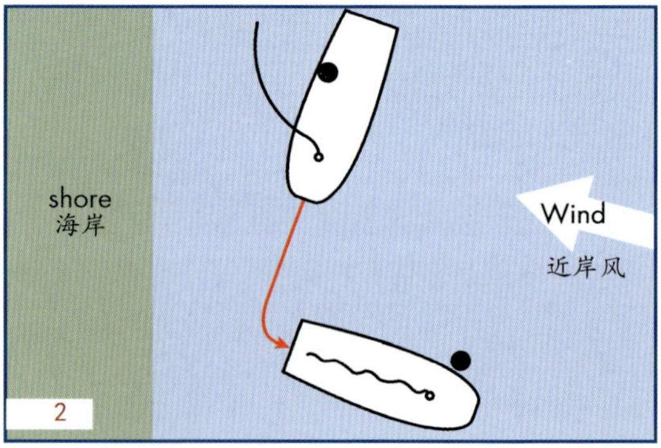

In surf, this method doesn't work! (The boat will probably swing broadside to the waves and get rolled up the beach.) The technique here is to pull up the rudder and daggerboard and sail fast through the surf, straight towards the beach. Keep going straight until the bow grounds, jump out and then drag the boat up the beach before the next wave arrives.
在大浪情况下，上述的方法就不行了！（船身会打横并且被浪掀翻到岸上）此时的方法是：收起稳向板和船舵，快速航行穿过浪头，直奔岸边直到船头触到沙滩底，马上跳入水中，在下一个浪头到来之前拖船上岸。

Landing on a lee shore 近岸风时上岸.

15 Care and maintenance 保养和维护

STORAGE 存放

With a hull depth of only 380mm, the Topper is very easy to store and takes up a very small space. If you are storing out of doors it is perfectly satisfactory to stand the boat on its gunwale against a wall; you can pull it against the wall by passing a rope out through the daggerboard case and tightening this on to a piece of timber set at right angles to the slot. If you have room to keep the boat flat, raise it off the ground a few inches to allow air to circulate. (The photographs below show the best support points.) There is no need to cover the boat – foul weather will have no detrimental effect at all on the polypropylene hull.

Topper船身的高度仅仅38厘米，因此很方便存放而且占用空间很小。如果在室外存放，最好是把船体立起来靠着墙。你可以用一根绳子穿过稳向板插槽并绑在一根和插槽呈直角的木头上。如果空间允许平放，在船体下面要留有几英寸的空隙以保证空气流动。（下面的图片说明了最佳的支撑点位置）没有必要把船身盖住，即使是恶劣天气对聚乙烯船身也不会造成破坏。

If you have the use of a garage, there is usually enough height to sling a Topper from the roof above the car. You can use the roof rack straps as slings and these should pass around the hull – forward beneath the mast step position and aft below the rear bulkhead. The easiest method of lifting the boat into the required position is to drive it into the garage on the car roof. This way you have the minimum of lifting to contend with!

如果你可以使用车库存放，一般可以把船吊挂在车子上面的屋顶上。你可以用车顶架绑带穿过船身进行固定——前面带子固定在桅杆插槽位置，后面带子固定在后挡水板位置。最简单的方法是把船放在车顶开进车库，这样你需要抬起的高度最小。

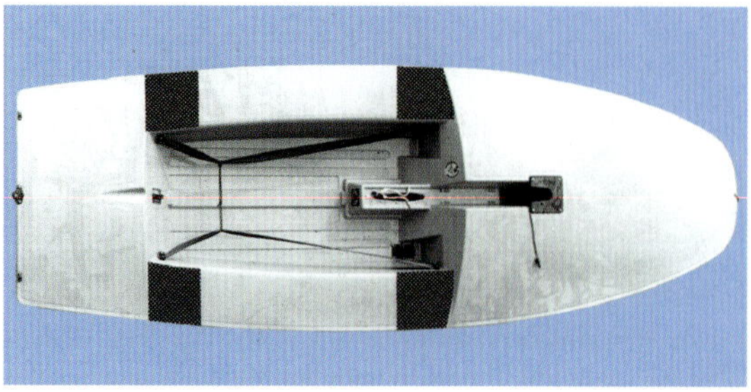

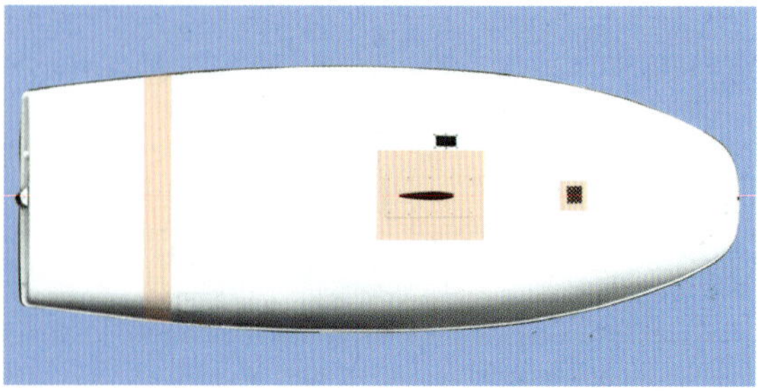

Strong points. The aft one is under the aft bulkhead.

适合支撑的位置。后部的带状区域位于船舱后挡水板下面。

ROUTINE MAINTENANCE 日常保养

Hull 船身

The material from which Topper hulls are moulded is extremely tough and is the same all the way through. So you are not concerned – as with a GRP hull – about damaging the gelcoat and allowing water to penetrate. However, polypropylene is a little softer than GRP and is inclined to scratch with harsh treatment. With sensible use and reasonable care, it is quite feasible to keep the bottom in good shape; minor scuffs and scratches can be removed with fine wet-and-dry paper, and a reasonable shine can be restored with a good cutting compound. More severe scratches are best tackled with a sharp cabinet scraper or Stanley knife blade. The material cuts beautifully but does not respond well to coarse sanding, which can leave a furry surface that will do nothing for your boatspeed. Major shunts – usually the result of a boat becoming detached from its roof rack – can result in a split hull. This can be satisfactorily repaired by a special hot-air welding process and the manufacturers will advise on your nearest specialist.

Topper的注塑材料非常结实并且贯穿全部船体。因此你完全不必担心会像玻璃钢船身那样会由于船体表面破损而进水。不过，聚乙烯材料比玻璃钢略为柔软一些，如果受到强烈撞击容易产生划痕。如果谨慎使用并认真保养，可以很容易地保持船底的形状。轻微的滑痕和磕伤可以用防水砂纸修复。用光滑剂可以让船体光亮如新。严重的划痕需要用刮刀或Stanley工具刀进行修复。修补材料易于切割但是不易用粗砂纸打磨，表面略显粗糙但对航速没有影响。如果船身从车顶架滑落，会造成船体上下部分脱离。你仍然可以采用热空气焊接方式进行修复。制造商会推荐你附近的专家来帮助你。

Spars 杆具

These should rarely require any maintenance although it is a good idea to check the riveted eyes for security – particularly if you are going out in heavy weather. Rivets have been known to break or work loose. Cleats can also break or 'burn out', but make sure you check the class rules thoroughly to ensure that you do not replace them with anything that could put you out of class.

杆具一般都不需要维修。当然当恶劣天气时出航前，检查一下铆钉孔是个好主意。铆钉是有可能破裂或松脱的。夹绳器也有可能破损或失效，如果要更换夹绳器，请仔细阅读级别规则以避免因超规改装而失去级别资格。

Rudder and daggerboard 船舵和稳向板

These are injection moulded in polypropylene, and glass-reinforced to give them the required stiffness and hard surface. No maintenance at all is required apart from keeping the tips smooth and free of indentations by the judicious use of wet-and-dry paper. Always check the rudder bolts for correct tightness – there should be no slop between the blade and the cast aluminium stock, nor should it be so tight so as to prevent the blade from retracting properly. Tiller extensions have been known to detach themselves at the least convenient moments so it is worth checking frequently that the rubber joint is not splitting.

船舵和稳向板是聚乙烯材料喷塑制造，并且加入玻璃纤维增加了强度和表面硬度。完全不需要保养，但注意使用水砂纸让侧边保持平滑避免凹陷。经常检查舵叶螺栓保持正确的松紧度——不能过松而导致舵叶和铸铝套托之间有水溢出，也不能过紧使得舵叶很难收起。经常检查副舵柄的橡胶万向节，避免因破损造成航行时副舵柄脱离。

Sail 帆面

This is the 'engine' of your Topper and if you race the boat it is absolutely essential to keep it in peak 'tune'. There is no doubt that all sails have a life-span, so according to how often you use your Topper you will have to replace the sail from time to time. Nevertheless, sensible treatment and care can extend this life-span considerably. Never crumple a sail into its bag after use – always fold it carefully, concertina fashion across the sail parallel to the boom, finally rolling it up as loosely as possible. An even better system is to roll the sail around a plastic pipe, which is slightly less convenient to transport but does totally eliminate creasing. Creasing will not ruin the sail, but could

make it that little bit less efficient.
Salt water will have no short-term ill-effects but always rinse the sail thoroughly in fresh water and dry properly prior to storage.
帆是你的Topper的引擎，因此绝对要使其调较在最佳状态。毫无疑问所有的帆都是有寿命的，所以取决于你使用帆的频次，你总是需要更换新帆，但通过细心呵护是可以大大延长年限的。每次收帆后千万不要胡乱地塞进帆袋，应该把帆小心地平行于横杆叠起来，像手风琴风箱那样漂亮，最终把它轻轻地卷起来。有个更好的办法是把帆卷在一根塑料管上，虽然运输起来稍微麻烦些，但是可以彻底避免折痕。折痕不会令帆面损坏，但是会减少帆效。海水虽然在短期内不会对帆面造成破坏，但是每次储存之前仍然用清水彻底冲洗。

Fastenings 紧固件

There are a number of machine screws on the Topper's hull and these are threaded into expanding brass inserts which work in a similar fashion to a rawlplug. They should be checked periodically for tightness but be careful not to overtighten.
Topper船体上有一些机制螺丝，安装在铜质膨胀套环上。需要不时检查松紧度，避免过紧。

Self bailer and mast gate 排水筏和桅杆插槽

These do not need lubrication but it helps to keep them operating efficiently if you rinse them frequently with fresh water to clear away any abrasive sand and grit that could shorten their lives.
这些都不需要维护， 但是要注意经常用清水冲洗，避免粗沙粒造成的磨损。

Tips on travel and storage 运输和存放的注意事项

Topper hulls distort when left for long periods of time. Try to store them upside- down. The decks seem to distort less than the hulls and anyway don't matter so much in a racing boat.
Choose a trolley that supports the hull under the back of the daggerboard case and under the mast step. It should also have a high handle to save your back and allow the boat to be stored on its deck. The original plastic trolley is very poor. Galvanised steel and lightweight aluminium ones are far better. The latter are "knockdown" which is great if you plan to car-top. A good top cover will also fit as a bottom cover but increasingly sailors are using undercovers as well. These should allow water to escape either by having mesh panels or be made of a material that allows water to seep through. Undercovers protect from the worst of road dirt but more importantly save abrasion.
Foil covers and spar bags are readily available and do make life easier. Trollies are available that fit the normal Laser combi base and this is a good move if you plan to move on to a Laser. There are lots of double and triple stacker trailers around.
如果长时间不被使用，Topper的船身可能会有变形。存放时尽量甲板朝下。甲板比船身的变形小些，但对于一艘竞赛型帆船这些都不是大问题。船车应该支撑在稳向板插槽和桅杆插槽下面的船底位置。有个加高把手，方便控制。船车也应该允许甲板朝下存放。最初的塑料制船车质量很差。而镀锌钢材和轻质铝材船车的性能就好多了。后者对于车顶运输更是独具优势。盖顶式船衣也可以用来保护船底部，但越来越多的人在使用包底式船衣。船衣使用打孔或透水材料排出积水。包底式船衣可以保护船身不被恶劣路面的灰土颗粒污染和磨损。箔片盖布和桅杆套带来很多方便。船车放置在标准激光拖车上，所以如果你想升级到激光船型依然可以继续使用同一个拖车。另外还可以选用双层或三层的专用拖架。

摄影：付琼鸽

16 The International Topper Class Association

国际Topper级别委员会ITCA

The Topper is one of the world’s fastest-growing dinghy classes and enjoys one of the best-supported and best-administered class associations.
The International Topper Class Association (ITCA) has divisions in many countries. Membership is mandatory to be eligible for ITCA events.
There are many benefits of belonging to ITCA: members receive free of charge the magazine Topper Times which gives full information and reports on Topper events, regattas and other social activities. The association defines (and polices) the rules of the class – making sure that racing is fair and that the older boats remain competitive. And, perhaps most important of all, the association will help you communicate with other Topper sailors and thus enjoy your boat to the full – whether you are a beginner or a budding World Champion!
The addresses of your National and International Secretaries can be obtained from the manufacturers:

Topper是世界上发展速度最快的稳向板级别之一。级别组织管理高效，提供很好的服务。国际Topper级别委员会ITCA在很多国家有分部。会员有资格参加ITCA的活动和赛事。成为会员有很多好处：免费得到“Topper时代“杂志，里面包含各种信息和各类赛事及社会活动的报道。该协会制定级别规则——保证赛事的公平性并且确保老旧船只依然保持竞争力。最重要的是ITCA会帮助你和全世界的Topper爱好者交流，无论你是初学者还是老牌冠军都可以享受Topper带来的乐趣。
我很高兴地得知中国Topper级别委员会已经在2016年8月正式成立，并得到了ITCA International的认可。
你可以从Topper 制造商那里获得你的国家和国际Topper组织的信息：

Topper International Limited
Kingsnorth Technology Park
Wotton Road
Ashford
Kent
TN23 6LN
England
www.toppersailboats.com

Also (amongst others):
www.itcaworld.org
www.gbrtopper.co.uk
www.irltopper.com

Part 2 第二部分

The Topper 4.2

摄影：张琦

Part 2 第二部分
The Topper 4.2

The 4.2 sail is nearly 20% smaller than the standard one. The sail area has been taken out of the leech (back of the sail) making the boat better balanced in a breeze. The end of the boom is three inches higher, so there is less tendency for the boom to hit the water when the boat heels on a reach. And if you do capsize, the boat is far easier to right because there is less sail area to drag through the water.

This rig is designed for lighter / younger sailors who find the Topper a handful. But all the feedback is that it is a great rig for everyone, and older sailors find it a delight in a blow. Indeed, in a regatta or series you can choose to use the 4.2 rig and sail against the standard boats provided you stick to your chosen rig throughout – the ‘single sail rule’. It might be worth considering this at a windy venue! In the UK we now have Topper 4.2 National and Inland Championships as well as regular regattas that run on their own courses. There is also a Topper 4.2 National Squad that has brought on the sub 45kg sailors in a way that was not possible with just the normal sized (5.3m) sail.

Apart from the sail, the rest of the gear is standard, including the mast. And the settings are the same, too. (But, because the sail is cut flatter, you may not need to put such huge amounts of tension on the control lines.)

4.2的帆比标准型帆的面积小20%。帆面的后部被切掉一块，让船在微风中的平衡性更好。横杆的尾部要高3英寸，因此横风航行时不易碰到水面。船体翻覆时也更容易回正，因为较小的帆面在水中的阻力也较小。

索具的设计让体重较轻或年龄小的选手也容易控制。所有的人都反馈良好，老年选手在大风中也可以获得乐趣。在比赛中如果坚持“单面帆原则”，可以选择4.2帆型和标准帆型进行较量。在大风的场地里更值得考虑使用4.2帆型。在英国已经有4.2级别的全国锦标赛和内湖比赛，并且使用专门的航线。甚至已经成立了4.2级别的Topper国家队，让体重轻于45公斤的选手获得了用标准帆型不可能得到的进步。

除了帆之外，其他的索具和桅杆都是标准的，配置也相同（不过由于帆型较平，你不需要让控制索具拉力过紧）。

The smaller 4.2 sail (left) in comparison to the reefed 5.3 sail (right).
4.2帆（左）与缩帆后的5.3帆（右）的对比。

The racers gather in their Topper 4.2's.
4.2 级别的选手集结在一起。

The Topper 4.2 is great for lighter racers!
4.2级Topper适用于体重轻的选手

Part 3 第三部分

Racing: the basics

比赛：基本技巧

摄影：Simon McIlwaine

Part 3 第三部分

Racing: the basics 比赛：基本技巧

Don’t forget that, beginner or not, you will be a very welcome addition to the fleet. Those who usually do well, the ‘hotshots’, will be only too pleased to come home having beaten a larger fleet. Those nearer the back will welcome the chance to perhaps beat someone! Don’t be disappointed if you finish last – just give it a go. Do remember that, particularly in the heat of the start, some competitors can get a bit excited and may shout at you if they think you are infringing the rules. Don’t let this worry you; they may not have had time to realise that you are a beginner and you will probably find that back in the clubhouse they are quite friendly. But do speak to them about any such incident afterwards, particularly if you are unsure of which rule you may have infringed. It’s a good chance to learn as well as make friends.

别忘了，不管你是否是初学者，都热烈欢迎你加入Topper船队。那些经常取胜的所谓“高手”，只有在一场更大的赛事中获胜才会满足。那些经常落后的人如果击败了某些人就会喜不自禁。即使你最后冲线也不要沮丧——坚持！你要记住，特别是在出发时的拥挤中，某些赛手会激动起来大声叫喊说你犯规了。不必介意这些，也许他们并不知道你是个初学者，而回到俱乐部后他们会变得很友好。不过你一定要和他们交流，搞清楚你违反了哪条规则。这是一个学习提高和交朋友的好机会。

THE RULES 规则

A full discussion of the rules is outside the scope of this book: see The Rules in Practice by Bryan Willis. For the cautious beginner, a few key rules will keep you out of trouble in most cases.

本书不会全面地讨论规则。您可以阅读Bryan Willis撰写的《实操规则》一书。对于谨慎的初学者，掌握一些关键规则就可以让你在大多数情况下避免陷入麻烦。

Boats meeting on opposite tacks
非同舷风的船相遇

A boat is either on a port tack or a starboard tack. It is on a port tack if the wind is blowing over its port side. In Figure 1, boats A, B and C are on port tack; boats D, E and F are on starboard tack.

A port tack boat must keep clear of a starboard tack boat.

D, E and F have right of way over A, B and C, who must keep clear.

船只航行时要么是左舷风要么是右舷风，当风从船的左舷吹来就是左舷风航行。在图1中，A,B,C三条船都是左舷风航行，D,E,F三条船是右舷风航行。**左舷风航行的船必须为右舷风船让路（左让右）**。因此A,B,C船必须把航线让给D,E,F船。

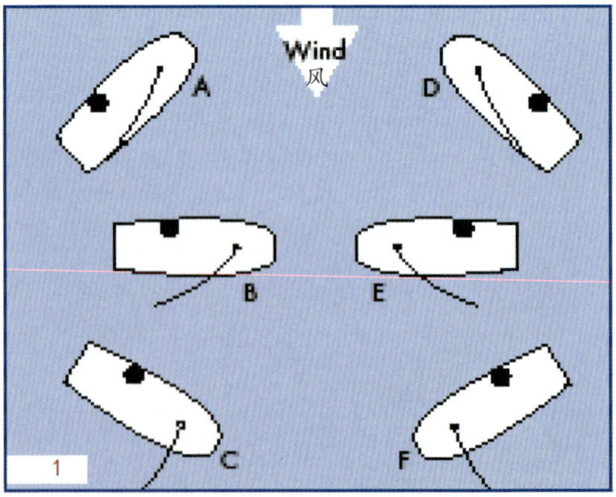

Boats meeting on the same tack
同舷风航行的船相遇

If the boats are overlapped (i.e. if the bow of the following boat is ahead of a line at right angles to the stern of the leading boat) the following rule applies:

A windward boat shall keep clear of a leeward boat.

In Figure 2, G must keep clear of H, I must keep clear of J and L must keep clear of K.

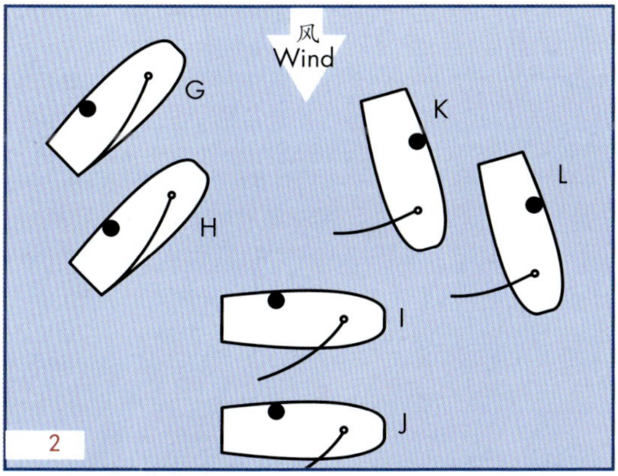

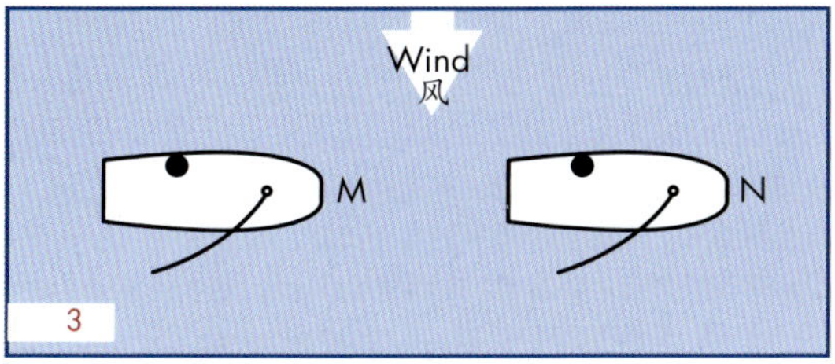

If the boats are not overlapped (Figure 3):

A boat clear astern shall keep clear of a boat clear ahead.

If M is sailing faster it is not allowed to sail into the back of N.

如果两条船重叠（也就是说，后面船的船头超过了前面船船尾的垂直线），规则如下：**上风船必须让行下风船（上让下）**。在图2中，G船必须为H船让路。I船必须为J船让路而L船必须为K船让路。如果两条船没有重叠（图3），**后面的船必须让行前面的船**。如果M船的速度更快，就不能驶入N船的后面。

Boats meeting at marks 船只在标区相遇

An outside boat shall give each boat overlapping it on the inside room to round or pass the mark.

P must give O room to go round the mark on the inside. O must get his overlap on P before P’s bow reaches an imaginary circle of radius three boat’s lengths from the mark (Figure 4).

Note that this rule does not apply at start marks

如果两船重叠，外面的船必须给里面的船足够的空间绕标或通过。P船必须给内侧的O船足够空间绕标（外让内）。O船必须在以标为中心，半径为三个船长的标区里和P船重叠（图4）。请注意这一规则并不适用于起航标。

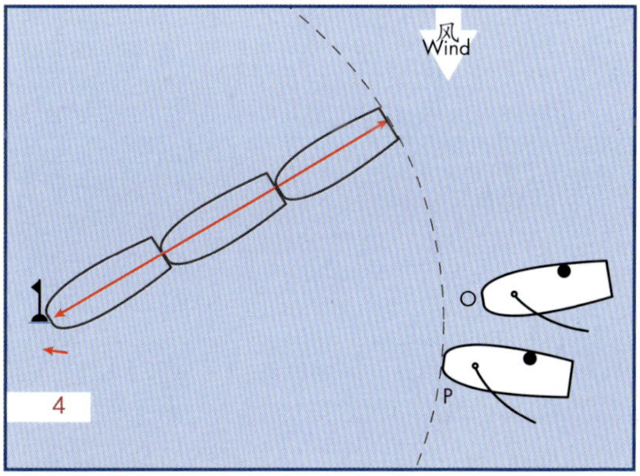

Penalties 判罚

If you hit a mark, you must sail clear and do a one turn penalty including a tack and a gybe (Figure 5) (see chapter 12). You have no rights while you are doing this penalty turn.

If you hit another boat and reckon you’re in the right, shout ‘protest’. Argue your case in the protest room afterwards.If you hit another boat and are in the wrong, you may exonerate yourself by sailing clear and doing a two turn penalty. (see chapter 12). You have to do two tacks and two gybes (Figure 6).

如果你碰到了浮标，你必须在空旷水域自行绕一圈，包括一个迎风转向和顺风转向（图5）（见第12章）。你在受罚绕圈时没有航行优先权。

如果你碰到了别的船并认为自己没有犯规，要大声喊“抗议”。之后要到仲裁室申请仲裁。如果你因为犯规而碰到了别的船，要自行到空旷水域绕两圈（见第12章），做两个迎风转向和两个顺风转向（图6）。

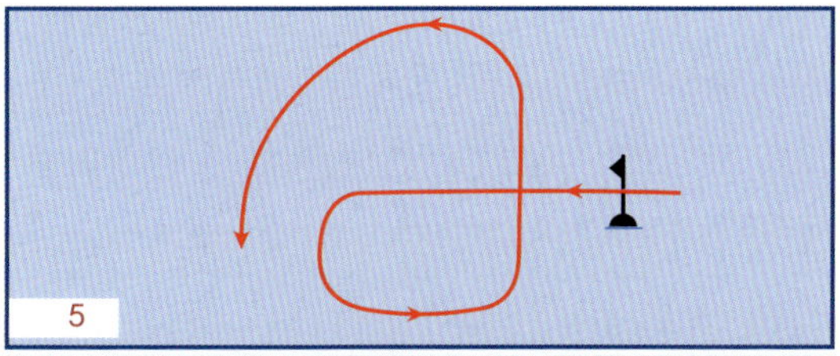

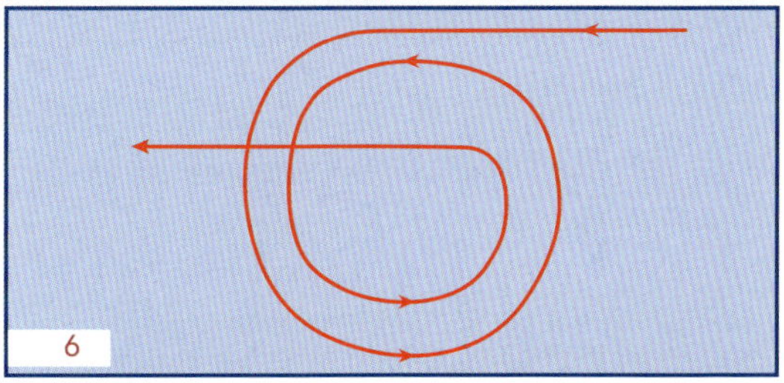

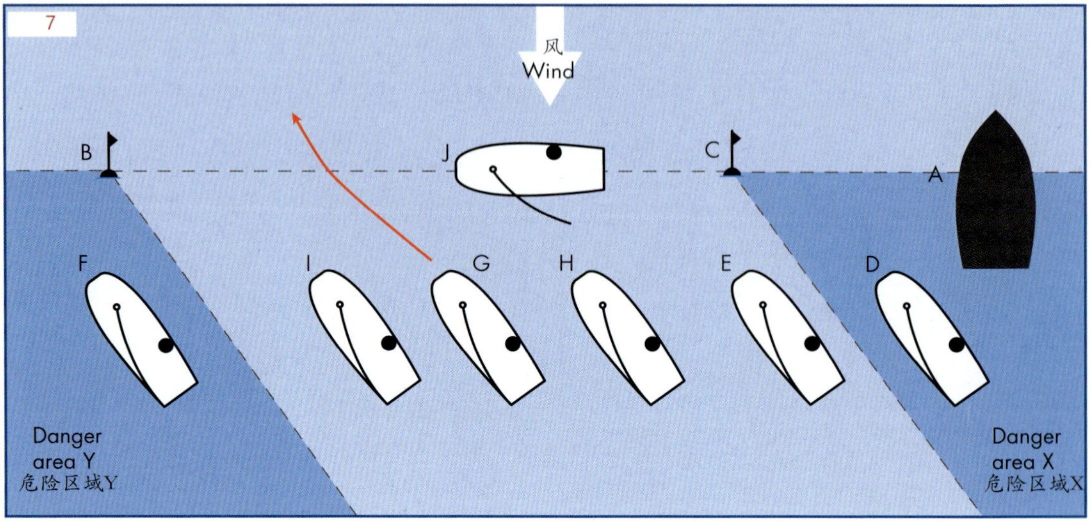

THE LINE START 起航线

The start is the most important part of the race. If you get a bad start, you have to overtake everyone to win – while you' re battling past the opposition, the leaders are sailing further ahead. If you get a good start, you' re sailing in clear air.

起航是比赛中最重要的部分。如果起航很糟糕，你必须超过所有的船才可能赢得比赛——当你拼命超越对手时，领先的船可能会越来越远。如果起航很出色，你就会在干净的风中顺利航行。

大部分的比赛都是迎风起航。竞赛委员会在裁判船桅杆(A)和起航浮标(B)（图7）之间设立一条想象的起航线。通常还会设立一个浮标(C)，不一定在起航线上。A和C之间不允许船只航行。一般在出发前五分钟会在裁判船升起级别旗并伴随着鸣号。出发前四分钟会升起蓝色P旗并鸣号。出发前一分钟蓝色P旗降下并鸣号。起航时，级别旗降下并鸣号。起航信号发出前，所有的船都必须在起航线之后。你的目标是在起航时正好压在起航线之后并全速前进。

How is a race started?
比赛如何开始？

Most races are started on a beat. The race committee sets an (imaginary) start line, usually between the mast of the committee boat (A) and a buoy (B) (Figure 7). They often lay another buoy (C), which does not have to be on the line. Boats are not allowed to sail between C and A.Normally five minutes before the start the class flag is raised on the committee boat and a gun is fired. Four minutes before the start the Blue Peter is raised and a sound signal is made.

One minute before the start the Blue Peter is lowered and a long sound signal is made.

At the start, the class flag is lowered and a sound signal is made.

Boats must be behind the start line when the starting signal is made. Your aim is to be just behind the line, sailing at full speed, at the start.

How can I get a good start?
如何成功起航？

Set your watch at the five-minute signal, and check it at the four-minute signal. During the last few minutes, avoid the ‘danger’ areas X and Y. From X you cannot get on to the start line because the boats to leeward have right of way. Boat D, for example, will be forced the wrong side of buoy C. In Y you are bound to pass the wrong side of buoy B. Boat F has this problem.

Don' t go too far from the line – 30 yards is plenty. A wall of boats builds up on the line in the last two minutes, and you must be in that wall. If you' re behind it, not only can you not get in, but your wind is cut off by the wall.

Aim to be six boat lengths behind the line with 45 seconds to go – closer if boats to windward are moving ahead of you. Control your speed with careful use of the mainsheet. Keep the boat moving forward slowly – most of the sail will be flapping but take care not to stop or you will have no steerage way. With ten seconds to go you should be two lengths behind the line. Pull in the mainsheet, sit out and start beating. You should cross the line just after the gun with full speed. Boat G has followed this advice.

在起航前五分钟设定你的手表倒计时。并在四分钟时检查。在最后几分钟里，避免驶入危险的X和Y区域。在X区域你无法到达起航线，因为下风船有优先权。比如说D船就可能被逼到浮标C的错误一侧。在Y区域你也会被迫从错误的一侧通过浮标B，F船就有这个麻烦。不要离起航线太远——别超过30码（约27米）。最后两分钟时，沿着起航线会形成一排船墙，你必须置身其中。如果你在这堵墙的后面，你不仅插不进去，而且你的风也会被船墙挡住。在45秒时要距离起航线6个船长——如果有上风船要挡在你前面，你就驶近起航线。用主缭小心地控制速度。保持船慢慢前进——大部分的船都会飘帆，但小心不要让船停止否则你将无法机动。十秒钟时你必须距离起航线两个船长。收紧主缭向外压舷并转向迎风。在起航号响起时你要提速并越过起航线。G船就是这样做的。

What about the other boats?
别的船怎么办？

It's important to watch out for other boats as you line up to start. G has right of way over H, but must keep clear of I. As you line up, keep turning into the wind a little. This keeps you away from the boat to leeward – it also opens up a nice 'hole' to leeward that you can sail down into at the start (for extra speed).

Don't reach down the line with 15 seconds to go like boat J. You will have no rights over G, H and I who will sail into you. If you're too early, let the sail out in good time and slow down.

你在排队起航时一定要注意旁边的船。G船对H船具有优先权，但必须让行I船。在起航线附近你要略微向上风靠一些，这样可以远离下风船并且在你和下风船之间留下一个“空洞”，可以让你在起航前向下风获得更好的速度。不要像J船那样在十五秒时就到达起航线，这样你必须为向你靠近的G,H和I船让行。如果太早到达，放出主帆降低船速。

Which end of the line should I start?
选择起航线的哪一端起航？

So far, the wind has been at right angles to the start line. As far as the wind is concerned it will not matter where on the line you start.

Usually, however, the wind is not at right angles to the line. You can find out what it's doing by sailing down the line on a reach. Adjust the sail so the front just flaps (Figure 8). Keeping the mainsheet in the same position, tack and reach back down the line. In Figure 9, the sail will now be too far in – you will have to let the mainsheet out to make it flap. This indicates the wind is blowing from the starboard end of the line – and you should start at this end.

理论上风向总是垂直于起航线，所以从风向的角度来说，你从起航线的任何一个点出发都可以。但很多情况下风向并不是垂直于起航线。你可以通过沿起航线横风航行来找到实际风向变化。调整主帆让帆的前部飘动（图8）。保持主缭的位置不动，转向回头，沿起航线横风航行。在图9中，你会发现主帆收得过紧，你必须放出主缭才能让帆飘动。这表明风从起航线偏右的方向吹来——因此你应该从右侧起航。

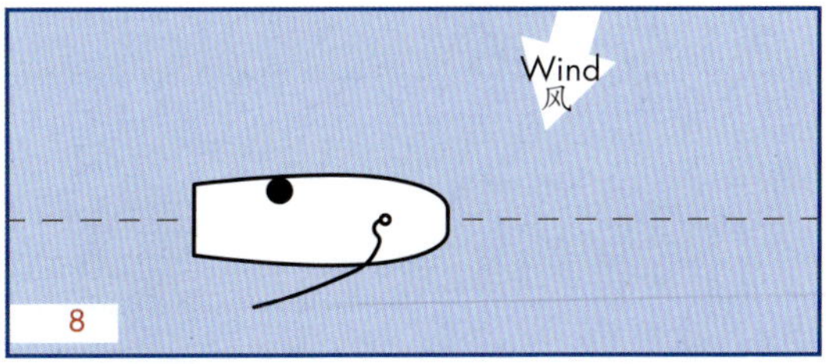

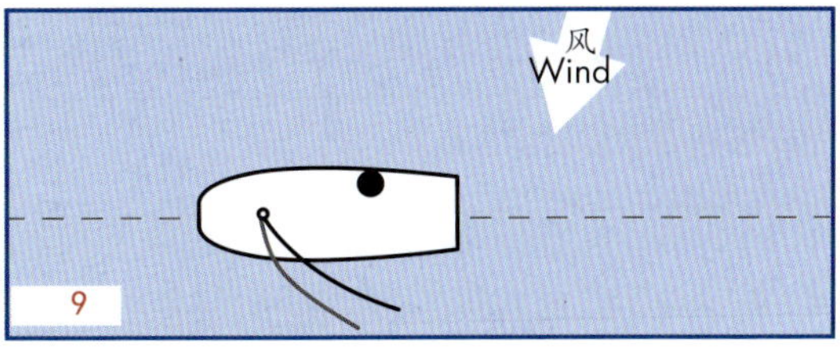

How do I make a starboard end start?
如何从起航线右端出发？

Sail slowly, and as close to the wind as possible, so you will reach the windward end of the line with the gun (Figure 10). Boats to windward have no rights and are forced out. Boats to leeward can't

touch you – you’re already sailing as close to the wind as possible.
慢速航行并尽可能上风，这样你就可以到达起航线的上风端（靠近裁判船一侧）（图10）。在你上风的船必须让行，可能被你逼出起航线之外。而你的下风船也不能碰你——因为你已经足够上风了。

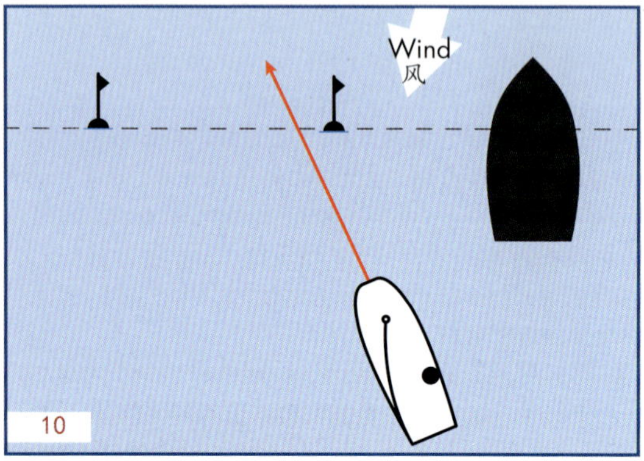

How do I make a port end start?
如何从起航线左端出发？

Keep near the port end of the line (Figure 11). Aim to cross as near the buoy as possible. Tack onto port tack as soon as you can clear the fleet.
如图11所示，尽量靠近起航线的左端，尽可能靠近浮标起航，然后迎风转向进入左舷航行，远离船队。

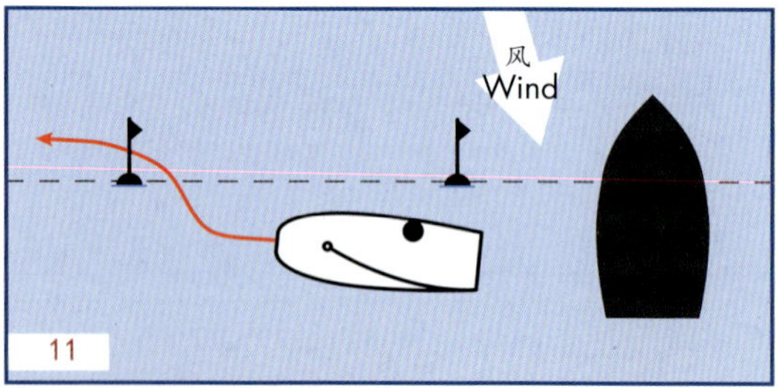

THE GATE START
门式起航

A gate start is made by crossing the wake of a boat called the pathfinder which is beating on port tack in front of the fleet. In theory everyone has an equally good start, because the earlier you start the further you have to sail. The pathfinder, who is selected by the race committee from among the competitors, waits near the committee boat while the usual sound and flag signals are made. About one minute before the start the pathfinder sets off on port tack, accompanied by two motor boats, the gate boat and guard boat, to protect it from overenthusiastic competitors (Figure 12). A few seconds before the start a free-floating buoy is dropped over the back of the gate boat to mark the port (left-hand) end of the line. After the start, competitors (on starboard tack) pass closely behind the gate boat (Figure 13). The line gradually lengthens, and boats start one at a time. A late start is no disadvantage, since the pathfinder is sailing up the beat for you while you’re waiting.
门式起航指在船队的前面安排一条左舷迎风航行的船（称作“探路者”），其他的船穿过“探路者”的尾迹。从理论上说每条船都可以做出同等漂亮的起航，因为你越早出发你的航线就越长。“探路者”是由竞赛委员会从比赛选手中选出，它在五分钟信号时在裁判船附近等待，倒计时一分钟时它在两条机动艇（称作门标艇和护卫艇）的保护下开始左舷迎风移动（图12）。几秒钟之后，门标艇扔出一个自由浮标作为左舷标（起航线左端），起航信号发出后，右舷风航行的选手们紧挨着从护卫艇后面穿过（图13），起航线逐渐延长，选手渐次出发。后起航的船并不吃亏，因为在他们等待时，“探路者”扫清了前方障碍。

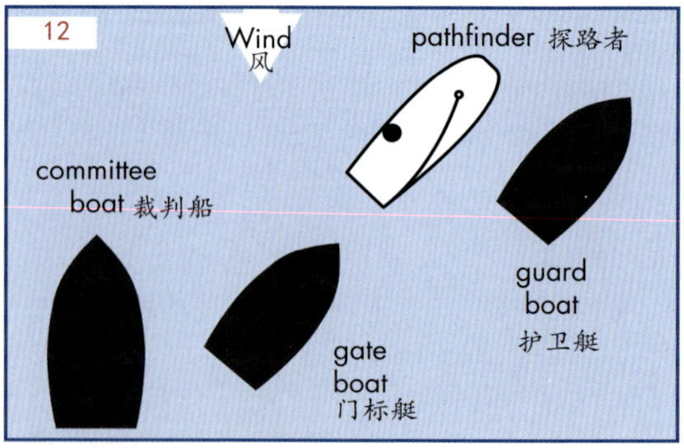

How can I get a good start?
如何漂亮地起航？

You need to know the course the pathfinder will take. So, with about four minutes to go, begin beating on port tack from the committee boat. After two or three minutes bear away onto a reach, then tack and wait with your sail flapping (like boat Y in Figure 13). Watch for the pathfinder, and control your speed so that you beat slowly up to the stern of the guard boat. As you go behind it, pick up speed by bearing away slightly and sitting out. Then beat, flat out, to pass just behind the stern of the gate boat.

NEVER reach towards the guard boat like boat X. You have no rights over boats D and E who will push you into the guard boat or gate boat. If you hit either, you will be disqualified. If you find yourself in boat X’s position, try to tack onto port and bear away. When you’re ready, tack back onto starboard and try again. If all else fails, point into the wind and stop!

你必须了解“探路者”将要行驶的航线。当四分钟倒计时左右，开始左舷迎风驶离裁判船。两三分钟后转向下风做横风航行，然后迎风转向并飘帆等待（如图13中的Y船）。观察“探路者”，控制船速慢慢迎风靠近护卫艇的船尾。当你来到护卫艇后面，稍稍下风并向外压舷，提速航行，刚好通过门标艇的尾部。千万不要像X船那样以横风状态靠近护卫艇，因为你对D船和E船都没有优先权，他们会让你被迫驶向护卫艇或门标艇。而如果你碰到了任何一艘艇，就会失去比赛资格。如果你已经处于X船的位置，要转向为左舷航行，然后转向下风。时机成熟时再转向为右舷迎风航行，尝试起航。如果这一切都无效，那就让船头正迎风并停下来。

How can I recover from a bad start?
起航不好如何赶上来？

If you start too far from the gate boat, your only option is to sail through the gate, then tack onto port and sail behind the whole fleet to the right-hand side of the course. If that turns out to be the best side, you could find yourself ahead at the windward mark!

如果起航时你离门标艇太远，唯一的办法是穿过起航门，然后迎风转向进入左舷迎风，在船队后面直奔航线的右端。如果运气好的话，你可以领先到达上风标。

Where should I start?
在何处起航？

Start late if you think you are slower than the pathfinder, if you think the pathfinder will hit a permanent header (see page 95) or if the tide is more favourable to the right of the course. Otherwise start early.

下列情况下要滞后起航：你的船速低于“探路者”，或者你判断“探路者”会撞到持续下风摆（见95页），或者潮流有利于航线的右端。其他情况下要选择早起航。

THE BEAT 迎风段

After the tension of the start, it’s important to settle down and concentrate on sailing hard.

在紧张的起航之后，要平静下来，专注于努力航行。

13

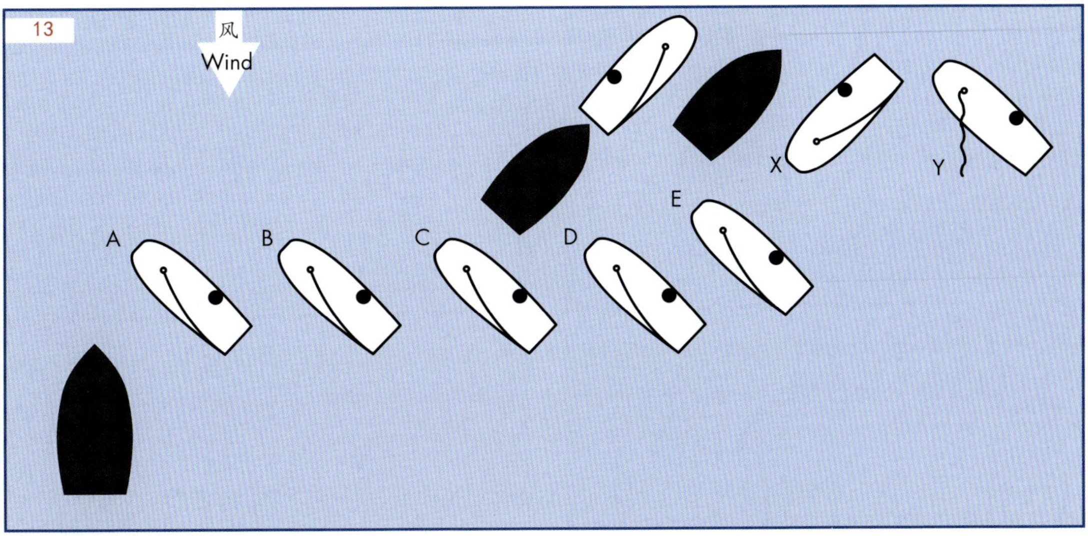

What about other boats?
其他船的影响

A boat when beating casts a ‘wind shadow’ – shown in Figure 14. It also creates an area of disturbed air to windward due to the wind being deflected by the sail; the air behind the boat is also disturbed. You should therefore avoid sailing just to windward of another boat, behind it, or in its wind shadow. In Figure 14, boat B should either tack or bear away to clear its wind. Boats D and F should both tack.

帆船迎风航行时会产生“风影”—见图14。同时由于帆的作用，在船的上风侧一片区域也产生风的扰动。船的后部区域的风也被扰动。因此你要避免另一条船的上风侧、正后侧及其风影区航行。在图14中，B船应该做迎风转向或转向下风，以获得干净的风。D、F船也都应该迎风转向。

Which way should I go?
我应该向哪里去?

You may have to modify your course to take account of tides and windshifts, but your first aim should be to make reasonably long tacks to start with, shortening them as you approach the windward mark.

在规划航线时应该考虑到水流和风摆。但首要的目标是在起航后走长一点的航线（然后转向），接近上风标时可以缩小每次转向的航程。

Don’t sail into the area indicated by the shaded part of Figure 15 – if you do, you will have to

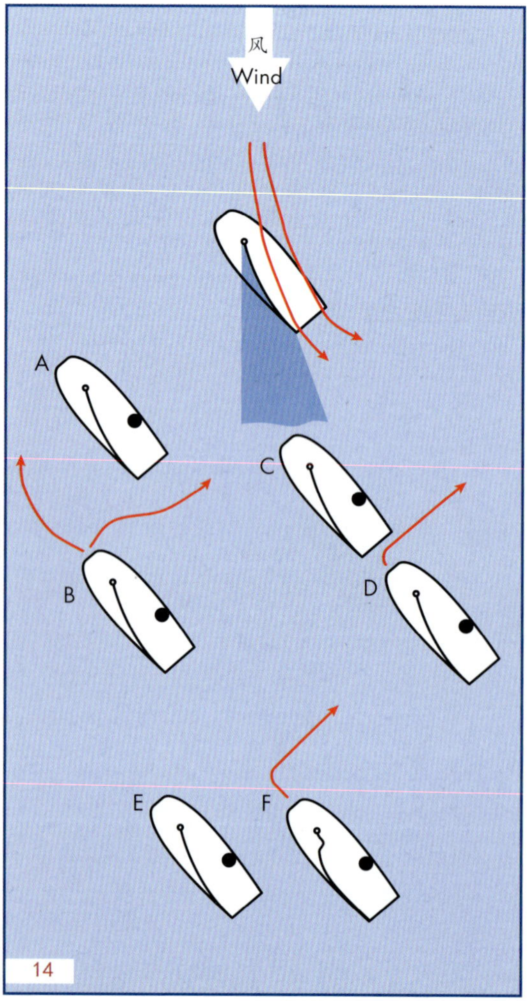

14

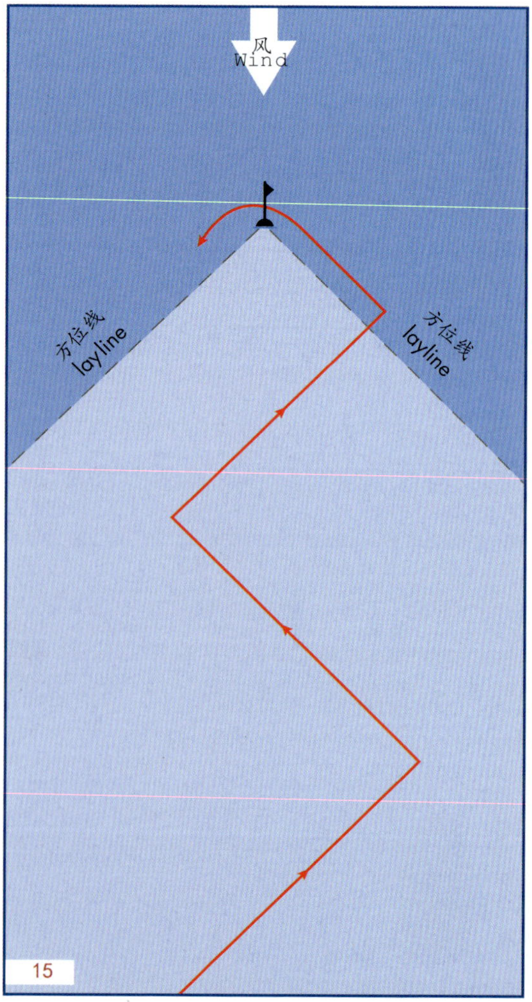

15

reach in to the buoy and will lose valuable time and distance. Stay inside the laylines – these are the paths you would sail when beating to hit the windward mark.
不要进入图15所标注的阴影区。否则你就要横风航行到上风标，因距离加长而浪费宝贵的时间。保持在基准线内侧，这是你迎风驶向上风标的线路。
When approaching the windward mark on the first beat in a big fleet it is advisable not to arrive at the mark on port tack. For safety' s sake make your final approach on starboard tack.
当你在第一个迎风段处在船队之中接近上风标时，建议你不要以左舷迎风方式到达。为安全起见接近标时要右舷迎风航行。

Windshifts 风摆

Once you are confident at beating and can tack efficiently, you are ready to start using windshifts.
当你已经可以自信地迎风航行并有效地迎风转向后，就可以开始利用风摆了。风的方向是随时变化的。有些风摆力度更大，持续更长——这是你需要有效利用的。
The wind constantly alters in direction about its mean. Some of the shifts are more pronounced and last longer than others – it is these that you have to spot and use. In shifty winds, stay close to the middle of the beat. Tack each time the wind heads you (forces you to alter course away from the mark). In Figure 16, the boat takes no account of windshifts. Note how little progress it makes

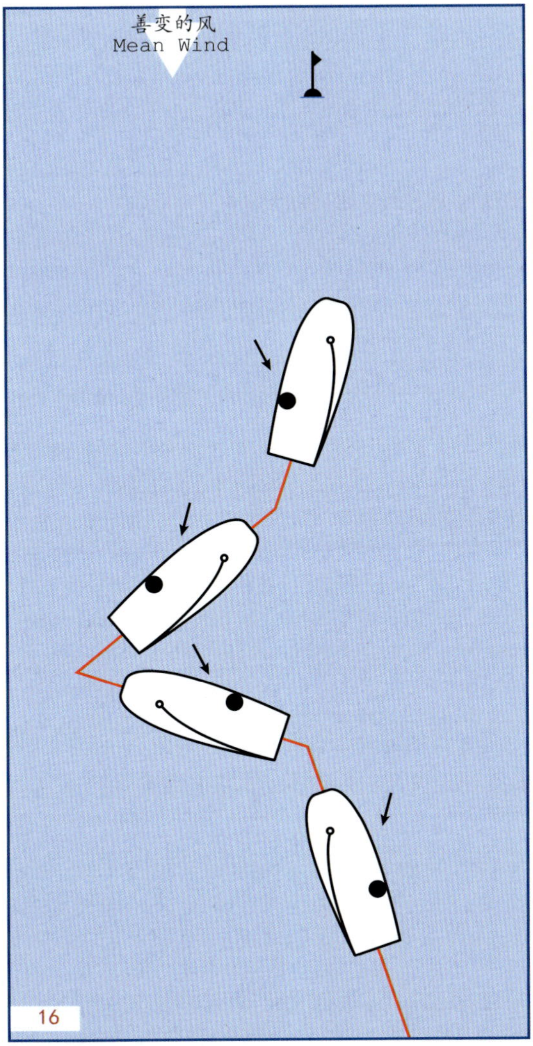

16

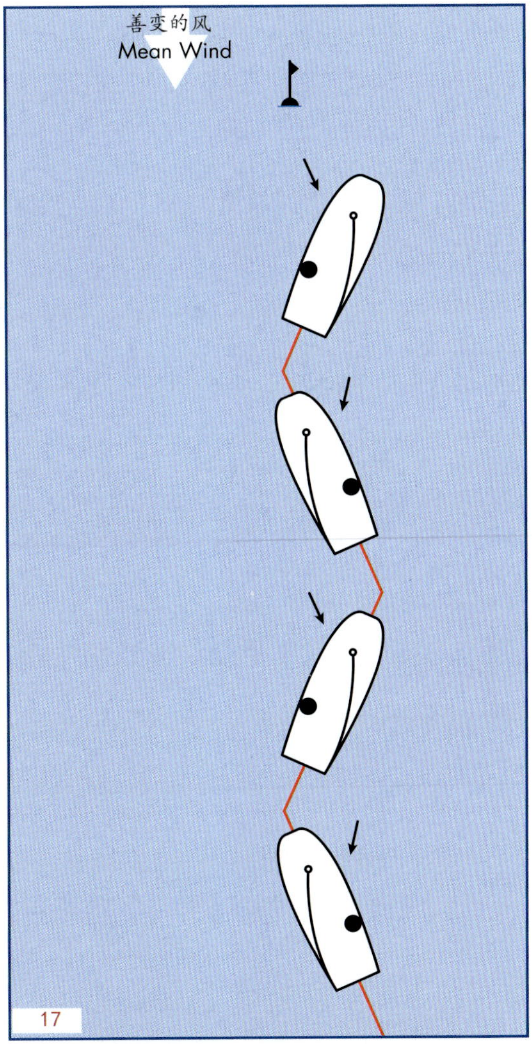

17

compared with the boat in Figure 17, which tacks each time the wind heads it.
The main problem is to differentiate between a real shift and a short-lived change in the wind. For that reason, sail on into each shift for five or ten seconds to make sure it’s going to last. If a header lasts that long, tack.
If you find yourself tacking too often, or are confused, sail on one tack for a while until you’re sure what the wind is doing. Remember that you lose at least a boat’s length each time you tack, so there has to be a good reason to do so. (see page 95)
当风摆频繁时，尽可能在迎风航行时靠近风。每当风把你推离目标时就做转向调整。在图16中，船没有针对风摆进行转向调整，而图17中的船则在每次风摆时都进行转向，

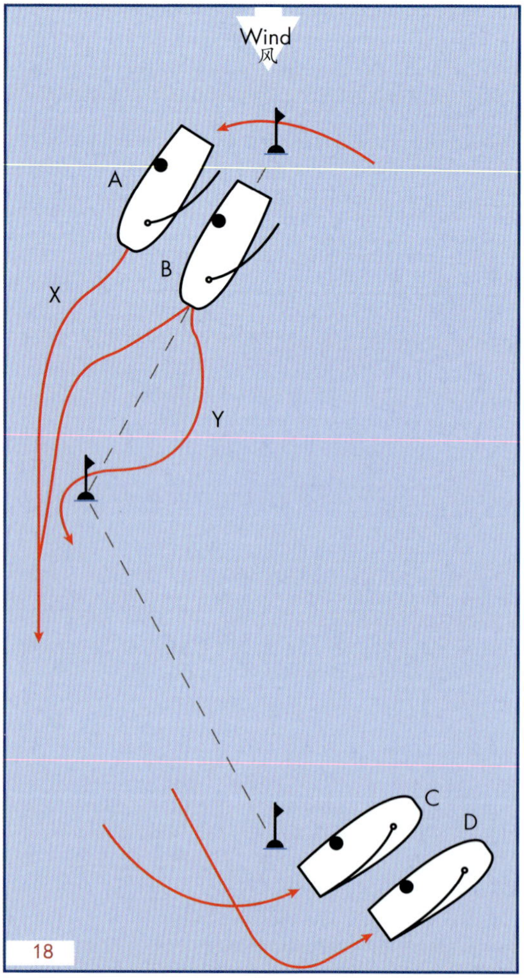

两者的结果相差很大。主要的麻烦是如何区分真正的风摆和短暂的风向变化。因此在每次风向变化时等待5~10秒钟来判断是否风摆是持续的，如果是就转向。如果你发现自己转向太过频繁或者有些茫然，就保持航向直到你确认风是如何变化的。要记住你每做一次转向就会损失一个船身的距离，所以一定要明确的理由才能转向。（见95页）

How can I get up the beat faster? 如何在迎风段提速？

- Keep your wind clear.
  保证你获得干净风。
- Watch for windshifts. 观察风摆。
- Keep near the middle of the course.
  保持在航线中间位置。
- Practise tacking. 干净利落地转向。
- Get fit – then you can sit out harder!
  保持好的体型——让你能够尽量向外压舷！

THE REACH 横风段

If it’s blowing hard, pull the daggerboard half up before you bear away round the windward mark. Turn slowly, moving your weight back and letting out the mainsheet.
如果风力较大，在绕标并转向下风之前把稳向板收起一半。慢速转向，身体向后移动并放出主帆。

What course should I steer? 选择哪种航线？

The quickest way down the reach is a straight line from one mark to the next. However, if your rivals let you sail this course, you’re lucky! The problem is that overtaking boats (e.g. A in Figure 18) push up to windward. The boats to leeward (e.g. B) get nervous about their wind being stolen and steer high also. The result is that everyone sails an enormous arc (X), losing ground on the leaders.
横风下行航段中最快的方式就是沿两个标的连线直线航行。当然，如果你的对手给你机会直线航行就太幸运了！麻烦是后面的船会试图从前船的上风侧超越（图18中的A船）处于下风侧的前船会担心风被后船盖住而被迫驶向上风，结果就是大家都走了一条大弧线（航线X），拉大与领先者的距离。

You have to decide whether or not to go on the ‘great circle’; the alternative is to sail a leeward path (Y). You have to go down far enough to avoid the blanketing effect of the boats to windward – but usually you will sail a shorter distance than they do. You can go for the leeward route on the second reach too, but this time you will be on the outside at the turn.
你必须要选择是否走这条大弧线。另一个选择是走下风航线（Y）。你要向下风偏转以避免上风侧的船形成的“风影效应”——这样你走的距离会比对手短一些。第二圈的时候你依然可以走下风航线，但这一次你应该走外侧。

How can I get down the reach faster?
如何在横风段快速航行？

- Follow the tips for fast reaching under ‘Going faster’ on page 44.
  按照44页的横风“快速航行”的要诀。
- Keep your wind clear. 保持干净的风。
- Sail the shortest route.
  尽可能选择最短航线。
- Go for the inside turn at marks.
  过标时争取内侧绕标。

Starting the next beat
开始下一段迎风航行

As you approach the leeward mark, tighten the downhaul and push down the daggerboard. Steer round the mark so that you leave it very close (like boat C). Don’t come in to the mark close (like boat D) or you’ll start the beat well to leeward of your rivals. Sit out and go!
接近下风标时，拉紧下拉索并把稳向板放到底。过标时尽量贴近标（像C船）。D船不要太贴近标，否则就会在迎风段被迫在对手的下风侧航行（处在风影中），向外压舷前进！

THE RUN 顺风段

In strong winds, take your time as you bear away on to a run. Pull the daggerboard half up, sit back and adjust the mainsheet as you turn. If the boat starts to roll, steer a straight course and pull in the mainsheet a little. Continue to bear away when the boat is under control.
在大风时，转向下风进入顺风段时要格外注意。将稳向板拔起一半，转向时向后坐并且调整主缭。如果船开始翻转，收进主缭直线航行一段，把船控制住后继续向下风转向。

What course should I steer?
选择哪种航线？

The quickest route is a straight line to the leeward mark (Figure 19). In very strong winds, you may not be able to control the boat on a straight downwind run. An alternative is to follow course Z, wearing round (see page 98) rather than gybing at the midpoint.
The presence of other boats may also prevent you steering a straight course. Boat F is blanketed by boat E – it can escape by steering to one side (course M or N). Other things being equal, N would be better since it gives the inside turn at the next mark.
Boat E is correct to blanket F in this way.
E can attack from a range of up to four boat’s lengths; it can sail right up behind F, turning to one side at the last moment to overtake.
E must, of course, keep clear of F during this manoeuvre. Watch out for boats still beating, especially when running on port tack. Alter course in good time to avoid them – a last minute turn could capsize you.
最快的线路是直线驶向下风标。在强风条件下保持直线顺风航行可能会控制不住船。可以选择航线Z，在航线中点绕一圈而不是做顺风转向（见98页）。其他船的存在也可能让你无法直线航行。F船的风被E船挡住，可以选择转向M或N航线来解决风影问题。航线N更有利些，因为你可以在过下风标时以内侧绕标。E船比F船更有利因为可以挡住对手的风。E可以在离F船4个船长的距离内开始超越，一直追到F船的正后方，在最后一刻转到F船的一侧进行超越。而E船必须要为对方让行。一定要观察在迎风航行的船，尤其是左舷顺风时。及时改变航线避开迎风船——如果仓促转向有可能造成翻覆。

What about crowding at the leeward mark?
在下风标挤成一团怎么办？

It often happens that several boats arrive at the leeward mark together. The inside berth is the

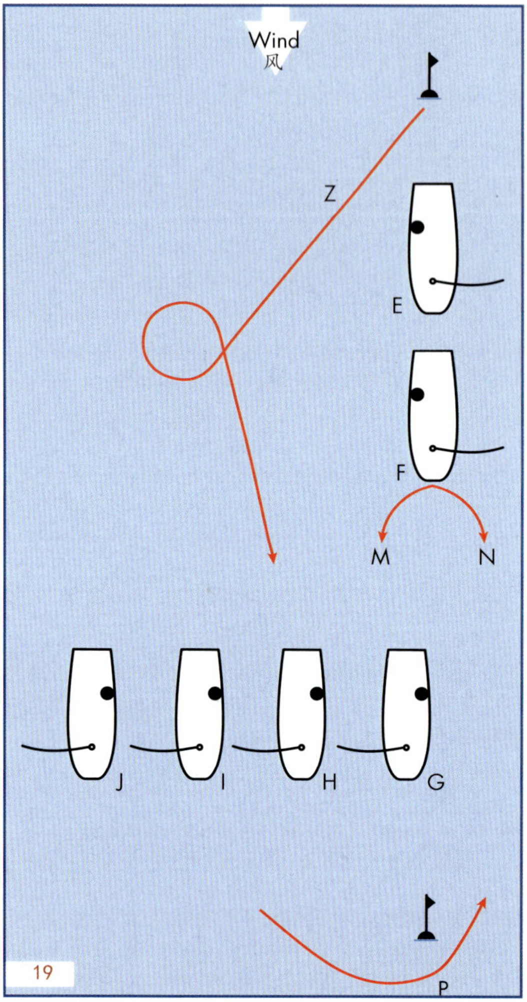

place to aim for – H, I and J have to give G room to turn inside them. If you're in J's position, it's better to slow down and wait to turn close to the buoy rather than sail round the outside of the pack. Try to anticipate this situation, and slow down and move across to the inside in good time. Try to get G's position.

As you get near the leeward mark, tighten the downhaul and push the daggerboard down. Turn slowly and aim to leave the mark close (course P). You will need to pull in a good length of mainsheet as you round the mark – pull it in using both hands as described on pages 41 - 42.

经常会发生几条船同时到达下风标的情况。尽量争取处在最内侧的位置——H,I和J都要给G留出空间绕标。如果你处在J的位置，最好减速等待，从下风标的近处通过而不要在船队的外侧远处过标。尝试着减速并及时贴到内侧。最好处在G的位置。接近下风标时收紧下拉索，把稳向板全部放下，慢慢地转向并贴近绕标（航线P）。绕标时需要收紧很长的主缭长度——按照41页、42页的要领用双手收紧主缭。

How can I get down the run faster?
如何在顺风段快速航行？

- Follow the 'Going faster' tips on page 61. 按照61页“快速航行”的要领去做。
- Keep your wind clear. 保持干净的风。
- Sail the shortest route. 选择最短航线。
- Go for the inside turn at the leeward mark. 在下风标处内侧绕标。

CURRENTS AND TIDES
水流和潮汐

When sailing, you must take account of currents and tides. Naturally, when sailing against the current you will look for a course where the current is weakest, and when you are sailing with the current you will go where it is strongest. The current is weakest in shallow water and near the shore (where friction with the land slows it down). Before you go afloat make sure you know the likely strength and direction of the tides across the race course.

航行时一定要考虑水流和潮汐的影响。在顶流航行时，你很自然地就会寻找水流最小的地方航行。顺流航行时肯定要在水流最强的地方。近岸的浅水区域的水流最弱（因为岸底的摩擦减小了流速）。下水之前你应该了解比赛航线区域的潮流速度和方向。

Beating against the tide
迎风顶流航行

Enormous gains can be made at the start over the majority of the competition who will disregard the effect of the tide. Get to the line early and stem the tide with the sail flapping – it is often possible to have a whole boat's length lead over boats around you in these circumstances.

在比赛中如果对手不考虑潮流的影响，你可以获得很大优势。及早到达起航线迎着潮流并飘帆——一般你可以获得一个船身的领先。

Beating with the tide
顶风顺流航行

Starting is difficult since in these circumstances the majority of the fleet will be early, resulting in many general recalls. You have no alternative but to keep in line with the front rank of starters.
Great gains can be made however on the beat and reach in wind-with-tide conditions. Figure 20 shows how easy it is to overstand the windward mark if you go to the normal layline; boat A expected just to lay the mark but is swept well upwind; boat B gets it right. You can gain many

Rounding the leeward mark. 绕下风标

Practising starting. 'Hang' near a buoy with the sail flapping, using the tiller to control your position. Then sheet in and start on the signal.
练习起航。靠近一个浮标并飘帆，用舵柄调整你的位置，然后收紧主缭在信号发出时起航。

places by keeping near the middle of the course, always tacking well within the laylines.

On the reach, helms unaware of the effect of the tide will sail a considerably greater distance (Figure 21). They may end up running into the tide like boat C – this is very slow! Boat D allows for the tidal effect and sails straight to the mark, even though her heading is well to leeward.

这种条件下起航会很困难，因为大多数船都可能抢航，经常会全部召回。你别无选择，只能保持在第一排而不要提前越线。当风与流同方向时，迎风和横风航行会非常受益。图20表现了顺流航向上风标时，如果沿着通常的方位线航行，很容易被推离标区。A船瞄准上风标航行却被潮流推向上风区域。B船的航线是正确的。如果通过转向来调整位置，保持在方位线附近就可以获得很好的位次。横风航行时如果不了解潮流的影响，航线会偏离得更远（图21）。可能会像C船那样船速很慢！D船考虑了潮流的影响，即使航向偏向下风，最终也能直线驶向下风标。

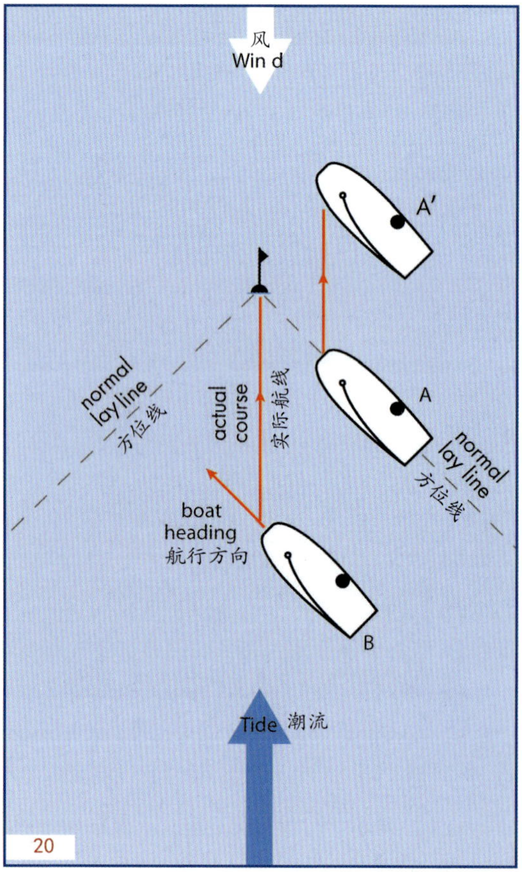

20

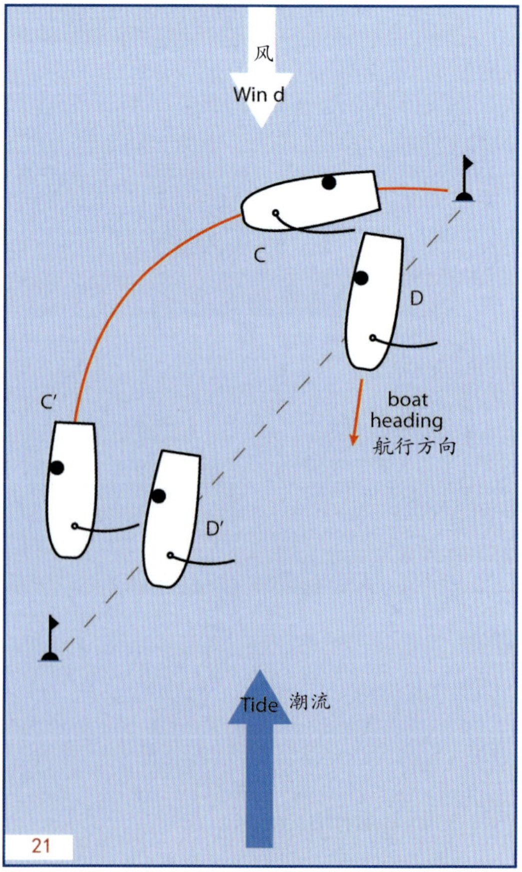

21

Part 4 第四部分

Masterclasses大师级别

摄影：Simon McIlwaine

Masterclass 1 大师级别1
Preparing yourself for success 做好准备获得胜利

I will often ask a group I am coaching "Who would like to win boat races?" and they will all raise a hand. The next question is "Who really wants to win boat races?" and most will say they do. The number of hands gets less when you ask, "Who is desperate to win boat races?" and of course that is understandable. Sailing can be enjoyed in so many different ways and the way someone enjoys it can change over the years.
我经常在训练时问队员们"谁想赢得比赛?"所有人都会举起手。问下一个问题"谁真的想赢得比赛?"时大部分人也会举手。当我问"谁渴望赢得比赛"时举手的人会减少,当然这是可以理解的。因为享受帆船有很多不同的方式,而且随着时间的推移,享受的方式也会变化。
These masterclasses will give you the best chance of winning by preparing your boat and understanding how it works to achieve your best speed, preparing yourself physically and mentally, by giving you pointers to good race tactics and race strategy and by touching on goal setting. They also seek to provide a little advice to parents on how to support their youngsters as they develop as racers.
Sailing is not rocket science. The super-star who wins a boat race is not superhuman. Every part of sailing can be learned, none is difficult, it's just that there are very many parts to learn and then be applied at the right time!
The aim is to prioritise the things you learn so most progress can be made in the shortest time. 这些大师级别的内容会指导你把船准备好,了解如何操控船以获得最好的速度,让自己在身体和精神上都进入最佳状态,提供比赛的战略战术以及如何设立目标。同时也给家长们一些建议如何支持孩子成长为一个帆船赛手。帆船航行不是火箭科学,赢得帆船比赛的明星也不是超人。航行的每一部分技巧不难,易于掌握。只是需要学习的内容比较多而且要保证在正确的时间应用这些技巧。你的目标是把所有内容按重要性排序,这样在短时间内就可以获得明显进步。
To win a particular boat race you must:
要赢得比赛你必须:

- Turn up!振作起来!
- Have a reliable boat (but a technically well-prepared boat is helpful).
  拥有一条可靠的船(一条装备精良的船很重要)。
- Understand the Sailing Instructions.
  懂得航行指令。
- Know the course.
  了解航线。

The most important techniques are:
最重要的技术是:

- Starting – the most important 60 seconds in any race.
  起航——比赛中最重要的60秒钟。
- Holding your lane off a start line - do not allow yourself to slip behind the boat to windward and to leeward.
  出发后保持你的航道——不要处在上风侧的船后面,也不要处在下风侧的船的后面。
- Upwind sailing – maintain clear air and look for the laylines.
  迎风航行——保持干净风并且注意方位线。
- Offwind sailing – clear air again but establish the transit
  顺风航行——保持干净风并且熟练地转换。
- Mark rounding – normally wide in tight out.
  绕标——一般是进入时与标保持距离,出来时与标紧贴,宽进窄出。

The most important boat handling/boatspeed techniques are:

操控船和保持速度的重要技术是:

- To think of the rudder as a brake – it stops you.
  要明白船舵相当于刹车——它令你减速。
- Use the shape of the boat and your sail to steer the boat.
  利用船的外形和帆来控制方向。
- Change your controls often and feel the results.
  经常调整控制索并且感受到效果。
- Practise, practise, practise and practise so that doing things well becomes automatic. Only then can you look outside the boat and take in the bigger tactical and strategic picture. This is where the biggest gains are to be made.
  练习，练习，练习还是练习，让所有的动作变成自动反应。只有这样你才能把注意力集中到船之外的状况，制定通盘的战略战术。这样才能使你获得明显的进步。

Attitude 态度

There is no doubt that the most important 150mm in any boat race is the space between the sailors right and left ears! You determine how successful you are going to be and it's not down to talent!
毫无疑问，在帆船比赛中最重要的150毫米空间位于选手左耳和右耳之间（态度）！你的成功取决于决心而不是智力。
It is said the three factors that determine success are talent, determination and funding but of the three I'd place determination the most important by far. Yes you need funding but if you are determined enough (and pleasant with it!) someone out there will help you, especially if you show you are prepared to help yourself as well.
据说获取成功的三要素是智力，决心和金钱，但我认为迄今为止最重要的因素是决心。当然成功是需要金钱支持的，但是如果你有足够的决心（并且以此为乐趣），能够充分地准备好帮助自己时，总会有人（在金钱上）帮助你。
Talent is useful but I'd back the determined sailor with less talent than a talented sailor with less determination. Clearly the top of the sport has talented sailors but they are talented sailors who also have determination – a wonderful combination!
智力当然很重要，但我认为一个决心坚定而智力一般的水手比一个智力过人但决心不足的水手更容易获得成功。在运动的金字塔尖上都是那些智力很高的水手，但他们同时也拥有坚定的信念——一个完美的结合体！
So do you like to win, do you really want to win or do you 'just have' to win? This will decide how much time and effort you will put in. The trick is to make the best use of the time you are prepared to spend.
因此，你是喜欢获胜，还是确实想获胜还是"不得不"获胜？不同的态度会决定你付出多少时间和努力。秘诀是充分利用你付出的时间。

Winning attitude 取胜的态度

The following was sent to me from a sailor who moved from dead last at a squad camp to top 5 overall at the next major event. The huge improvement in results was not because of a change in her sailing skills but because of a change in her attitude.
下面这段话是我在一个特训营的女学员写给我的。她从一开始的持续垫底成长到一个重要赛事的总成绩前五名。这种巨大的成长源自她态度的转变，而不是技术上的提升。
"I think the biggest thing I learnt from this weekend is that I have to accept before I start that if I don't work my absolute, absolute, absolute hardest, then I'm going to finish completely annoyed with myself, and I decided in all the races on the weekend that I was going to work harder than everyone else. Maybe not that I'd win or anything, but I promised myself no-one would work harder than me."
"我在这个周末学到的最重要的东西是：如果在比赛前我没有绝对，绝对，绝对刻苦地训练，那我一定会在结束时彻底把自己恶心了。我决定在周末的每一场比赛中都要比别人更刻苦。也许我不会因此而获胜或得到什么别的回报，但我向自己保证我一定是练得最苦的那一个。"

Mental toughness 坚强的意志

Mental toughness is all about being able to perform under pressure, in the race. Lots of sailors lack confidence in their ability and this stops them getting the results they deserve. Confidence is not about brashness, which too often shows itself for the veneer that it is when things get difficult.

Confidence develops over a period of time, based on adding to your abilities in all the many aspects of the great sport of sailing. I like the idea of a confidence bag, a place where all your process skills are collected. Knowing that you have these skills gives you the inner confidence to trust your ability and the knowledge that if you' re having a bad day that' s all it is – a bad day – which is not the same as being a bad sailor. Results follow and these reinforce your confidence – a virtuous circle!

坚强的意志能够让你在比赛的压力下做出良好表现。很多水手对自身实力缺乏自信，这样就阻碍他们获得本应有的成绩。自信不意味着鲁莽，否则在困难条件下会经常让你陷入困境。建立自信是需要时间的，取决于你在伟大的帆船运动中各方面能力的累积。我喜欢“自信袋子”的说法，装满了你全部的技能。要懂得拥有这些技能会给你内在的信心，让你相信自己的能力和知识。这样即使你有一天表现很差，这也只是一个倒霉的日子而已，绝不意味着你是个差劲的水手。不断地获得好成绩能够加强你的自信——一个正能量的循环！

In the zone 最佳状态

When things are going well it' s often referred to as being 'in the zone'. You feel good, the boat is fast, you' re not concerned about the way others are going and the wind strength is just perfect for you. Being 'in the zone' is great, getting back there when things are not so good is the aim. Start by recognising how you react under pressure. Do you get 'hyper' and throw all your toys out of the cot (often associated with feeling tense and irritable and making rash decisions)? Do you close down and feel lethargic (often associated with not making any decisions and not being forceful enough)? Somewhere in between is where your best performance can be found. Hyper types need to calm down; lethargic types need to be stimulated.

当一切顺利时我们会说“最佳状态”。你的感觉好，船速快，不用担心周围的情况，而风力也很理想。处于“最佳状态”是很重要的，如果情况不顺利，一定要尝试回到最佳状态。要分析你在压力下是如何反应的。你是那种把玩具扔的到处都是的“亢奋型”吗（经常感觉紧张和急躁并且匆忙做出决定）？或者你是“慢热型”（经常不做出决定并且缺乏执行力）？在两者之间找到平衡可以让你做出最佳表现。亢奋型的人需要更冷静，慢热型的人需要被激发。

I' m definitely the hyper type and amongst other things grip the tiller extension so hard I can' t read what it' s trying to tell me. I find the phrase 'soft hands' helps me remember what it' s like in the zone and I find myself back there. Others tell me they sing when things are going well and they have particular songs for getting back in the zone for different conditions. Great idea – but you haven' t heard my singing!

我绝对是亢奋型的，总是紧紧握住舵柄以致于无法感觉到它给我的信息。但当我“轻握”它时，就可以帮我回到最佳状态的感觉。有人告诉我他们在不同的条件下回到最佳状态时，会唱特定的歌。真是个好主意——但我从来没唱过歌！

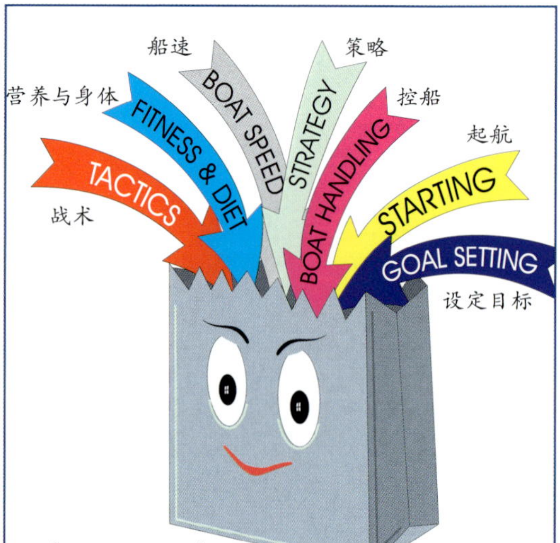

A "confidence bag".
“自信袋子”

Things do go wrong in boat races and it' s common to dwell on what' s happened. In different situations you can find yourself thinking 'what if?'. What if I finish the race in this position? What if I capsize at this gybe mark? What if I lose the protest? None of these thoughts are useful. The aim is to concentrate on the next 100m, on the next decision, on the next boat-handling task. Don' t dwell on the past or even

anything beyond the end of the race; aim to make everything you do the best it can be and the results will follow.
在比赛中总是会出状况的，你也只能去接受它。在不同的状况中你经常会想“如果……会怎样……”，如果我就以这个名次结束比赛会怎样？如果我在这个下风标翻船会怎样？如果我被抗议判罚会怎样？这些想法全都于事无补。你应该集中精力在下一个100米，再下一个决定，再下一个动作。不要停留在过去的事情和其他与完成比赛无关的事。专注于把每一个动作做到最好，自然会得到好的结果。

Goal setting 目标设定

Fail to plan and you plan to fail. Goal setting is a way of maximising the time you spend trying to improve as a sailor. All elite athletes set goals.
如果不做计划，你就不会成功。目标设定是一种方法，让你的时间最大化，提升你的帆船水平。所有优秀的水手都会设定目标。

Long term, inspirational, goals 长期的激励性目标

These are your dreams, the things you want to achieve in any field of human activity. They may well change as you go along but without them you are going nowhere.
这是关于你的梦想，你在某一人类运动领域想获取的成绩。这些目标可能会随着你的成长而改变，但没有了目标你将一事无成。

Medium term goals 中期目标

These are associated with the coming season, the events you want to attend and the results you would like to achieve, and the squad you hope to be invited into. They will help you sort out the logistics for the year.
这些目标包括在下一个航海季想参加的赛事和想获得的成绩，或者是你想进入的代表队。这将激励你在下一年中做好物质准备。

Short term goals 短期目标

These are process goals – e.g. aiming to improve leeward mark roundings. Goal setting makes the difference and so few sailors do it effectively. I love this quote from Ed Moses:
这些都是阶段性的目标，比如改进下风侧绕标技术等等。目标的设定会让事情变得不一样，因此很少有人能做好。我喜欢Ed Moses说的一段话：

“Ain’t no use worryin’ bout things beyond your control, cause if they’re beyond your control, ain’t no use worryin’…………”
“在你能力之外的事情，你担心也没用，因为你控制不了……”

“Ain’t no use worryin’ bout things within your control, cause if you got them under control, ain’t no use worryin’…………”
“在你能力之内的事，你也不用担心，因为你本来就能控制……”

Knowing what you can control and what you can’t is the key here. You can’t control the weather and I hear sailors complaining that it’s not their conditions and that they hate it. Like everyone I prefer 12 knots and sunny with a nice swell running but the trouble is everyone else loves it as well, can sail well in it and it’s more difficult for me to win. No-one prefers 3 knots and rain with a nasty tide because it’s difficult. If you remind yourself that others are hating it and can persuade yourself that you love it (or at least hate it less than them!) then psychologically you’ve got them beat. You get in the zone more quickly and you concentrate longer. The result is you find yourself doing well in these conditions and, as if by magic, you find that you do like these conditions. Equally, when it’s really windy, don’t think, ‘I’m too light for these conditions’. Remember that everyone’s hurting; keep going a little longer and again good results will come.
搞清楚哪些可控哪些不可控是很关键的。比如你无法控制天气。但我时不时听到有人抱怨这不是他们喜欢的天气或者恨这天气之类的。像大家一样我也喜欢晴朗的天气并且在12节的风中舒适地航行。糟糕的是所有人也喜欢这种条件，所以我很难取胜。没有人会喜欢下雨天，风力只有3节还伴随着恼人的水流，因为这种条件下航行太难了。如果你能说服自己乐于在这样的条件下航行（或至少不像别人那样恨这天气！），那么在心理上你就赢了。你可以更快地进入最佳状态并且专注得更持久。结果就是你在这样的条件下可以做得更好，并且像魔术一般，你开始喜欢这样的天气。同样地，如果风很大，不

SHORT TERM GOALS BASED ON MY PREVIOUS EXPERIENCE
基于我的能力的近期目标

MY GOAL 我的目标	WHAT I INTEND TO DO 我想做到什么	HOW I'M GOING TO DO IT 我将如何去做	WHEN I INTEND TO DO IT 何时去做	HOW IT WENT 做得怎么样

要总想着“我体重太轻压不住船”之类的。要记住每个人都一样很痛苦，坚持下去就会有好的收获。

Your short term goals will be process based – improving tacking in light winds say or even better improving the entry phase of a roll tack or even better positioning your feet during the entry phase of a roll tack. Get it? – it's better to be specific. There are loads of ways of setting this out in sailing.But which process to improve on to get the most benefit? Use the chart above to help decide.

短期目标都是阶段性的——改进小风时的迎风转向，改进滚动转向的进入阶段技术，或者改进你的脚的位置。改进了吗？目标越细越好。帆船航行有很多的小技术可以改进，但哪方面的改进对提升成绩最有效呢？用上面的图表帮助你决定。

An example of how you might use the chart to achieve your short term goals:

下面举例说明如何用这个图标来达到短期目标：

- **My goal** - Maintain my speed when tacking in light winds.
  我的目标——小风时迎风转向不失速。
- **What I intend to do** - Understand how to Roll Tack.
  我想做什么——懂得如何滚动转向。
- **How I'm going to do it** - Read the Masterclass in The Topper Book about Roll Tacking and then put into practice what I have read!
  我如何做到——阅读Topper手册中的大师级别。
  关于滚动转向的内容，然后进行练习。
- **When I intend to do it** - The forecast is for light winds on Saturday. I'll miss one of the club races and practise the technique.
  我什么时候做——天气预报显示周六是微风，我决定放弃俱乐部比赛，专心练习这项技术。
- **How it went** - OK but I do need to practice more. Now where did it say about the entry into a Roll Tack?
  进展如何——还不错，但还需要更多练习。现在，该开始练习滚动转向的进入动作了。

Let's say you decide the starting problem is associated with not being able to hold your boat still on the line. Go out and practise. Find a fixed mark and play around it until you can control your boat in any conditions close to the mark without moving.

再比如说你决定解决起航的问题，因为你不能把船停止在起航线上。出海练习吧。绕着一个固定浮标直到你可以在任何条件下在它附近停住不动。

Perhaps it's a boatspeed problem and for this you need a friend. Sail close to each other until one boat is clearly ahead. Look at the settings on the faster boat and change the slower one to suit. When both boats are at the same speed then the real gains can be made. Make a change to one boat and see the effect: if it's faster change the other to suit, if it's slower then try something else.

也许你想解决船速不够快的问题，这时你需要一个朋友一起航行。两条船同向航行直到有一艘船明显领先。落后的船要按照领先船的帆索控制进行调整，当两条船速度一致时，就获得了真正的提升。调整其中一条船的设置然后观察效果，如果船速加快就调整另一条船，如果船速减慢就尝试调整别的。

Mental rehearsal 意念演习

Sometimes it is difficult to get on the water and another technique becomes useful. Mental rehearsal is where you run through an action in your mind, from memory, often in a quiet place and with your eyes closed.
当无法下水练习时，其他的一些技巧就派上用场了。你可以找一个安静的地方闭上眼睛，把你要做的动作在脑子里过一遍，这就是意念演习。

- Imagine a start in a big fleet. I mean it, imagine you are really there! Try to experience it in the most realistic way you can and go though the sequence. The pressure should feel just like the real thing and you will get a little more used to it.
想象你和很多船一起准备起航，想象你确实在那里！像真的一样按顺序做每一个动作，你会感受到和真实情况一样的压力，逐渐变得适应。
- Imagine a downwind leg in 15 knots and a great wave pattern. Feel the wave lift the back of the boat. Rehearse pumping the sail, imagine your body movements, feel the increase in speed and look ahead for the wave pattern, which will allow you to hop onto the next wave.
想象你正航行在顺风段，风力15节并伴随着大浪。感受浪峰把船的后部抬起，模拟把帆鼓满，想象你在移动身体，感受到加速航行并且观察前方的涌浪，腾跃到下一个浪峰。

Physical preparation
身体上的准备

Top sailors are physically very fit. If you aspire to Olympic sailing you will want to grow the body you will need in ten years time! Fitness gained in youth is important. This does not mean you have to go to the gym each day as Olympic sailors do, but it does mean the following:
顶级的水手身材都很标准。如果你渴望成为一个奥运级别的水手，大概需要用十年的时间来打造你的身体！年轻时保持身体状态极为重要。这并不是说你要每天去健身房锻炼，但是要做到下面这些：

- Eating healthily. There is plenty of information on diet especially on the use of complex carbohydrates to sustain performance over a long event. One useful trick is to eat carbohydrate within the first hour of finishing any physical activity; your body is keen at that stage to replace lost energy.
健康的饮食。有很多有关营养的知识特别是关于碳水化合物如何能让你在长时间的运动时保持体力。一个有用的窍门是在每次运动后的一个小时内补充碳水化合物，因为这时身体急需补充能量。
- Drinking plenty of fluid especially during physical sessions. A 2% drop in body fluid has been found to affect performance by 20%. Plain water will go straight through the system so a hydrating fluid is better. The easy solution (if you' ll excuse the pun!) is a drink of 1/3 fruit juice, 2/3 water and a pinch of salt. If you feel lethargic at the end of a race ask yourself if you drank enough.
在运动过程中多喝水。研究发现身体含水量降低2%会使竞技状态下滑20%。纯水会直接从消化系统中流过，所以喝运动饮料效果更好。一个简单的方法是1/3的果汁，2/3的水并加一勺盐。如果比赛结束时你筋疲力尽，很可能是饮水不足造成的。
- Sleeping well, especially leading up to an event.
睡个好觉，特别是比赛之前。
- Warming up cold muscles before you leap in a boat and blast off from the shore. Even before you lift a boat off the roof of the car and strain cold muscles! A very gentle 5 minute jog followed by mobility exercises is the minimum. Do this on arrival and then jog to the boat to re-warm before you go afloat. The added benefit is increased brain activity, which is useful in a sport that requires a lot of important decisions to be made.

The National Squad warm up.
国家队赛前热身

在跳上船离岸比赛之前一定要热身。即使你只是把Topper从车顶搬下来也要先活动一下肌肉。最低限度是5分钟慢跑加上动态练习，你到达场地后就要做这些，然后慢跑到船边再次预热。这样做的额外好处是可以增加脑子的活力，这对于从事一项要经常做出重要决定的运动是非常有用的。

- Stretching down. Having worked so hard, a warm down jog is needed too. Remember, if you' re not doing this and your competitor is then there will come a day when you are injured whilst he/she is not and then who has the last laugh!
  恢复运动。大运动量之后，需要做些慢跑来恢复。记住如果你懒得做恢复运动而你的对手坚持做，总有一天你会受伤而你的对手会笑到最后。

STORAGE 储存

This is a big issue for Topper sailors. It has always been tricky stowing stuff in the boat so what can you do?
储存对Topper的使用者是个大问题。在船上存放东西是需要动一番脑筋的。

Fluids 饮水

This compass bracket can incorporate a bottle holder. It is easy to get to, low down and out of the wind. The bottle holds 700 cc but this is not enough fluid for back-to-back races. An additional bottle can be attached to a thin bungee cord that is secured to the neck of the bottle and then to the boat. Pull the cord to drink, release to stow.

Site the drinks bottle here. 把水瓶放在此处

这个罗盘支架可以包含一个水壶套，很容易存放水壶并且避风。水壶容量700毫升但对于背靠背的比赛仍然不够。额外的水壶可以用细的弹力绳的一端绑住瓶口另一端固定在船上，喝水时拉过来，松手后恢复原位。

Food 食物

Some kind of storage bag is useful, like the one in the photo (opposite). Sandwiches will get soggy so put them in a plastic bag as well. Clearly, these bags will be useful for spares too.
有些储物袋是有用的，比如对面照片所示。三明治很容易浸水因此要放在塑料袋中。其他备用品也需要用袋子存放。

In the support boat 保障船

Three litres of fluid for three back-to-back races, each lasting one hour, would be difficult to handle. A support boat should be provided so that you can stow additional supplies. These dry bags are big enough to hold additional spares and an extra item of clothing.
三场背对背的比赛，每场持续一个小时，如果只有三升水肯定不够。因此需要一艘保障船提供额外的给养。这种防水袋足够储存额外补给和装备。
The trick here is not to go over the top but be sensible and be prepared. Will you need to protect against the sun or a sudden cold patch? Food and drink matter, cost very little compared to the cost of big events, and have a big effect.
要细心地准备而不要简单地把袋子塞满。你是否需要防晒保护或低温防护？食物和饮水非常重要，而成本比你为比赛付出的费用少得多。

BACK TO YOU 回到你自己

Final thoughts on you - and do remember that you are the most important part of any particular performance – not your boat, not your parents, not your coach, not your friends. It' s you that matters, it' s you that has to want to compete and above all it' s you that has to enjoy yourself. This is not to belittle what the support structure, like parents, do for you. Far from it, they need to be appreciated and even be thanked occasionally!
最后思考你自己——记住你自己是任何一场表演中最重要的因素，而你的船、你的父

Storage bag for spares and food. 存放配件和食物

A dry keg and water bottle for spares in the support boat.
在保障船上的防水袋和备份水瓶

母、教练或朋友都不是最重要的。你是最要紧的，是你要去竞争，最重要的是你去享受这一切。并不是要忽略其他因素比如父母对你的帮助，恰恰相反你应该经常地对他们感恩并表达谢意。

It’s worth knowing what elite athletes are like. Research has looked at the best in a whole range of sports and it was discovered that **elite athletes are:**

值得了解一下杰出的水手是什么样的。对于运动领域的研究发现杰出的运动员**具备下列特征：**

- **Fit** 身材良好
- **Mentally tough** 意志力强
- **Determined** 果敢
- **Dedicated** 投入
- **Skillful - at sailing** 航海技术熟练
- **Skillful - at competing** 比赛经验丰富
- **Good at setting goals** 善于设定目标
- **Honest with themselves** 客观面对自己
- **Able to put in 10,000 hours of practise**
  至少进行一万小时的训练
- **People who recognise that the past doesn’t matter**
  不会沉迷于过去而是勇敢向前

Masterclass 2 大师级别2

Preparing your boat for success 装配好船以获得胜利

Finding the right boat

找到一只正确的船

There are over 40,000 Toppers out there somewhere so finding one should not be too difficult. Finding a boat suitable for racing is more of an issue. All the Toppers ever made have come out of the same mould so they should all be the same and they are pretty well indestructible.

全世界有四万条Topper，因此不难找到一条来用。但找到一条适合比赛的船就不那么容易了。所有的Topper都是用同一套模具制造的，因此每条船都是一样的并且很难损坏。

Alternatively look for a boat used as a race boat and it will come with race controls and be well looked after. Perhaps the best boats are ones left in a boat park for years and years. The grass may be growing around them but a quick power-wash and they will look (almost) as good as new.

尽量寻找那种一直比赛的船，因为这种船装配了竞赛型索具并且保养良好。也许最好的船已经躺在船库里很多年，四周长满杂草，但是强力冲洗后它们会和新船一样。

What to look out for

如何检查船只

Check that the mast cup, at the base of the mast, is not worn through and that the transom plate bolts can be fully tightened. Make sure the spars are straight and the sail has some service left in it. All spares are available and there is not a lot to go wrong in truth. Hulls and decks can be welded and leaks can always be stopped.Check that the hull is not too scratched or distorted.

Maintenance is straightforward and a little time spent brings a lot of rewards:

检查桅杆插槽底部没有被磨损，桅杆固定槽板的螺丝紧固。所有杆件平直，帆面具有弹性。备件充足。船身和甲板焊接良好无渗漏。船身没有重大划痕和变形。维护工作很简单，不会花费很多时间但会收获很大：

- Tighten all screws but be careful not to overtighten.
  把所有螺丝上紧，但不要过紧。
- Clean the hull with bathroom cleaner and a plastic scouring pad. Deep scratches can be improved with 'wet and dry' glass-paper.
  用浴室刷和冲洗垫清洗船身。较大的刮痕可以用水砂纸修复。
- Hose down with fresh water if sailing on the sea to slow down corrosion and to maintain the performance of the moving parts.
  在海上航行后，用淡水冲洗，减少盐分腐蚀并保持移动部件的性能。
- The rivets on the mast and boom are stainless steel or monel. Check and, if necessary, replace them regularly.
  桅杆和横杆上的铆钉是不锈钢或镍合金材料，经常检查，如果必要就更换。
- If water is getting into the watertight hull check the following by pumping the boat up a little (lung pressure will do) and applying washing up liquid and water to:
  如果船体和甲板之间的水密空间进水，要把船抬起来（可以用充气垫），用冲洗剂和水清洗，然后进行下面的操作：

1. The self-bailer. This is best removed and re-bedded with Sikaflex or silicon sealant. There is a gasket between the deck and the hull in this area that can also be replaced with Sikaflex.

排水筏。最好把它拆下来，再用聚氨酯密封胶或者硅胶重新粘合。在船身和夹板之间有一个垫圈，最好也用聚氨酯密封胶重新粘合。

2. The transom plate. The captive nut on the inside plate can become detached preventing the bolts being tightened. Replacement of this nut is difficult (but not impossible) because hatches are not allowed under class rules.
   船尾板。板内侧的螺帽可能会松弛，导致螺栓不能夹紧。更换螺母比较困难但是能办到的，因为级别规则不允许在船体上留洞口。
3. The mast cup at the foot of the mast has a bolt that pulls the hull and deck together. This cup should be replaced occasionally to prevent damage to the deck as it wears away. Behind it there is also a seal that may need replacing. The bung should be sealed and possibly replaced.
   桅杆底部的插槽位置有一个螺栓，用来把船身和甲板两部分扣紧。如果插槽磨损严重就需要更换。插槽后面的密封条也需要检查更换。塞子应该是密封的，如果不行也要更换。
4. The seal at the top of the plate case. Sikaflex and the use of negative pressure in the hull, using a vacuum cleaner, will cure this!
   如果船体甲板之间的密封出了问题，可以用聚氨酯密封胶和真空吸尘器产生的负压来修复。

It is rare to find that the deck-to-hull seal leaks but they can.
船体和甲板之间的密封发生渗漏的可能性很小，但仍然是可能的。

HULL 船体

Toppers are made of polypropylene and this must be taken into account. They are often mistreated by non-racers because they are so difficult to destroy! Racers need to take special care. Hulls must be stored upside down or they take on a ‘set’ (wavy hulls are not fast!). Scratches are difficult to remove from the hull and oh so easy to put in! You can scrape them out but I prefer using a sharp blade as a scraper followed by ‘wet and dry’, starting with a rough grade and finishing off with 1000 grade and plenty of water. A good quality trolley that supports the hull in the right places is essential. A high handle position on the trolley will save your back as well as the transom of the boat.
一定要记住Topper是由聚丙烯塑料制造的。这种材料的坚固性使得很多非专业选手很不爱惜船，因为它太难以损坏了。真正的帆船选手应该对船非常在意。船身应该反过来存放或者要有一个支座（变形的船身永远不可能跑得快）。船身很容易被划伤而且清除很困难。我习惯使用锋利的刮刀来除去刮痕，然后用1000度水砂纸打磨。一定要用高质量的船车来放置船并且妥善存放。船车上的加高扶手可以保护你的后背和船的尾部。

DAGGERBOARD 稳向板

Topper daggerboards are pretty well indestructible and not a bad hydrodynamic shape. However they are rather a sloppy fit. So:
稳向板不易损坏，拥有漂亮的流体力学外形。不过由于自身比较薄，因此：

1. Remove the hull plate and then the all-important daggerboard mouldings (bladders).
   卸下稳向板，注意保护边刃。
2. Clean up the inside surfaces of the daggerboard mouldings.
   保持稳向板插槽的内部清洁。
3. Attach Pro Grip to both of these surfaces – self-adhesive is best but if this is not available glue it with a contact adhesive.
   可以用绑带粘在稳向板和插槽内部—两者之间最好有自黏力，否则就需要用接触性材料（如绑带）来产生黏力。
4. Feather the edge of the Pro Grip with glasspaper or a file.
   用砂纸或锉刀把绑带的端部磨成羽毛状。

The daggerboard will now be a much tighter fit and has two additional advantages:
现在，稳向板装置更加稳定，带来两点好处：

1. It prevents the vertical scars found on almost all used daggerboards.
   防止稳向板上出现竖向划痕。
2. The daggerboard stays in the raised position without too much tension on the retaining elastic.
   稳向板可以固定在升起的位置而不需要给弹力绳附加太多拉力。

Ideal foil shape. 理想的片状部件截面

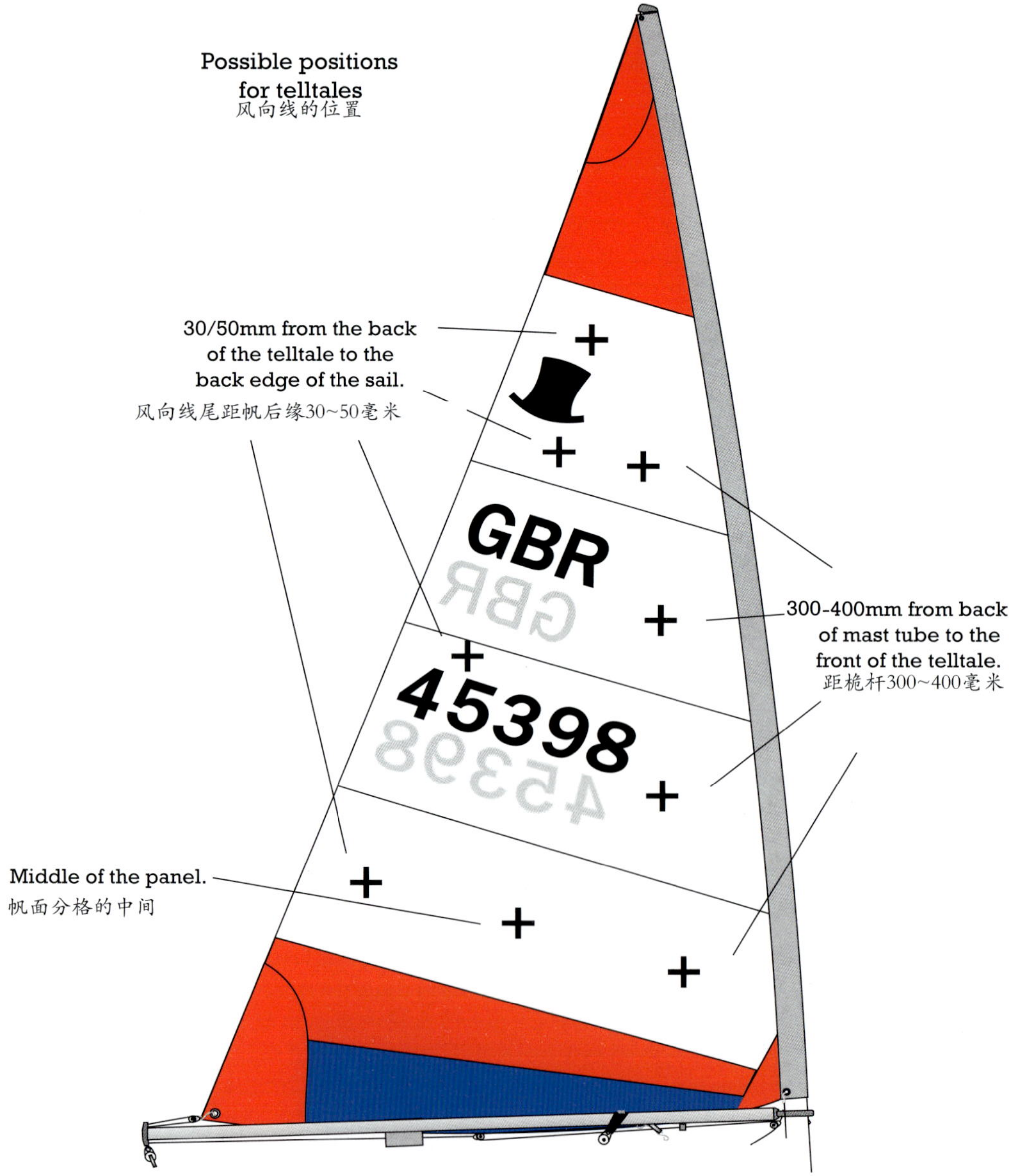

RUDDER & STEERING GEAR
船舵装置

The steering gear, as standard, is really sloppy so tighten and pack out as best you can. A new top pintle is now available and racers should fit them (please see 'How the Topper has changed', pages 10-12). It will remove most of the slop.
舵是标准的方向控制装置，舵叶非常薄所以要尽量保持紧固压紧。现在有一种新的顶部舵拴可供赛手们使用（请参见第10~12页“Topper如何改进的”），保证舵叶不会滑出。
I must say if you are going to spend time smoothing any part of your boat then do it to the rudder and daggerboard. They are under more pressure than the hull and much more inclined to stall out. You can spend the best part of a day 'wet and drying' a set of foils!
我的建议是如果你想花时间打磨你的船，要优先考虑舵叶和稳向板。因为它们比船体承担了更大的压力，更容易在使用中失效。你应该用一天中最好的时间来仔细打磨这些片状部件。

FOIL PREPARATION
片状部件的准备

Rudder blades and daggerboards really matter. Badly-prepared foils will adversely affect a boat's performance far more than the hull (although the very back of a boat has a pretty big effect).
舵叶和稳向板是非常重要的，如果状况很差就会大大影响船的表现。虽然船身底部对于航行的影响很明显，但也没有舵叶和稳向板的影响大。
In an ideal world foils should be stiff, light and a perfect aerofoil shape with a nicely-shaped elliptical front, an even curve that flattens out towards the back and finishes in a squared-off trailing edge perhaps 2mm wide. Topper foils will never be ideal but then we have all got the same foil so it doesn't really matter.
理想的片状部件应该是坚硬、轻盈的，断面如同飞机机翼：前部是非常漂亮的椭圆线条由曲变直延伸到后部，以2毫米宽的窄面作为结束。Topper的片状部件造型从来不会如此理想，但每条船的部件都是一样的所以也无所谓了。

You are allowed to 'repair' foils and you should spend a lot of time on them:
你可以对片状部件进行“修理”，但这需要很多时间：

- Reproduce the shape of the bottom of both foils if they have been damaged. This may include the use of a blade acting as a scraper, file and rough glasspaper followed by ever- decreasing grades of wet and dry paper until it is very smooth.
  如果片状部件的底部有损坏，就需要进行修补。可以使用刮刀和锉刀，最后用不同度数的水砂纸把底部打磨细滑。
- Check the front edges are chip-free and as elliptical as they were first intended.
  检查前部边缘确保没有磕碰，并且断面保持原始的椭圆状。
- Smooth out any damage on the sides by using abrasive paper wrapped around a long flat piece of wood – thick MDF is great. Finish with 1200 grade wet and dry with lots of soapy water to wash away the particles being removed.
  两边侧面如果有损伤，可以用粗糙研磨纸卷在一个木块上进行打磨，最后用1200度的水砂纸结合肥皂液清洗，冲掉残留颗粒。
- On no account round off the back edge. As produced it is already too rounded.
  后部不需要再磨圆，因为出厂时已经很圆滑了。
- It is often necessary to smooth the moulding marks on the sides of the daggerboard. Fill with an epoxy filler and sand off.
  稳向板两侧的注塑标志需要磨平，用环氧树脂填充后用砂纸打磨。

This 'perfect' shape is impossible to achieve but at least you know what to aim for!
Of the two foils the rudder blade is more important. It is more likely to stall out because it is asked to work through bigger angles when the boat is being steered. A perfect shape diminishes stalling.
得到“完美”的形状是不可能的，但你至少要知道追求的目标。在稳向板和舵叶之间后者更重要。因为在航行中舵叶经常要保持更大的角度所以更容易出故障。完美的外形会降低故障发生几率。

The front of the toestrap is held up by elastic. At the back one piece of elastic holds the toestrap up and the sidestraps in.

中央压舷带的前部有一根弹力绳扎住抬起，后部也有一条弹力绳将其抬起并把两侧压舷带束紧。

SPARS 杆件

The spars are generally good, especially the anodised ones. The upper mast should be packed out with tape so it is a tight fit into the lower mast. This makes the mast bend as evenly as possible. Check and replace the rivets regularly.
杆件的状态通常都不错，特别是做过阳极处理的产品。桅杆的上段应该缠些胶带以保证牢固地插进桅杆下段。这样令桅杆尽可能均匀弯曲。经常检查并更换铆钉。

MAIN HALYARD 主帆升帆索

Replace with a non-stretch rope and rig a 2-1 loop near the halyard cleat, or better still use a halyard loop. Please see 'How the Topper has changed' (pages 10-12).
用非拉伸型绳索，在升帆索羊角附近打一个2-1套结，或打一个升帆套，请参见"Topper是如何改进的"（第10~12页）。

AFT MAINSHEET SYSTEM 后置主缭系统

Ball bearing blocks and auto-ratchets are great here but much more important is that the mainsheet is at least 10m long so the boom will extend beyond 90 degrees for that essential running by the lee technique downwind. Smart sailors have a knot in the rope so when the boom is at the optimum angle, and they are in the right position in the boat, the knot is in their hand. Rope as thin as 6mm is used to allow the system to run smoothly, although 7mm is more usual.
滑轮器和凸轮夹绳器非常有效。但更重要的是主缭长度至少要10米才能在顺风段采用下风航行技术(running by the lee)时保证横杆放出超过90度。聪明的水手会在缭绳上打个结，这样当横杆处于最佳角度并且水手也坐在正确位置时，绳结正好握在手里。6mm的缭绳可以保证顺滑地运转，当然7mm的缭绳更为实用。

OTHER TRICKS 其他的秘诀

Like all simple boats that are being pushed beyond their original intended use, their helms have a thousand little tricks to make them work better as a race boat.
很多简单的帆船都从原来的简单功能发展而来，产生了成百上千的操控技巧令这些船有更好的竞技表现。

Use the following as a checklist:
下面是项目检查表

Hull 船体

- Rinse regularly, especially the mast cup.
  定期清洗，特别是桅杆插槽。
- Clean with bathroom cleaner and (if necessary) a plastic scourer.
  用卫生间洗洁剂洗刷，有必要可以用塑料刷。
- Bed down the hull plate by removing the top of the inserts.
  拆除甲板上的所有物件，把船体甲板朝下放置。
- Tape the join between hull plate and hull with 50mm waterproof tape.
  用5厘米宽的防水胶带贴在船身和甲板的接缝处。
- Tape the head of the mast cup screw.
  用胶带贴住桅杆插槽的螺帽。
- Check the positioning of the foam block in the rear tank.
  检查后部水堵位置。
- Check all screws for tightness but don't overtighten.
  检查所有螺丝的紧固，但不要过紧。
- Centre toestrap held up with elastic front and back.
  中央压舷带的两端都有弹力绳固定。
- Side straps as short as possible.
  两侧压舷带尽可能短。
- Store the hull upside down.
  把船体底朝上放置。

Foils 片状部件

- Clean regularly. 定期清洗。
- Smooth with wet and dry, especially the front edge.
  用水砂纸擦拭，特别是前侧。
- Maintain a sharp squared-off back edge.
  保持后侧锋利的小窄边。
- Tighten bolts on tiller and rudder stock.
  上紧舵叶和舵柄的螺栓。
- Tape the top pintle to remove slack or fit the new pintle fitting.
  用胶带缠住顶部舵拴，把舵杆放松，或者换新式舵拴。

- Pro Grip the daggerboard bladders.
  用胶带扎住稳向板边刃。
- Take the daggerboard elastic to the front of the boat. 把稳向板弹力绳放在船的前部。
- Aluminium/carbon tiller extension of maximum length (975mm).
  碳铝制造的副舵柄最大长度为975毫米。

Rig 支索

- Wash all fittings and fastenings regularly.
  定期清洗支索并上紧。
- Check the boom and mast straps for loose rivets.
  检查桅杆和横杆的捆扎带铆钉是否松脱。
- Check the lower mast for cracks around the strap.
  检查下部桅杆的捆扎带附近是否有裂纹。
- Pack out the upper mast with parcel tape to achieve a tight fit.
  上部桅杆的下端用胶带环绕，保证与下部桅杆插接紧固。
- Provide a backup rope for the mast strap.
  桅杆捆扎带需要一条辅助绳索。
- Velcro clew tiedown strap.
  捆扎带的尼龙搭扣压实扣紧。
- Sail stored by rolling around a tube.
  帆面存放时要卷在圆管上。
- Additional telltales attached.
  多贴几条风向线。

Controls 索具

- 3:1 kicker with fiddle block and cleat.
  用滑轮和羊角把斜拉索保持3:1机械力矩比
- Triple block 6:1 downhaul.
  下拉索为三重滑轮组保持6:1机械力矩比。
- 4:1 outhaul with pull from forward.
  后拉索需要在前部拉紧保持4:1机械力矩比
- 2:1 traveller using dyneema or 'Spec 12' and roller Clamcleat.
  滑车索使用迪尼玛或'Spec 12'索具和转轮夹绳器。保持2:1机械力矩比。
- 2:1 halyard using dyneema, halyard loop or new webbing strap.
  升帆索使用迪尼玛索具，配置顶部套索或新式绑带保持2:1机械力矩比。
- 7mm mainsheet 10m length (or 12.5m for the centre main).
  主缭直径7mm，长度10m (中置主缭为12.5m).
- Handles or loops on control ropes.
  控制索具都装配手柄或套索方便调整。
- Rope lengths adjusted to minimum.
  把绳索长度调较到最短。
- Measurement strip on boom for outhaul and mast for downhaul.
  在桅杆和横杆上标注下拉索和后拉索的长度标记。
- Measurement marks on kicker rope.
  在斜拉索上标记长度标志。
- Dry lube mast to allow sail to move easily.
  桅杆上润滑剂保证主帆移动顺滑。
- Dry lube controls for ease of use.
  索具上润滑剂保证使用平顺。
- Dry lube boom to allow slide to move easily.
  横杆上润滑剂保证滑动顺畅。

Other 其他

- Compass. 罗盘
- Burgee and/or wind indicator.
  燕尾标或风向标
- Drinks bottle. 水瓶
- Bag for spares and food. 零件和食物袋

TOESTRAPS 压舷带

The outer toestraps should be as tight as possible to keep them out of the way.
Pad the centre straps for comfort and grip. 'Kiwi – style' is good because it prevents the padding rotating. Use elastic to hold up this toestrap – the elastic at the front is shown opposite. At the back, loop the elastic around the outer straps and under the centre one.
外侧压舷带应该尽可能拉紧避免松脱。中央压舷带要加软垫保证使用舒适并钩紧。可以用"新西兰方式"来防止软垫翻转。用弹力绳把压舷带捆紧（对面的图片显示了前部的固定方法），两侧压舷带的后部用弹力绳穿过中央压舷带下部束紧。
A new system is available that allows the centre-strap to be adjusted for length on the water and with outer straps that hold an additional bag and

water bottle holder. Please see ‘How the Topper has changed’ (pages 10-12).
新设计的中央压舷带可以在使用中调整长度，两侧压舷带附带一个储物袋和水瓶托。请参阅第10~12页“Topper是如何改进的”。

TILLER EXTENSION 副舵柄

Use the longest tiller extension that the class rules allow - 975mm - and use the new rubber universal joint that won’t lock up.
建议使用级别规则允许的最大副舵柄长度：975毫米。使用不会锁止的新式橡胶万向节。

And one final point about the mast. With the new halyard loop, when the downhaul is loosened off downwind the two halves of the mast can jump apart and pinch the sail in between.
关于桅杆的最后一点：使用新式升帆索套顺风航行时，由于下拉索放松导致桅杆的上下两段松弛会导致帆面被夹住。

- File the ends of the mast tube.
  用锉刀把桅杆端部打磨粗糙。
- Keep the two halves from coming apart by taping them or use an off-cut from an old bike inner tube.
  用胶带绑扎桅杆端部或使用老式自行车上的一段套管来防止上下两段桅杆脱开。

Masterclass 3 大师级别3
Advanced control lines 加强版控制索具

You will need better ropes and more purchase if you want to race successfully.
如果要获得好的比赛成绩，你需要更好的索具，并购买更多的设备。

WORLDS kit 世锦赛装备	Dia (mm) 直径（毫米）	Type 材料	Length (m) 长度（米）	Colour 颜色
aft mainsheet 后置式主缭	7	Polylite 超轻聚乙烯	10	black or blue 黑色或蓝色
centre mainsheet 中置式主缭	7	Polylite 超轻聚乙烯	12.5	black or blue 黑色或蓝色
outhaul front 前部后拉索	4	Dyneema 迪尼玛（超高分子量聚乙烯纤维）	0.45	blue 蓝色
outhaul middle 中段后拉索	4	Dyneema 迪尼玛（超高分子量聚乙烯纤维）	2.1	blue 蓝色
outhaul back 后部后拉索	3	Pure Dyneema 超轻聚乙烯	2.2	blue 蓝色
6:1 downhaul top 上部下拉索	4	Dyneema 迪尼玛（超高分子量聚乙烯纤维）	0.8	yellow 黄色
downhaul bottom 底部下拉索	4	Dyneema 迪尼玛（超高分子量聚乙烯纤维）	1.6	yellow 黄色
kicker 斜拉索	5	Dyneema 迪尼玛（超高分子量聚乙烯纤维）	2.25	red 红色
traveller 滑车索	4	Pure Dyneema 超轻聚乙烯	3.25	yellow 黄色
halyard 升帆索	4	Dyneema 迪尼玛（超高分子量聚乙烯纤维）	6.5	blue/green 蓝色或绿色
halyard loop 升帆套索	4	Pure Dyneema 超轻聚乙烯	0.75	blue 蓝色

CLUB RACE LEVEL 俱乐部竞赛级别	Dia (mm) 直径（毫米）	Type 材料	Length (m) 长度（米）	Colour 颜色
aft mainsheet 后置式主缭	8	Polyester 聚酯纤维	10	white/blue 白色或蓝色
centre mainsheet 中置式主缭	7	Polyester 聚酯纤维	12.5	white/blue 白色或蓝色
outhaul front 前部后拉索	4	Polyester 聚酯纤维	2.1	blue 蓝色
outhaul back 后部后拉索	4	Polyester 聚酯纤维	2	blue 蓝色
3:1 downhaul top 上部下拉索	4	Polyester 聚酯纤维	0.4	yellow 黄色
downhaul bottom 底部下拉索	4	Polyester 聚酯纤维	1.6	yellow 黄色
kicker 斜拉索	5	Polyester 聚酯纤维	2.25	red 红色
traveller 滑车索	4	Dyneema 迪尼玛（超高分子量聚乙烯纤维）	3.25	yellow 黄色
halyard 升帆索	4	Dyneema 迪尼玛（超高分子量聚乙烯纤维）	6.5	blue/green 蓝色或绿色

STANDARD 标准级别	Dia (mm) 直径（毫米）	Type 材料	Length (m) 长度（米）	Colour 颜色
aft mainsheet 后置式主缭	8	Polyester 聚酯纤维	9.5	white/blue 白色或蓝色
outhaul 中置式主缭	4	Polyester 聚酯纤维	4	blue 蓝色
1:1 downhaul 下拉索	4	Polyester 聚酯纤维	1	yellow / orange 黄色或橘色
kicker 斜拉索	5	Polyester 聚酯纤维	2.5	red 红色
traveller 滑车索	5	Polyester 聚酯纤维	2.5	red 红色
halyard 升帆索	4	Polyester 聚酯纤维	6.5	blue 蓝色
painter 船头绳	6	Polyester 聚酯纤维	2	yellow / blue 黄色或蓝色

MISC. 其他索具	Dia (mm) 直径（毫米）	Type 材料	Length (m) 长度	Colour 颜色
centre strap 中央压舷带	50	webbing 尼龙带	0.95	blue 蓝色
outer straps 中央压舷带	50	webbing 尼龙带	1.27	blue 蓝色
front strap elastic 前部弹力绳	6	shock cord 减震绳	0.4	white / red 白色或者红色
back strap elastic 后部弹力绳	4	shock cord 减震绳	1	white / red 白色或者红色
daggerboard elastic 稳向板弹力绳	6	shock cord 减震绳	0.6	white / red 白色或者红色
d.board elastic to front 稳向板前部弹力绳	6	shock cord 减震绳	1.5	white / red 白色或者红色
PVC tubing for handles PVC塑料手柄	8 ID	PVC tubing 聚氯乙烯管	0.33	clear 透明

SHEET HORSE (TRAVELLER)
主缭滑车

This is often overlooked but it is essential that the traveller is very tight in all but the lightest of conditions, so that the mainsheet blocks stay on the corner of the boat when going upwind and that the blocks do not come together before the mast has been bent by a sufficient amount. Choose non-stretch rope such as 4 or 5mm Dyneema. Replace the plastic Clamcleat with an aluminium roller version to prevent slippage.

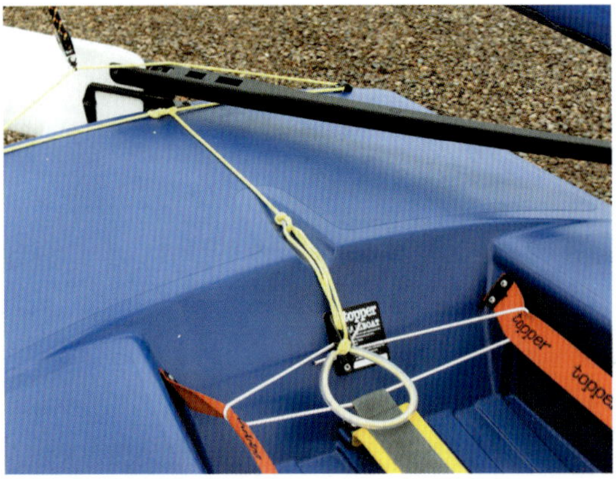

The traveller on a top-end race boat.
顶级赛船的滑车索

滑车总是被过度关注，最基本的要求是迎风航行时（除了小风条件下）滑车都要保持拉紧，让滑轮保持在船后角位置，这样即使桅杆大幅弯曲也不会让滑轮碰到一起。选择4或5毫米直径的迪尼玛非弹力绳索。把塑料转轮夹绳器更换成铝合金转轮夹绳器以防止绳索打滑。

Make a purchase as shown in the photo and diagram: class rules allow a 2:1 system. Use a rounded (forged) shackle between the bottom mainsheet block and the traveller so that it slides better. Only decrease the traveller tension if the shackle won’t cross the tiller in light winds.

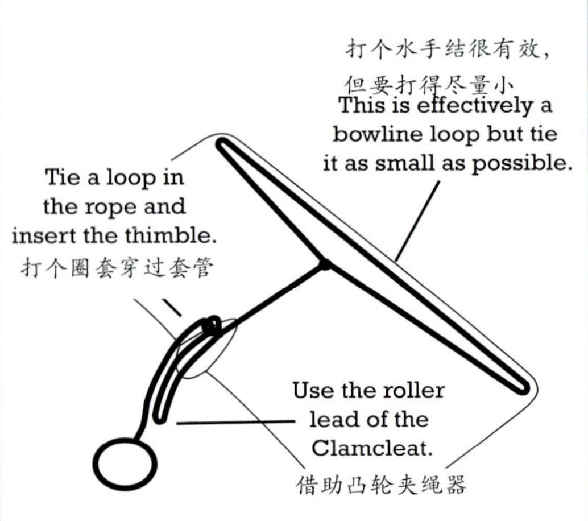

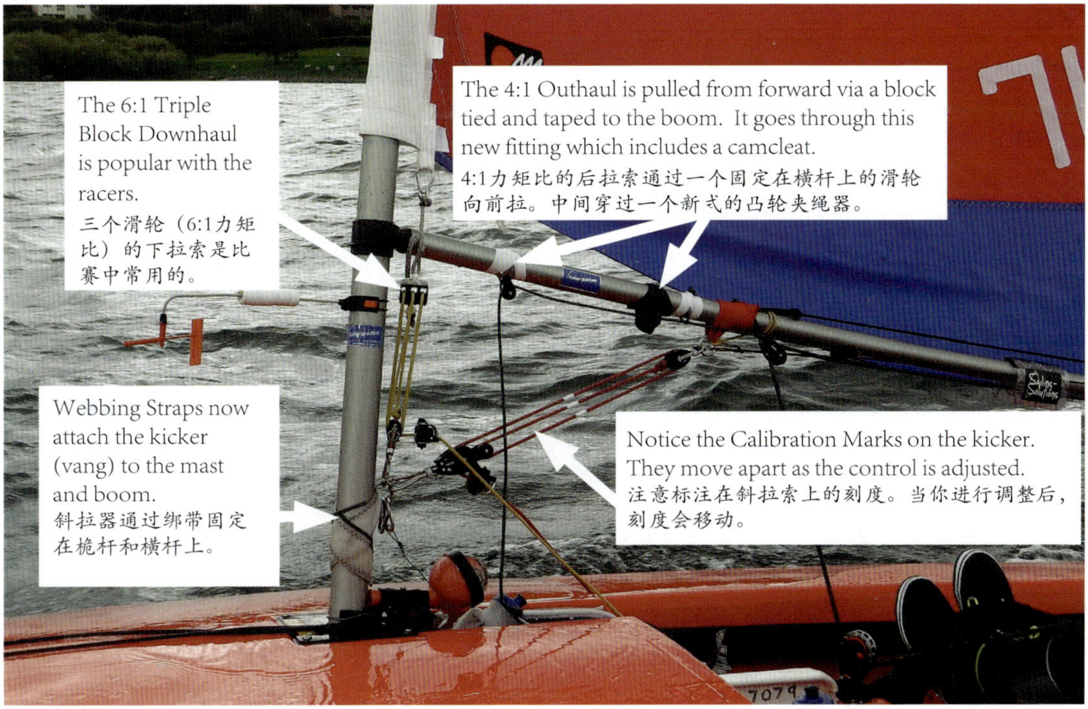

按照照片和图示制作滑轮组：级别规则允许制作2：1的滑轮系统。用圆形快挂连接主缭底部的滑轮和滑车以保证滑动顺畅。如果在微风时快挂不能移过中心线，就把滑车放松。

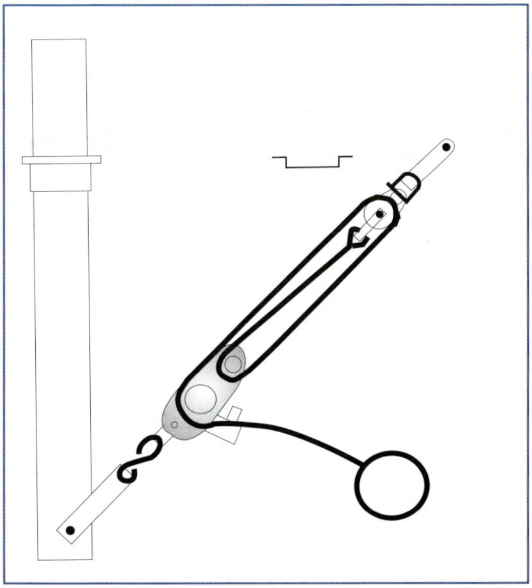

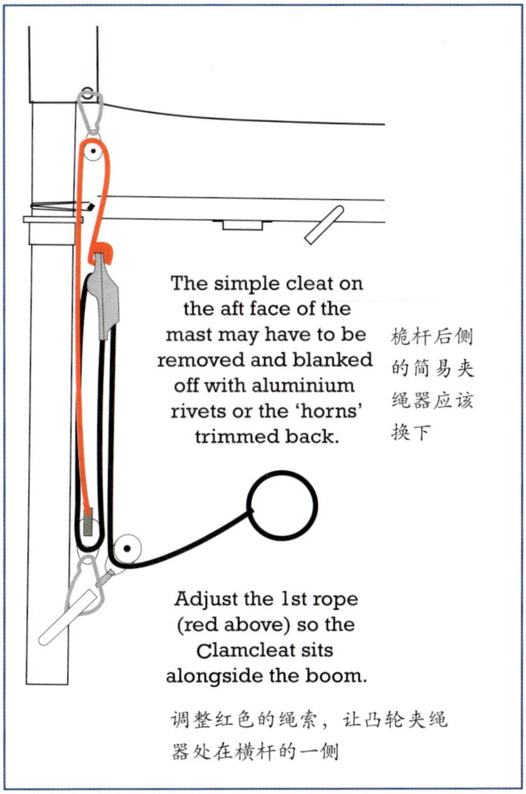

KICKING STRAP (VANG) 斜拉索

The original 2:1 'v cleat' system needs upgrading and a 3:1 with a fiddle block is universally used. Set the kicker at its minimum tension and then adjust the rope length so the handle is at the cleat. That way it becomes much easier to use your legs to apply the required force. You will have to push down on the boom in order to attach the kicking strap to the mast.

早期的2:1V形夹绳器需要升级为通用的3:1Fiddle滑轮组。把斜拉索的松紧度调到最低，然后调整绳索让绳套保持在夹绳器位置。这样你可以很容易用脚来调节斜拉器。安装斜拉索绑带时可以把横杆向下压。

Pull in the mainsheet so that the blocks are 150mm apart and take up the slack in the kicking strap. Now make marks, in line, on all three ropes. This gives a good reference for setting the kicking strap tension.

收紧主缭让滑轮之间保持150毫米的距离并把绑带绑紧，这时你可以在三条绳索上做记号，为调节斜拉索绑带的松紧度作参考。

DOWNHAUL 下拉索

Use the 6:1 triple block downhaul system in the photograph opposite. Pull on the tension upwind to bring the fullness forward which improves the balance of the rig and decreases the power of the sail. This control is very important in the Topper. Sailing upwind when it's breezy the fast setting is to have the front of the sail touching the boom. Lubricating the mast with drylube will allow the sail to return to its original position when the control is let off for downwind legs.

使用上页照片所示的6:1力矩比三滑轮下拉索系统。迎风航行时要拉紧下拉索以保持船体前倾并改善索具平衡，减少主帆受力。下拉索对于Topper的航行非常重要。大风条件下迎风航行时最简便的方法是让帆的前部碰到横杆。顺风航行时索具都被放松，如果在桅杆上使用干式润滑剂可以让主帆回到应有位置。

HALYARD 升帆索

If you use the old-style halyard there is no point in having an effective downhaul if the halyard stretches. 4mm Dyneema is an excellent choice of rope. Form a loop in the rope as it exits the sail sleeve so a 2:1 mechanical advantage is obtained. A bobble at the head keeps the sail, and therefore the boom, nice and high.

如果你使用旧式弹力升帆索，对下拉索进行控制就没什么意义了。4毫米的迪尼玛绳索是非常好的选择。在绳子穿出帆套之后打一个圈套，这样升帆时可以省一半的力量。顶部的卡球可以让帆型和横杆更漂亮并高举。

OUTHAUL 后拉索

A 4:1 system is allowed and the one in the diagram works well. Replace the 'V cleat' with a camcleat and add a turning block at the mast. Tie a loop in the free end as a grab handle.

允许使用4:1力矩比滑轮系统，图示中的形式工作得很好。用转轮夹绳器代替V型夹绳器，并在桅杆处加一个回转滑轮。在绳索的尽端打一个圈套结方便抓握。

Note that there is a hook or bobble on the first part of the system that needs to be released when reefing.

注意在滑轮组的第一部分有一个挂钩或卡球，如果缩帆时需要解下来。

The outhaul controls the fullness in the bottom of the sail. It really is hard to see the depth of your sail when sitting in the boat so apply measurement strips by one of the blocks to replicate fast settings.

后拉索控制着帆的底部是否充分受力。当你坐在船里时很难观察帆的弧度因此最好在一个滑轮组上做一些记号以快速调整索具。

Better still use a halyard loop
最好使用升帆套索。

Please note that the upper mast has been turned so the crane faces forward.
请注意转动桅杆上段，使桅顶扣盖向前。

1. Feed the halyard loop up through the front hole in the mast crane.
把做好的升帆套索穿进桅杆顶部扣盖。

2. Down the back hole. 从扣盖后部的孔中穿出。

3. Through the eyelets of the sail and back up the back hole (which might need enlarging slightly with a drill).
穿过帆面顶部的吊孔，再从扣盖孔中穿回（可能需要用螺丝刀帮忙）

4. Loop the end over the bobble at the front. 把套索绕到橡胶球上。

5. So that it tucks under the bobble. 橡胶球把套索卡住固定。

6 & 7. Pull the rope both sides of the crane and up into the groove on top of the mast-crane. This will tension the rope and so lift the sail.
从杆顶扣盖两边拉紧套索，并嵌入扣盖顶部的卡槽，这样会将套索拉紧并提起主帆。

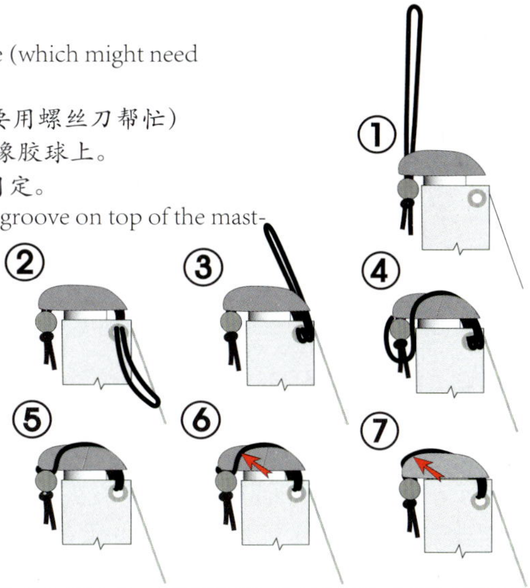

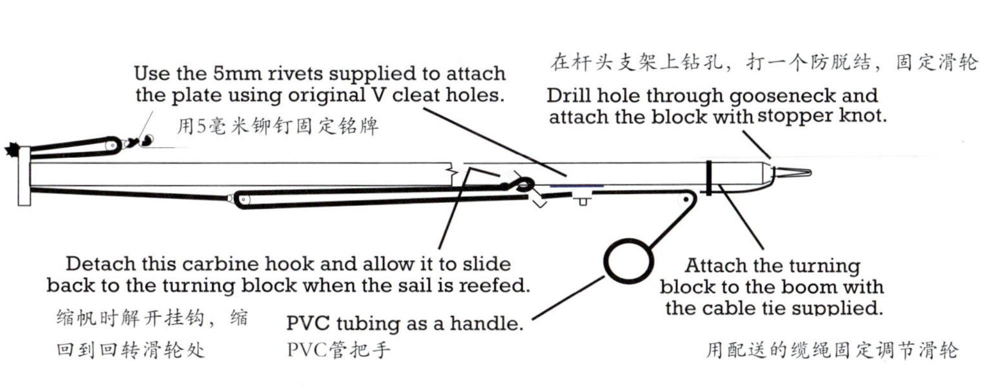

Masterclass 4 大师级别4

Boatspeed and boat handling for success

提高船速并控制船只以获得胜利

The principle here is that you should work with the elements rather than against them.
关键点是你必须和船的各个部分融为一体而不是和它们作对。

1. HEELING ON A BEAT 迎风压舷

This illustration shows the sort of sailing that is the opposite of what we’re after.
The wind is strong and the sailor is fighting the elements. The boat is heeled despite the sailor breaking their back trying to keep the boat upright.
Because it’s heeled the boat wants to round up into the wind (the curved side of the boat causes this). The sailor is pulling hard on the tiller to keep the boat travelling in a straight line and therefore the rudder blade acts like a brake because it’s across the water flow. The wind is sliding out of the top of the sail, which de-powers the rig, but the boat is slipping sideways because

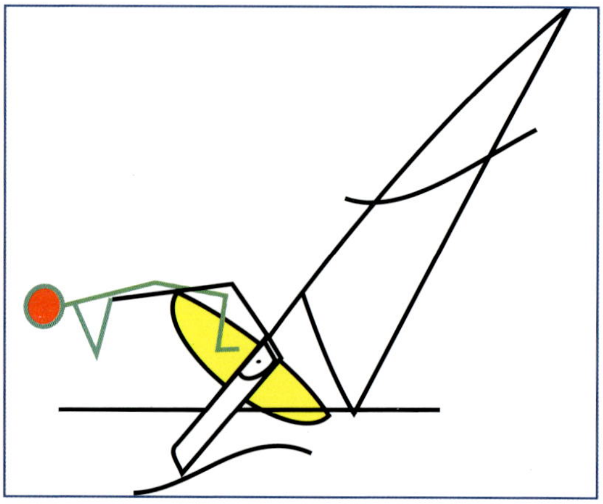

the dagger-board is angled. To make matters worse the wind is getting under the hull and pushing it over and the weight of the mast and sail is acting against the weight of the sailor.
这张示意图表现了一种不可取的航行方式。在大风下选手试图和各种因素作对：虽然他拼命向外压舷但船身仍然极度倾斜，这种倾斜造成了船体会转向迎风（这是弧形的船身造成的），选手因而奋力拉舵以保持航向直行，这样一来由于舵叶倾斜产生了阻力而降低船速。风从帆的顶部滑过减少了索具受力，但是由于稳向板倾斜造成了船体横移。更糟糕的是风作用在船体的底部令船更加倾斜，这样桅杆和帆的重量会抵消选手压舷的体重。
All the sailor needs to do is let out the sail! The boat comes upright and all these negatives disappear. Sailors tell me they are too light but if you are light you don’t need the same power to go as fast as the heavyweights. It’s about technique.
选手应该做的是把帆放出去！船身会保持平直而那些负面的效果烟消云散。很多选手告诉我说他们的体重太轻，那么你不需要使用和大体重选手相同的重量来提高速度，而是要运用技术。

2. STEERING BY HEELING 用压舷控制方向

When you are learning to sail, your rudder is your friend. When you start to race think of it as your enemy. Use it as little as possible and you maintain your speed.
刚开始学习帆船时，舵是你的朋友。但如果你要参加比赛了，要把舵想象成敌人。前进是尽量少用舵。

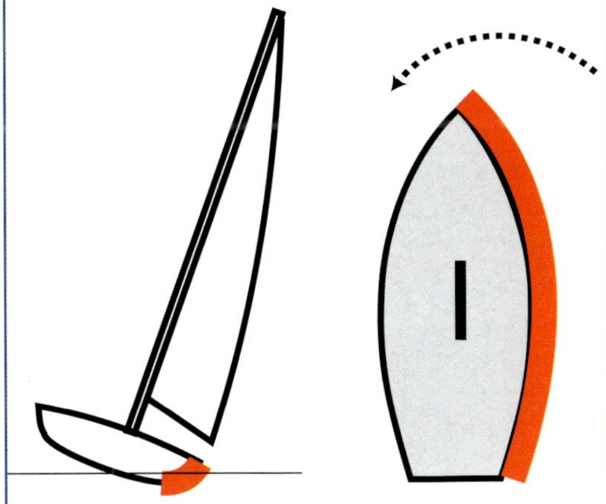

Steering by Heeling -
- Lean to leeward and the boat heads up.
- Lean to windward and the boat bears away.

通过船身倾斜控制方向
- 向下风向倾斜，船头转向上风
- 向上风向倾斜，船头转向下风

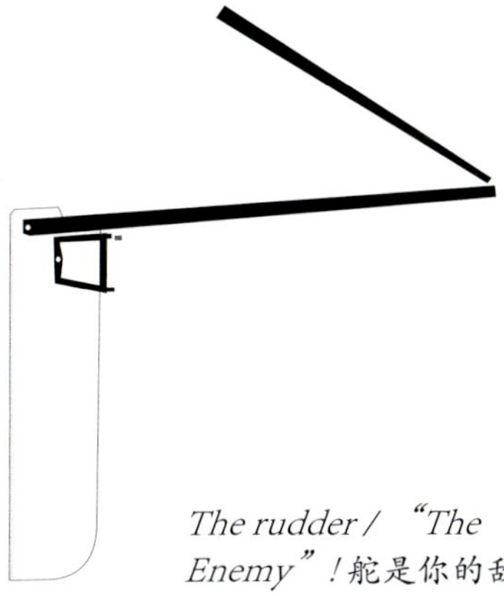

The rudder / "The Enemy"! 舵是你的敌人!

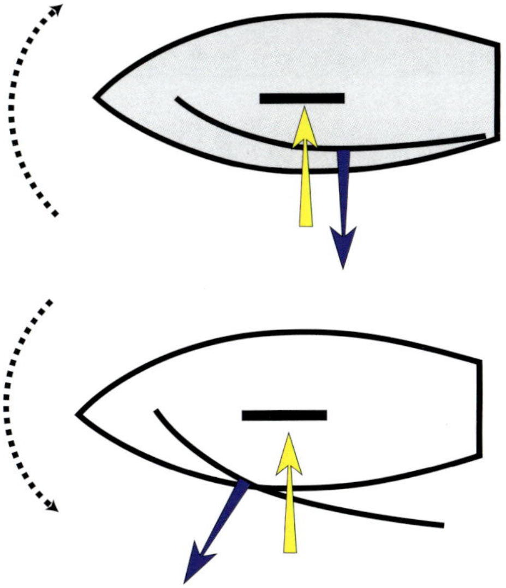

Steering with the sail
- Sheet in and the boat heads up.
- Let out and the boat bears away.

用帆控制方向
- 收紧帆，船头转向上风
- 松开帆，船头转向下风

3. HEELING ON A RUN
顺风压舷

Single sail boats should be heeled to windward when running. If they are sailed upright the point of effort on the sail spins them to windward and the helm will have to steer with the rudder to keep the boat tracking in a straight line. Heeling brings the point of effort directly over the point of pivot (the daggerboard) and the boat maintains a straight line without using the rudder 'the enemy'. You will know the correct angle of heal if you let the tiller extension just rest on your hand; if it's still you have set it up perfectly. There are two added advantages to this:

单面帆的船在顺风航行时应该向上风一侧倾斜。如果船身平直，则帆的受力中心会造成船体向上风侧偏转，导致选手需要用舵来保持直线航行。船身倾斜会令帆的受力中心与船的中枢点（也就是稳向板）重叠，这样不需要使用舵就可以保持直线航行。找到最佳的倾斜角度的方法是：把副舵柄轻轻放在手上，如果它保持不动就是最佳船体倾角。还有两个附加的好处：

- The amount of contact between the hull and the water is decreased and that reduces friction.
  船体和水的接触面减小，降低了摩擦力。
- The sail is raised into the air where the wind is less disturbed and a little faster.
  帆面的空气扰动减少，可以略微提高船速。

Once your boat is prepared and has controls that work you need to know how to use them.
一旦船只和控制索具准备就绪，你必须懂得如何使用。

4. DEPOWERING/POWERING UP 卸力和加力

Flatten the sail 保持帆面平整

Easy really, a deep sail will give you power whereas a flat sail will give you less power. Lighter sailors will have to use all their strength to pull the controls on hard enough to flatten the sail. Fit the best controls you can, get the rope lengths just right and use your leg muscles to pull them on.
深凹的帆面比平直的帆面提供的力量更大。体重轻的选手要拼命拉紧索具以保持帆面平直。要尽可能把索具调整到最佳受力并用腿部肌肉帮助收紧索具。

The principle – use the kicker, mainsheet and downhaul to bend the mast. A bent mast pulls the sail material forward which has the effect of flattening the camber in the sail, thus reducing the power.

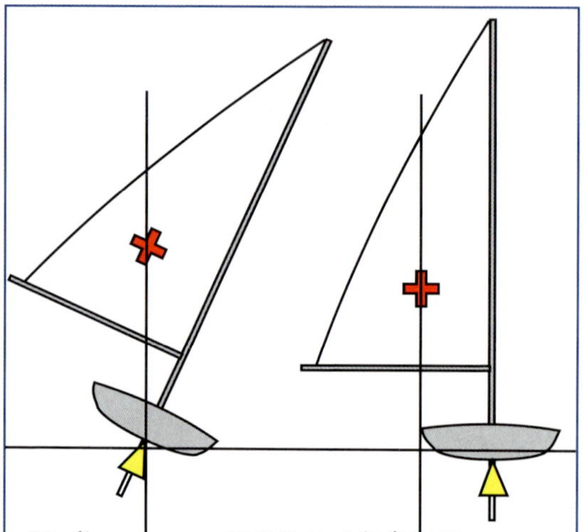

Heeling on a run 顺风航行时船身倾斜

基本原理——使用斜拉索、主缭和下拉索使桅杆弯曲。弯曲的桅杆可以把帆面拉平，降低弧度并减少受力。

The mainsheet – pulls down the back of the sail, which bends the mast by pulling on the tip. Be prepared to let the sail out if the boat heels. If you are pulling hard on the tiller extension then you are almost certainly heeling too much, trying to bear away when the heeled side of the boat is trying to make it head up.
主缭——把帆的后部下拉，使桅杆顶部受力而弯曲。如果船身倾斜就放出帆。如果你需要用力拉舵就意味着船身倾斜过度。如果船头向迎风偏转就尝试向下风走走。

The kicker – does the same as the mainsheet. In addition it drives the boom into the mast, which bends it. It also keeps the mast bent when the mainsheet has to be let out in gusts; otherwise when the mainsheet is let out the sail would become fuller and therefore more powerful which is bad news!
斜拉索——作用和主缭一样。另外它使横杆顶在桅杆上造成桅杆弯曲。当阵风时放出主缭也会令桅杆弯曲，否则帆面会鼓满而受力过大，这可不是好消息。

The downhaul – acts like a bowstring. It pulls the top of the mast down without pulling on the back of the sail. This makes it especially effective because the wind can escape more easily when the back of the sail is not pulled tight. Importantly, as well, it pulls the fullness in the sail further towards the mast, which counteracts the wind’s effect of taking the fullness further back.
下拉索——作用类似船头绳。不用拉动帆后部就可以令桅杆顶部弯曲。即使帆的后部没有拉紧也可以使风迅速通过帆面。重要的是这样做可以令帆的受力中心靠近桅杆，防止帆面后部过于受力。

The outhaul – makes the bottom of the sail fuller or less full. It will also need to be pulled tight but don’t overdo it or the sail will be too flat and have little forward drive.
后拉索——调整帆底部的受力。应该拉紧但不能过度，否则因帆面太平而缺少向前的推力。

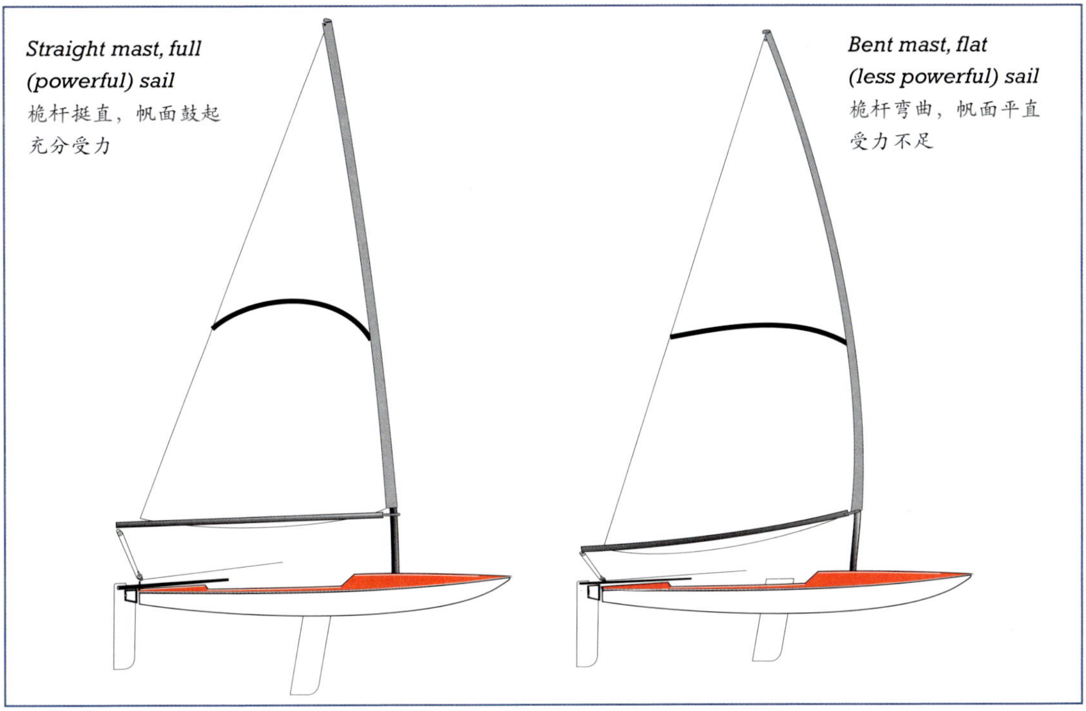

5. OTHER TIPS FOR WINDY CONDITIONS
大风条件下的其他技巧

Lift the daggerboard about 150mm when beating; it will take the harshness out of the boat. Conversely, leaving a little more down when on a run will steady the boat by damping the roll. Remember to tighten the daggerboard elastic to save the board dropping out of the slot if you do turtle. (This is important.)
迎风航行时把稳向板提起150毫米，这样可以减少船身阻力。在顺风航行时就要把稳向板放下多一些，防止船身翻转。一定要把弹力绳系牢以防止翻覆时稳向板滑出插槽。（这个很重要！）

Give yourself more time and space to make manoeuvres. KISS (Keep It Simple Sunshine) is a great tip at all times but especially in a blow. Keep looking towards the direction the wind is coming from so that you are ready to react before the gusts arrive rather than a split second later when it’s already too late.
在做机动练习时给自己留够时间和空间。任何时候都要保持微笑是很好的习惯，即使大风天也要如此。始终注意风吹来的方向以保证在阵风时采取措施而不是由于分心而造成动作迟缓。

On a reach be prepared to bear away with the gusts (stronger wind) and try to come up in the lulls (lighter wind).
大风时横风航行，随时准备在阵风到来时驶向下风；小风时就要向上风走。

On a run sit well back and if you are still nose-diving put on more kicking strap (vang). Pulling the sail in more will steady the boat down but will make it slower (not as slow as upside-down of course!). Bearing away and sailing by the lee also reduces nose diving.
顺风时尽量向后坐防止船头入水，如果不行就拉紧斜拉索。把帆收进可以保持船身稳定但会降低船速（当然不会比翻船还慢！）转向下风并且帆保持在上风一侧（sailing by the lee）也可以减少船头入水。

In flat water you can decrease the power on the beat by pinching higher than you would normally. You can feel the boat heel towards you as you overdo it. Weave a tight course that just keeps the boat flat when you are hiking hard. This will not work in waves because you need more speed to punch through them.

在平静的水面迎风航行时你可以比平时更向上风来减少受力。如果过度上风船身会倾斜加剧。如果你压舷太辛苦就可以多走“之”字形航线来减少船身倾斜。在有浪的情况下就不能这样做因为你需要更大的速度从浪头之间穿过。

On the reach sit further back and keep the boat very flat. When gybing just go for it – the faster you go into it the better chance you' ve got of coming out upright! Don' t turn too sharply though and aim to be on your new side before the boom has crossed the boat. Wear hiking shorts but make sure they fit correctly.

横风航行时尽量向后坐，保持船身平衡。顺风转向时尽量保持速度，船速越快就越容易在转向之后保持船身姿态平直。转向角不能太小，保证在过帆之前做到新的一侧。

Tacking 迎风转向

Toppers, like a lot of single-handed boats, are difficult to tack in very strong wind.

Topper和大多数单人艇一样，在强风时迎风转向是困难的。

A few tips:几个提示：

- Be bold. Go into the tack with plenty of speed (you may want to crack off a little as you approach the tack).
  鼓起勇气，在高速航行中果断进行转向。(也许你想在转向时略微松帆减速)。
- Cross the boat very fast, easing the sheet.
  快速换舷，松开主缭。
- Land on the new side and hike hard to bring the boat flat (or even heeled to windward).
  坐到新的一侧，尽力压舷把船身平直（甚至可以向上风侧倾斜）。
- If there are waves aim to be starting the tack as you go up the face of the wave. You will then be tacking at the top of the wave when both ends of the boat are out the water and speeding down the wave when you need to go faster.
  如果有涌浪，要在沿浪上行时开始转向，在浪尖上船头船尾都离开水面时实现转向最佳这样沿浪下行时可以获得最快速度。

If you do get stuck 'in irons' raise the daggerboard, sit further back, ease the kicker and let the sail out. Tease the sail in and as you start to move forward push the tiller away slowly and whip it back really hard. Repeat the latter several times to keep the boat off the wind.

如果你不幸顶风停船，收起稳向板，身体尽量向后坐，松开斜拉索并放出帆。向内收帆并且人向前移，同时轻轻推舵然后快速拉回。重复几次就可以驶出顶风区。

6. REALLY LIGHT WINDS 微风

In strong winds you need to be physical and do expect it to hurt – why should you feel different from everyone else! It' s different in light winds. Imagine a cat, the way it stalks – complete concentration and total control. Still and ready to pounce into action when the time is right. This is just the way to sail in light winds. You can let the boat take you around the race course but it will be a lot faster if you are proactive.

强风天气时你一定要准备好付出体力，而且肯定会浑身疼痛，其实别人也一样！微风时就不同了，想象一只猫在行走——全神贯注，保持状态，时机一到马上开始行动。这就是微风下航行的方式，你可以被动地绕标，但如果积极主动先发制人就可以更快。

The wind is always lazy, looking for the easiest route to follow but this is even truer as the wind speed decreases. It is not happy to travel around a deep sail and the merest jolt will knock it off course.

风总是很懒惰，你可以采用最容易的航线，风力减弱时更应该如此。如果帆没有收紧，很可能一个轻微颠簸就会让你失去航线。

These things help:下面的建议会有用：

- Heel the boat so gravity is pulling the sail into the right shape. Heeling the boat also decreases the wetted surface area and so lowers friction.
  保持船身倾斜，重力会使帆保持好的形状。同时船身倾斜也可以减少接触水的面积，减少阻力。
- A boat down by the stern will drag its transom, which slows it a lot. Try sitting well forward and see how much better it goes.
  船尾下沉会产生拖拉阻力降低船速。尝试尽量向前坐看看有多少改善。
- Move carefully but be prepared to spring into action when you need to – like in a roll tack for instance.
  小心地移动，一旦时机成熟要果断行动——比如在滚动转向时。

7. ROLL TACKING
滚动迎风转向

Stage 1 - Initiating the tack
第一步，开始转向

- **Lean into** the boat and sheet in more than usual. This will make the boat want to tack itself.
  把身体收回船内并比平时更加拉紧主缭，这样可以让船自身转向。
- Wait until the boat approaches head to wind, by which time it is slowing down.
  Wait longer than you think!
  直到船头迎风，船速会降低，继续等待！

Stage 2 - The middle bit
第二步，中间段

- Throw yourself out to the old windward side. This pulls the sail through the wind and gives you a pump just as the boat needs extra speed.
  身体保持在原来的上风侧，这样可以促使主帆换舷，在船需要速度时提供一个助推力。
- The main will come across. Once it has, let out the mainsheet a little.
  主帆换舷之后，略微放出主缭。
- **Wait** until the sail is on the new leeward side (it should be behind your head). You are still on what will become the new leeward side. The boat will be right on top of you (very scary!).
  继续等待主帆来到新的下风一侧（位于你的头部后面）你依然处在新的下风一侧。船身正位与你的上方（挺吓人的）。

Stage 3 - Coming out of the tack
第三步，结束转向

- Come across the boat (by standing up!) to the new windward side. Hike out no further than you were doing on the old windward side.
  站立起身换舷，做到新的上风一侧，向外压舷。
- As you move back across bring the main back to the position it was on the old tack.
  换舷后把主缭带回原来的位置。
- Pull the boat up slowly (the second pump) and powerfully but leave extra heel for the fiddle factor.

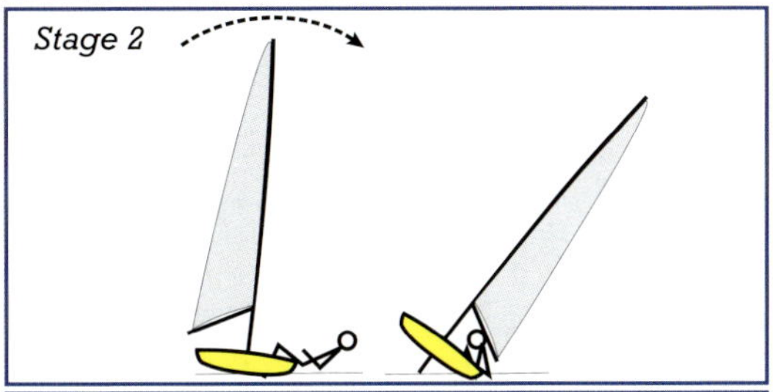

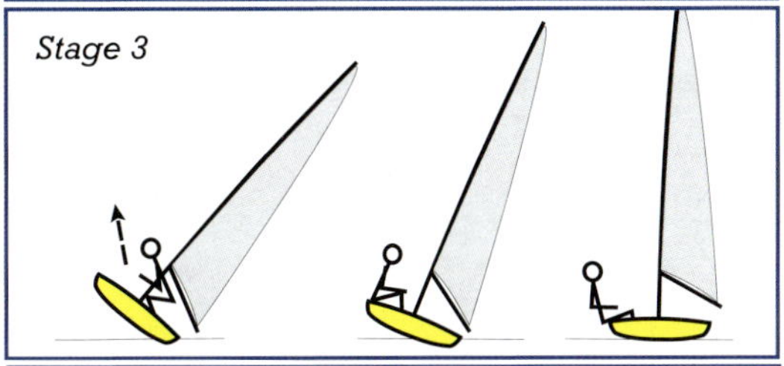

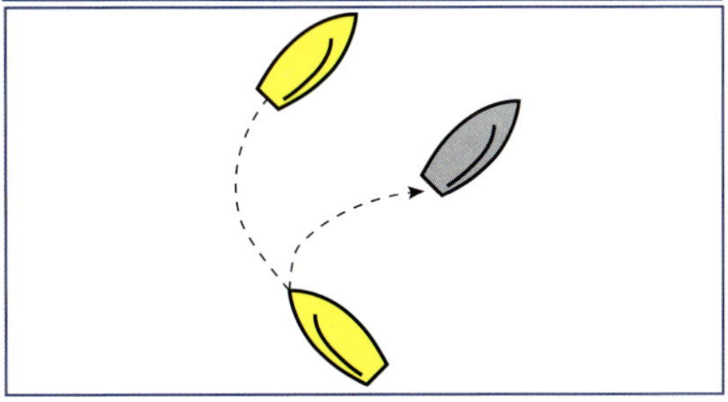

  慢慢让船向上风行驶（二次加力），但可以让船体多倾斜以便做细微调整。

Use the ‘fiddle factor’ to correct the new direction of travel – if you need to luff allow the heel of the boat to head you up. If you need to bear off (which will have slowed you down) pull the boat upright, to increase speed, as you bear away.
运用"细微调整"让新的航线更为精准——如果想走向上风就可以调整船体倾斜度来实现。如果想走向下风(会令你减速)就把船身调平，然后加速。

Use as little rudder as possible
尽可能减少用舵

Use the extra push of the two pumps to spend as much time as possible heading towards the wind rather than speeding up, because coming out of a tack faster than going in is not allowed. A long curve through the wind is what is needed.

The rule says you cannot exit a tack faster than you go into it. Use the extra push from two rolls to move further to windward rather than breaking the rule by coming out faster.

尽可能延长驶入迎风的时间以利用两次加力，因为转向结束的过程比开始的过程时间短是不允许的。最好是沿一个大弧线穿过风。规律表明在转向时你不能结束的比进入得快。尽量运用两次滚动时产生的额外推力前行，而不是急于结束转向。

As I said this is difficult to describe but keep trying. I won an Open Meeting once, not because I was the best sailor but because I was the best roll tacker. We had to beat up a narrow river in light wind. The only way to make progress was to tack up the banks out of the current. In three races we did about 650 roll tacks. (We counted them in the last race and worked it out.)

说起来容易做起来难，坚持练习吧！我曾经赢得过一次公开赛，原因并不是我是最好的赛手而是因为我的滚动转向技术最好。在比赛中我们需要在狭窄的河道里迎风航行（风很小），我们只有在快到河岸边时一次一次地转向以避开水流。在三场比赛中我们做了650次滚动转向！

8. ADJUSTING THE SAIL FOR UPWIND迎风时的调帆

The principles 原则

In light winds a flat sail is needed. Achieve this with a tight(ish) outhaul. Do not use downhaul. In medium winds it is best to have a full sail, achieved by using no downhaul, only a little kicker/vang and by having the outhaul at its loosest setting. In strong winds it is best to have a flat sail, again achieved by using lots of downhaul and lots of kicker/vang but keeping some shape in the bottom of the sail with the outhaul.

小风时需要让帆面平直。拉紧后拉索，不用调整下拉索。风力中等时尽量让帆面鼓起来，下拉索不用动，微微拉紧斜拉索，并且放松后拉索。大风时最好让帆面平直。拉紧下拉索和斜拉索，调整后拉索让帆的底部具有一定的弧度。

Very little wind – below force 2
微风——2级以下风

Kicker – sheet in the mainsheet so the mainsheet blocks are 200mm apart. Take up the slack on the kicker.

斜拉器——拉紧主缭，让两个滑轮之间间距为200毫米。放开斜拉索。

Downhaul – none.下拉索—不动

Outhaul – tight but not so tight that there is a crease in the foot of the sail.

后拉索——拉紧但不要过紧以致反面下部产生褶皱。

Traveller – tight but just loose enough that the shackle can slide across the tiller without catching.

滑车——拉紧但要保证快挂能够顺滑地滑动。

Hunting for maximum power – force 2-4
2～4级风时捕获最大力量

Kicker – sheet in the mainsheet so the mainsheet blocks are 75mm apart. Take up the slack on the kicker plus a little more.

斜拉索——收紧主缭，让两个滑轮之间间距为75毫米。进一步放开斜拉索。

Downhaul – none. 下拉索——不动

Outhaul – so there is a maximum distance from the boom to the sail of about your finger length.

后拉索——让帆底与横杆之间的距离为一个手指长度。

Traveller – very tight.

滑车——非常紧。

Overpowered – force 5 and above
风力过大——5级以上

Kicker – as much as you can pull on.

斜拉索——尽可能拉紧。

Downhaul – as much as you can pull on.

下拉索——尽可能拉紧。

Outhaul – maintain the curvature of the sail.

后拉索——保持帆面弧度。

Traveller – very tight.

滑车——非常紧。

These are a guide only. Much depends on your experience, weight and strength.

这些都是基本原则。更多地要依靠你的练习并结合体重和力量条件。

Settings 调校

The settings in the table overleaf are in more detail but are also offered in the right spirit. You cannot sail by numbers. Develop your sense of speed and adjust controls around these suggested start points.

Note that settings on a reach are somewhere between the Upwind and Running settings depending on wind speed and direction. For a close reach or when reaching in high winds, set up the controls nearer the Upwind settings. For a broad reach or when reaching in light winds, set up the controls nearer the Running settings.

在次页的表格中的调较设置比较详细但都是一些原则。你不能依靠数字进行航行。要努力培养对速度的感觉，并在建议的设置基础上进行调整。要注意到横风时的调较基本介于迎风和顺风之间，同时要考虑风速和风向。在上横风时的调较要接近迎风时的状态；下横风或横风时要接近顺风式的状态。

Many experienced helms talk about getting feedback from the tiller extension. Grip it loosely and it will tell you things. Make a change to a setting and feel the effect.

很多有经验的舵手会谈到从副舵柄得到反馈的经验：轻轻握住，会告诉你很多事情。你可以尝试改变船的设置来感受效果。

9. ON THE WATER JUDGES – AND RULE 42
水上裁判——第42条规则

All sports need rules. In fact without rules there is no sport. What rig would you choose to put on your Topper if the rules didn’t limit you to the one we use?

The main difference between sailing and most other sports is that we are asked to police the rules ourselves. Boats are only measured at major events and on-the-water rules are policed by the sailors on the race course. This is why doing turns is so important and why I would encourage you to protest any sailor who breaks the rules. Protesting shouldn’t be seen as an emotional business and the outcome should be accepted by both parties with a shaking of hands – we all need an inspirational goal! The alternative is that we allow the cheats to gain advantage which none of us want.

所有的运动都需要规则。实际上如果没有规则就没有运动本身。如果规则没有对船的装备进行规定，你如何选择装什么呢？帆船和其他大部分运动的主要区别就是我们要自律地遵守规则。只有大型的比赛才会对船只进行测量，而水上竞赛的规则是由选手们自己来维护的。这也是为什么做转向如此重要而且我会鼓励大家去抗议那些违反规则的人。抗议并不是一种情绪化的行为，而当事的双方也应该友好握手并接受仲裁的结果—我们都需要一个激励人心的目标！否则我们就会让欺骗行为收益，这是大家都不愿见到的。

What do judges look like?
裁判是什么样子？

Clearly, on the water judges are on the water! They will be in a RIB but be warned, just because you can’t see them doesn’t mean they are not watching you! You will also see them at the briefing where they will be letting the sailors know what they are looking for.

很清楚，水上裁判就呆在水上，他们在橡皮艇上，就算你看不到他们并不意味着他们看不到你！你在赛前准备会上也会见到他们，他们会告诉你裁判会关注什么。

What are they looking for?
他们关注什么？

Principally they are looking for sailors who break Rule 42, which is all about illegal propulsion. You can read the cold facts in the ISAF rule book.

他们最主要的是关注是否有人违反第42条规则，这是关于非法推进的规则。在世界帆联的规则手册中你可以看到那些严厉的案例。

42.1Bsic Rule 基本规则

Except when permitted in rule 42.3 or 45, a boat shall compete by using only the wind and water to increase, maintain or decrease her speed. Her crew may adjust the trim of sails and hull, and perform other acts of seamanship, but shall not otherwise move their bodies to propel the boat.

除规则42.3和45规定的情况外，比赛中的帆船只能利用风和水来提高、保持或降低速度。船员只能调整帆和船体并运用其他的合法手段，但不允许移动身体来推进船前进。

Medium winds and flat water: (hiking fully but not overpowered) 中等风力，水面平静（充分压舷但不要过度）		
Control 控制部件	***Upwind*** 迎风端段	***Running*** 顺风段
Mainsheet 主缭	*Almost block to block* 滑轮非常接近	*90°+ Run by lee - in gusts bear away* 帆放出90度+下风侧顺风航行——遇阵风就偏向下风
Traveller 滑车索	*As tight as possible* 尽可能收紧	*As tight as possible* 尽可能收紧
Kicker 斜拉索	*Take up slack + a little more* 不可松垂+略收紧	*Less - leech just able to flick* 略放松直到帆后缘略微摆动
Outhaul 后拉索	*Sail a finger length from boom* 帆下缘和横杆相距一根手指	*Hand length from boom* 帆下缘和横杆相距手掌长度
Downhaul 下拉索	*Off or very little* 略微放松	*Off* 完全放开
Daggerboard 稳向板	*Down* 全部放下	*3/4 up* 升起3/4
Balance 船身平衡	*Flat* 水平	*Heeled to windward - neutral helm* 向上风侧倾斜——舵叶居中
Trim 前后平衡	*As far forward as possible* 尽可能向前坐	*As far forward as possible* 尽可能向前坐

Medium winds and waves: (waves tending to upset the boat upwind) 中等风力和浪（船有可能被浪打翻）		
Control 控制部件	***Upwind*** 迎风段	***Running*** 顺风段
Mainsheet 主缭	*Almost block to block* 滑轮非常接近	*90° - play the waves* 帆放出90度+切浪航行
Traveller 滑车索	*As tight as possible* 尽可能收紧	*As tight as possible* 尽可能收紧
Kicker 斜拉索	*Take up slack + a little* 不可松垂+略收紧	*Less - leech just able to flick* 略放松，直到帆后缘略微摆动
Outhaul 后拉索	*Looser than flat water* 比平静水面时略松驰	*Slightly tighter than on flat water* 比平静水面时略紧
Downhaul 下拉索	*Take out some of the creases* 尽量减少帆面褶皱	*Off* 完全放开
Daggerboard 稳向板	*Down* 全部放下	*1/2 to 3/4 up* 升起1/2到3/4
Balance 船身平衡	*Slight heel to leeward* 略向下风侧倾斜	*Heeled to windward - neutral helm* 向上风侧倾斜——舵叶居中
Trim 前后平衡	*250mm further back* 向后移动250毫米	*Forward and back - ride the waves* 根据船和浪的相对位置向前或向后坐——骑浪而行

Looking for more power
追求更多力量

Control 控制部件	*Upwind* 迎风段	*Running* 顺风段
Mainsheet 主缭	*300mm off block to block* 滑轮相距300毫米	*90°+ and by the lee* 帆放出90度+下风侧航行
Traveller 滑车索	*As tight as possible* 尽可能收紧	*As tight as possible* 尽可能收紧
Kicker 斜拉索	*Take up the slack* 不可松垂	*Less - until leech starts to flick* 略放松，直到帆后缘略微摆动
Outhaul 后拉索	*Width of wrist from boom* 帆下缘和横杆相距一拳	*Length of hand* 帆下缘和横杆相距手掌长度
Downhaul 下拉索	*Slack* 放松	*Off* 完全放开
Daggerboard 稳向板	Down 全部放下	*$^1/_2$ to $^3/_4$ up* 升起1/2到3/4
Balance 船身平衡	*Very slightly heeled to leeward* 微微下风侧倾斜	*Heeled to windward - neutral helm* 向上风侧倾斜——舵叶居中
Trim 前后平衡	*Forward* 向前坐	*Forward - stern out of water* 向前坐——船尾出水

Overpowered: (fully hiking and having to let out mainsheet upwind)
过度的力量（完全向外压舷，顺风时把帆放出）

Control 控制部件	*Upwind* 迎风段	*Running* 顺风段
Mainsheet 主缭	*Block to block - let off* 放开滑轮距离	*As far out as you dare. 80° max* 看你的胆量了，帆最大放出80度
Traveller 滑车索	*As tight as possible* 尽可能收紧	*As tight as possible* 尽可能收紧
Kicker 斜拉索	*Take up slack + lots more!* 不可松垂+收紧	*As much off as you feel safe with!* 在你感觉安全的范围内尽可能放松
Outhaul 后拉索	*Width of wrist from boom* 帆下缘和横杆相距一拳	*Hand length from boom* 帆下缘和横杆相距手掌长度
Downhaul 下拉索	*Loads - until front stops backing* 放松	*Off* 完全放开
Daggerboard 稳向板	*$^1/_4$ up* 升起1/4	*$^1/_2$ up* 升起1/2
Balance 船身平衡	*Flat* 水平	*Heeled to windward - neutral helm* 向上风侧倾斜——舵叶居中
Trim 前后平衡	*250mm further back* 向后坐250毫米	*Well back - prevent nosedive* 向后坐——防止船头扎水

Looking for any power at all! (very little wind) 微风中获得力量

Control 控制部件	Upwind 迎风段	Running 顺风段
Mainsheet 主缭	*300mm off block to block* 滑轮相距300毫米	*90°+ and by the lee* 帆放出90度+下风侧航行
Traveller 滑车索	*Tight - but allow block to travel* 拉紧但允许滑轮滑动	*Tight - but allow block to travel* 拉紧但允许滑轮滑动
Kicker 斜拉索	*Take up the slack* 不可松垂	*Less - until leech starts to flick* 略放松-直到帆后缘略微摆动
Outhaul 后拉索	*Reasonably tight - finger length* 略紧-帆下缘和横杆相距一指	*Reasonably tight - finger length* 略紧—帆下缘和横杆相距一指
Downhaul 下拉索	*Off* 放松	*Off* 放松
Daggerboard 稳向板	Down 全部放下	*$^1/_2$ to $^3/_4$ up* 升起1/2到3/4
Balance 船身平衡	*Heeled to reduce wetted area* 船身倾斜以减少贴水面积	*Well heeled to leeward* 尽量向下风侧倾斜
Trim 前后平衡	*Far forward* 尽量向前坐	*Sit on bulkhead* 坐在船舱前端

Sailing is about··· well sailing! It' s not about air rowing and those who body pump, fan, scull, and pump inappropriately need to join another sport. Governed by IARF (International Air Rowing Association!) rather than by ISAF (International Sailing Federation) no doubt! Actually windsurfers are allowed to air row!

It would take too long to set out in this section exactly what is allowed (sailing) and what is not allowed (air rowing) but here is a taste:

帆船就是一项绅士运动！不允许划动空气、跳动身体、摇扇、摇橹，否则你就去干别的运动吧！可以加入IARF（国际空气划动组织）而不是ISAF (国际帆联，现在叫世界帆联)。事实上帆板运动允许划动空气！

如果要把所有允许和不允许的动作列出来会是一个长长的单子。下面是些基本要求：

Sailing (allowed) 合法行为

- Roll tacking and gybing.
  滚动迎风转向和顺风转向。
- Adjusting the sail when the boat changes direction.
  航向改变时调整帆。
- Moving your body weight in or out to help steer the boat.
  内移或外移你的身体来帮助调整航向。
- Using the rudder to steer the boat.
  使用舵来调整航向。
- Moving the mast over the vertical at the completion of a tack or a gybe.
  在迎风转向和顺风转向时调整桅杆垂直度。
- Torquing (upper body movement) to change the fore-and-aft trim of the boat in phase with the waves, provided it does not result in pumping the sails, especially flicking the leech.
  在过浪时移动身体上部来调整船身前后平衡，但前提是不会摇动帆，尤其是引起帆的纵缘震动。

Air rowing and other illegal propulsion (not allowed) 划动空气和其他非法推进（不允许）

- Coming out of a roll tack or roll gybe faster than you went into it.
  滚动转向的结束过程短于进入过程。
- Repeated tacks or gybes unrelated to wind changes or tactical considerations.

反复迎风转向，并不是由于风向的改变或战术的考虑。

- Pumping the sail (rapid movement) except to promote surfing (once per wave or gust and even then you must succeed in surfing).
  摇帆（快速移动帆），除非在滑浪（每个浪头或每次阵风只允许一次，而且你必须成功地滑浪）。
- Any sculling (two or more similar movements of the rudder, however small) that does not result in a clear change of direction (especially once beyond close hauled when the sail can fill).
  任何一种摇舵动作（两次以上的相同的舵叶转动，即使动作很小），这种动作没有明显改变航向（特别是在最小迎风角之外进行摇舵以促使帆鼓满）。
- Violent body movements like ooching (sudden forward body movement, stopped abruptly).
  剧烈的身体移动(急动急停)。
- Paddling! This includes any part of the body and movement of the boat in any direction (you can't stop by putting your hand in the water, for instance).
  划桨！包括用身体或船体的任何部分在任何方向进行划动（比如你不能把手放进水里把船停下来）。

The above is only a taste and you would be best to read the rules and talk to coaches and umpires.
以上只是一些经验，你最好仔细阅读规则并且和教练和裁判交流。

The above should not stop sailors being active in a boat. I think of it as being 'on your toes' and you can tell a talented sailor by the attitude that sees them constantly checking their settings, looking around and changing their position in a boat as the situation demands. They are far more proactive rather than being reactive. The latter often results in over-exaggerated movement, which will be penalized.
上面这些不能阻止一个选手的积极进取。你可以观察选手是否随时检查设置，四处观察并且及时改变在船上的位置来辨别是不是一个好选手。好的选手一定是主动应变而不是被动改变，后者往往是过度移动而受到处罚。

Three pointers三点提示

- When you watch a fleet all the boats are being moved by the waves, unless it is very calm, at much the same frequency. The boat that is not being moved in the same way as the rest is clearly doing something wrong/different.
  当你观察到整个船队都以相似节奏随着涌浪移动，如果有个别船的动态明显不同，就一定发生了什么事情或者错误。
- Judges will look closely at the leech of the sail. If it is flicking (opening and closing repeatedly), irrespective of any action by the sailor, then clearly something is wrong.
  裁判会观察帆的纵缘，如果不是因为船员的动作就产生拍打（重复地开合），就一定有什么问题。
- When boats are lining up for a start, and therefore manoeuvring at slow speeds, the temptation to scull is high. It may surprise you how little movement judges will allow. Sculling is the most penalised crime of all.
  当船队列队准备出发时船速都很慢，这时候摇橹的欲望很高。你会吃惊地发现裁判对于摇橹动作的容忍度很低。在帆船比赛中摇橹是所有的违规动作中被判罚最重的。

What happens if I break Rule 42?
如果违反了第42条规则怎么办？

The judge will let you know that you have broken the rule by blowing a whistle and pointing a yellow flag at you. Don't argue. Having spent a day with Carol Haines at the Inlands I know she was watching some sailors over a period of time and from a fair distance. By the time we motored up they were being very good (so they knew!) but it was already too late.
裁判将吹哨并把一面黄旗指向你通知你犯规了，这时你不要争辩。我在内陆湖面上和Carol Haines（著名裁判）曾经度过了一天，她经常在远处观察一些选手，当我们开船接近时这些人会表现得很乖（说明他们明白规则），但这时已经晚了！

The first time you are caught at the event you must do a two turns penalty promptly (and without sculling or coming out of the manoeuvre faster than you went in or you will be penalised again!). The second time (and this may be another race at the same event) you have to retire from that race (and if you don't retire you will be disqualified

and have to count the result towards you final score). If you are daft enough to do it a third time you could be disqualified from the whole event. This has happened at the Topper Worlds in the past, by the way. But do check Sailing Instruction to see if this has been altered in any way.
你首次被判罚时，必须迅速地原地转两圈（不许摇橹或者结束过程短于进入过程，否则会被再次判罚！）。如果第二次被判罚（可能在同一个赛事的不同场次），你就必须退出当次比赛（如果你拒绝退出则会被判为没有完成比赛DSQ并被记入总成绩）。如果你疯狂到第三次被判罚，你就会被排除出整个赛事。以前的Topper世锦赛曾经发生过这样的事。建议你仔细阅读航行规则看看这一规则是否已经被修改。
This is pretty fierce stuff. Judges don’t want to penalize you but they are there to see fair play so we are going to have to learn how to stay within the rules.
这确实有点残酷。其实裁判并不想处罚你，但是他们必须保证比赛是公平的，因此我们必须学习如何掌握规则。

How can I get it right?
如何正确地比赛？

Ask! Coaches can help but the most important source of knowledge is the judge. They will hang around on the water between races and are keen to talk to sailors about what they did wrong and why they were yellow flagged. Even if you didn’t get penalized and want to check a technique they will be happy to help – use them. Equally they are there after racing has finished and are very approachable.
去问！教练会帮助你但是最重要的知识来源还是裁判。他们比赛间隙会在水上巡游并且愿意和选手交流哪里犯规和为什么被判罚黄旗。即使你没有犯规而愿意探讨技术问题他们也很愿意帮忙。比赛结束后他们仍然会在水上，依然可以交流。

10. A FEW MORE TIPS!
几个新的提示

- **Sheeting in quickly**快速收缭绳

Sheeting in quickly is especially important at the start but also at the leeward mark. With the centre sheeting, start by reaching down to the ratchet block with your front hand (the one not holding the tiller extension), then grab the rope and pull until your hand is over your head. Drop the rope carefully into the boat at the same time as you hinge the extension down and pick up the rope with your back hand. Hinge the extension upwards (the trick here is to do this without steering in the wrong direction!) to allow you to pull the rope as you reach down with the front hand for the next pull. I often see sailors with a lap full of rope because they didn’t place it carefully after a pull!
出发时和绕下风标时快速收缭绳非常重要。如果是中置主缭船型，出发时要用前臂够到棘齿滑轮，然后抓住缭绳用力拉直到手臂挥到头顶上方。然后把缭绳小心地放在船底同时把副舵柄放低并用后手臂抓起缭绳，把副舵柄抬起（注意一定要保持正确航向！）给前臂留出空间在下一次继续收紧缭绳。我经常看见选手的膝盖上乱糟糟的一堆绳子，因为在收紧后没有小心地放置缭绳。

- **Responding to a sudden lift**
如何应对风摆

In a sudden lift you want to turn quickly into the new wind but it is impossible to turn that fast. Instead let out the mainsheet quickly (so that the sail is trimmed to the new wind). Then pull in the mainsheet again as you luff smoothly up to the new wind direction. The boat will spurt forward.
在风向突然变化时你肯定希望马上恢复最佳迎风角度，但你不可能很快转向。可以快速放出主缭（主帆会和新的风向形成好的角度），然后收进主缭慢慢靠向上风找到最好角度，船速会提升。

- **Beating – another technique**
迎风航行——另一种技术

Earlier in this book we taught you to beat by luffing until the front of the sail begins to flap, then bearing away until it stops flapping. A more subtle way is to sail by heel:
在本书的前面我们建议在迎风时慢慢走向上风，直到主帆前缘开始飘动，然后向下风走直到飘帆停止。一种更精巧的方式是利用压舷航行：

A. Get ‘on the wind’ and sit out (hike) so that the boat is almost flat. The exact angle of heel will be determined by the conditions, but you shouldn’t have much weather helm.
上风航行并且向外压舷，保持船体平直。准确的船身倾斜角度取决于各方面条件，但是不能有太多的上风舵。

B. Now luff gently whilst sitting out (hiking) the same amount. Eventually the boat will roll on top of you.
现在慢慢地走向上风并且向外压舷，最后船身会滚动到你的上方。

C. Now bear away until you are sailing at the same heel as in step A.
然后走向下风直到倾斜角度与步骤A相同。

Keep repeating this technique and you will find that you can sail the ideal upwind course (without continually watching the sail) but instead taking in all that is happening around you.
重复练习这个技术你就会学会掌握理想的迎风航线（不需要总是观察帆），并且利用上所有的周边条件。

摄影：何则通

11. THE FINAL WORD
最后的话

Improving boatspeed and developing boat handling will improve results in small fleets. Practise them until they become second nature. Make them so automatic that even in stressful situations you still do things the right way. Even more important, make them so automatic that you don’t have to think about them. When that happens you can concentrate much more on the bigger picture – on what other boats are doing and which is the best way to go. This is what will give you good results in big fleets.

不断地提高船速和改进控船水平可以让你在小型的比赛中取得好成绩。持续地练习直到成为你的第二天性并且成为自动的反应，即使处在各种压力下你也可以操控自如。更重要的是让这种反应不需要通过思考就自动做出来。当各种状况出现时你仍然可以专注在更重要的事情上——其他船的动向以及你的最佳航线。这样可以让你在大型的比赛中获得好成绩。

Keep the boat upright like this, by hiking hard. Pull in the mainsheet until the blocks are close together.

像这样尽力压舷，保持船身平直。收进主缭直到两个滑轮贴在一起。

Excellent beating. Sit well forward unless the waves are breaking over the foredeck.

非常好的迎风航行。除非浪头涌过前甲板，否则要尽量向前坐。

摄影：何则通

Masterclass 5 大师级别5 Tactics and strategy for success 制胜的战术与策略

Before the start 起航前

A boat race begins long before the start sequence. Time on the water, long before the first sound signal, will affect your result. Top sailors have a routine and so should you. The following is offered as a possible framework because preparation in this stressed period is very individual.
帆船比赛的竞争在起航之前很早就开始了。起航号响起之前的表现将会对最终成绩产生影响。顶级的选手都有一套固定程式，因此你也应该有。下面是一些可能的框架，在这个紧张的阶段，准备活动是非常个人化的。

- On arrival take a look at the conditions and compare them with the forecast you already have. Check the geography of the land: will it affect the wind on the race course?
  到达比赛场地后观察比赛条件，和你预期的状况进行对比。注意岸上的地形，判断是否对比赛航线上的风产生影响。
- Get on the first rank ashore so your launch times are not controlled by others.
  尽量处在岸上的前排下水，这样你的下水时间就不会受到别人影响。
- Launch early.
  尽早离岸。
- As you sail out be observant of wind and tide. Has the race team set the course?
  离岸后观察风和潮汐，赛事方是否已经设置好航线？
- Sail the first beat against a friend and see which side, if any, is favoured.
  测试一下迎风航行，最好有一个朋友选择不同的方向出发，比较从那一边出发更有优势。
- This is a good time to set up the boat for the conditions.
  这时候应该把船的各个部分根据外部条件调整好。
- Determine the headings on your compass and see if the windshifts are oscillating or if there is a windbend.
  在罗盘上确定航向角度，观察风摆是否振动或者风向是否呈曲线。
- Windbends are best checked as you sail back downwind to the start area.
  当你顺风航行回到出发区域时，是观察风向是否呈曲线的好时机。
- Once the line is set, check the bias and take a transit.
  一旦航线确定，观察风的偏角并进行航线角度转换。
- Work with your friend or coach to determine your tactics and strategy.
  和你的朋友或教练一起确定战术和策略。
- Keep focused and warmed up as you recheck conditions up the course and the position of the line.
  保持注意力和热身，同时观察航线上的状况和航线位置。

Starting 起航

Once you can race a boat reasonably well the ability to start is probably the most important thing to get right. So how can you improve your chances of making a good one?
一旦你可以顺利地进行比赛，起航的能力是所有因素中最重要的。因此你如何能改进并漂亮地起航呢？

A SAFE START 安全地起航

If you are inexperienced and a little nervous about starting, especially in big fleets, try this:
如果你欠缺经验并且对起航略感紧张，尤其是身处大量起航船之中时，建议你：

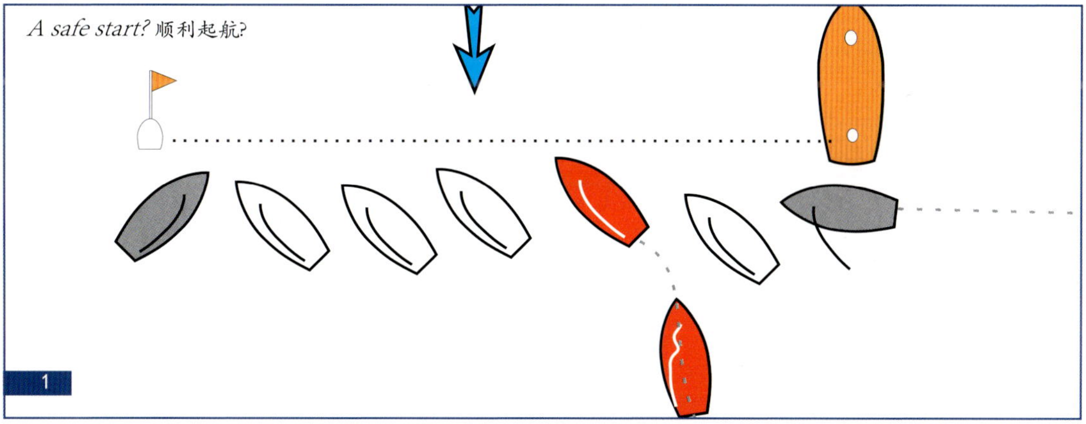

The rules say that the red boat (Figure 1) can luff up as far as head to wind as long as it gives the boat to windward room to keep clear. Approach the line slowly and try to create a space to leeward. The grey boat reaching in at speed is about to remove everyone’s wind indictors and the grey boat on port is also in trouble!

图1的红色船按照规则可以向上风走直到船头顶风，这时船的上风一侧留出了空间并且没有障碍。慢慢地靠近起航线，努力在下风一侧也留出空间。右侧横风航行的灰色船速度太快，即将和别的船碰撞，左侧的灰色船也一样有麻烦。

WHERE ON THE LINE?
如何选择在起航线上的位置？

Well certainly on the line, there is no point in being two lengths behind it or going the wrong way at the start signal! You will know, though, that the choice of position on the line can give you an advantage. The Race Officer will usually try to set a line that just favours the port end to counteract the advantage of being on starboard tack. If he/she doesn’t make the port end ‘biased’ all the boats start by the committee boat – nightmare! However the wind rarely behaves so you need to check.

保持在起航线附近，千万不要离起航线太远或者在起航信号响起时选择错误的航向。竞赛官员总是在设置起航线时让左侧起航的船具有些优势来抵消右舷起航船的优势。如果不把起航线左端略作偏转，所有的船都会挤在裁判船所在的右侧起航，那简直就是恶梦！虽然风不太容易变化，你还是要观察确认。

HOW CAN YOU TELL WHICH END IS BIASED?
如何确认起航线哪一端有偏转？

There are a number of ways:

有几个方法：

1. Reach along the line, or its extension, using your previously determined transits (Figure 2). Let out the sail until half of it is lifting. Keeping the mainsheet in the same position, tack or gybe and sail the line in the reverse direction. If the sail is now flapping more you are heading towards the upwind end. If it is flapping less you are sailing away from the windward end. This is the best method for determining the upwind end when the bias is only slight.
   沿起航线或其延长线横风航行，按照你事先确定的路线走（图2）。放出主帆直到一半的帆面受力。保持主缭在同一个位置并转向沿原路返回。如果此时帆面飘动更厉害就意味着你在朝向上风一端航行。如果飘动减少就意味着你在驶离上风一端。这是在风向偏转微小时判断哪一侧是上风端的最佳方法。
2. The yellow boat in the diagram has luffed head to wind. With the sail flapping along the centreline your bow is pointing towards the upwind end of the line.
   图中黄色的船偏向上风并顶风，帆面沿着船的中心线飘动，这时你的船头就是指向起航线的上风一端。
3. Get a friend to do a dummy start at one end of the line while you try the other (Figure 3). The one who passes ahead of the other has come from the upwind end.

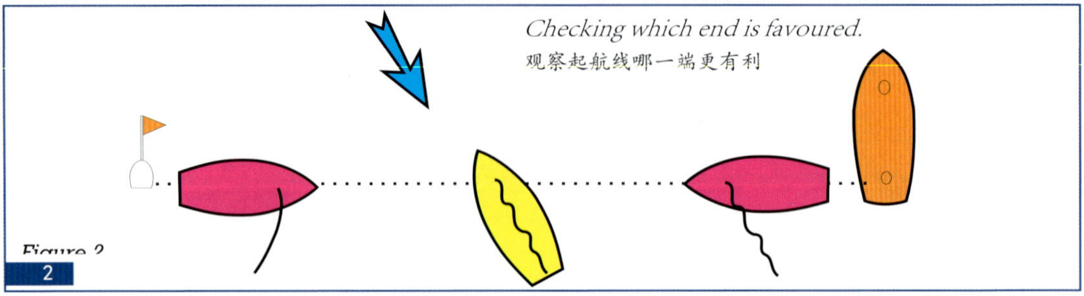

Figure 2
2

找一个朋友一起做一次模拟起航，你和他分别从起航线两端起航（图3）。先从另一只船前面穿过的船就来自上风一端。

BIG FLEETS 大批船出发

In big fleets with long lines watch out for ‘line sag’ (Figure 4,).

Close to each end sailors can tell they are on the line. Further away from the ends it’s more difficult to tell, so boats tend to play safe, especially if it’s a ‘black flag’ start. The smart sailor knows where the line really is and you can imagine the advantage gained and the cries that come from the rest of the fleet when they believe you are over the line! The grey boats are still being donkeys!

大批船出发意味着起航线很长，这时候要小心“中间塌陷”（图4）。

离两端近的选手会知道自己正在起航线上，离两端远的人因为难以判断位置，安全起见就会退后（特别是在黑旗起航的条件下）。聪明的选手知道起航线的实际位置并且可以获得优势，即使其他人认为他们已经越线而喊叫，图中的灰色船处于困难境地!

Remember to consider which side of the beat you want to play. Even if the line is port biased, if you want to go right up the beat, starting at the port end may be a bad idea.

记住你要选择从哪一边迎风起航。即使起航线朝左边偏转，如果你想径直走迎风，左舷起航可能是个坏主意。

3
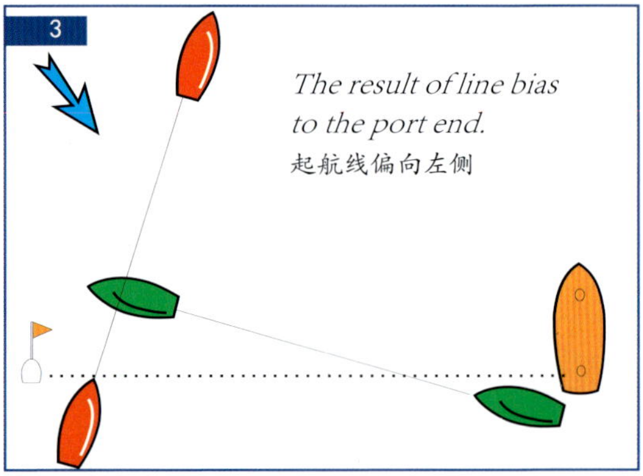

PLOTTING THE LINE 划定起航线

If only the Race Committee would paint the line on the water! But they don’t so how can the black boat tell? What you need is a transit. Look along the line (from outside either end) and find a fixed feature that lines up (Figure 5).

如果竞赛委员会能够在水面上画出起航线该多好！事实上他们不会画线，那如何辨别呢？你需要一条虚拟参照线。从起航线任何一端的外面向起航线望去，找到一个固定物体作为参照物（图5）。

Sometimes there are no transits visible. Try this alternative, the ‘tiller method’: When you think you are on the line point the bow of the boat at one end and centralise the tiller. Look along the tiller (still centralised) and, if you are on the line, it

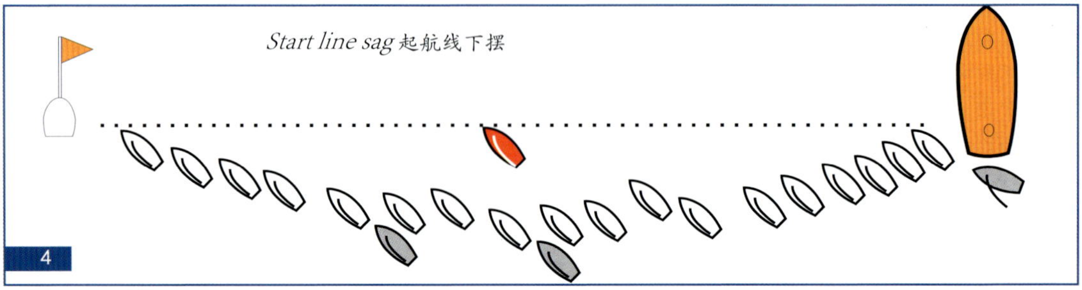

4

will be pointing at the other end. If you are behind the line (often the case!) the tiller will be pointing behind the line. If you are over the line it will be pointing ahead of the other end. It is remarkable how often you think that you are over the line when you are not.

有时候没有任何可视参照物就可以尝试“舵柄方法”。当你感觉处于起航线上时，让船头指向起航线的一端，然后把舵柄放置在船身中间与船体中线重合，沿着舵柄向另一方望去。如果你正位于起航线上，舵柄会正指向另一端的物体（裁判船或起航标）；如果你在起航线之后（经常如此）舵柄会指向另一端的后面；如果你已经跨过起航线，舵柄会指向另一端的前面。有趣的是你会经常认为自己越线了而实际上并没有。

OTHER IMPORTANT POINTS
其他的重点

- Allow for the current (Figure 6 **overleaf**).
  考虑潮流的方向并留足空间（下页图6）。
- Also, you still need to have a reliable stop-watch and know how to use it and trust it! Particularly on long lines when you are at the opposite end from the committee boat, start when your watch tells you and not wait until the sound signal reaches you.
  同时你还需要一块可靠的航海表，学会使用并相信它！尤其是你在长距离起航线远离裁判船的位置，在航海表倒计时结束时马上出发而不必等待起航号声。
- Good boat control is essential. You must be able to speed up and slow down, manoeuvre in tight corners and have a good idea how long it takes to cover a particular distance in a particular time.
  优良的船只操控是基础。你必须自如地加速或减速，在狭小的空间里腾挪，胸有成竹地按时完成每一个航段。

TOP TIPS FOR FIRST BEATS!!!
首个迎风段的最佳技巧！！！

- Know the settings that give you boatspeed in particular conditions.
  在不同条件下熟练地调整帆具索具以获得最大速度。
- Have a plan based on wind and tide but be prepared to change it. One way of checking this

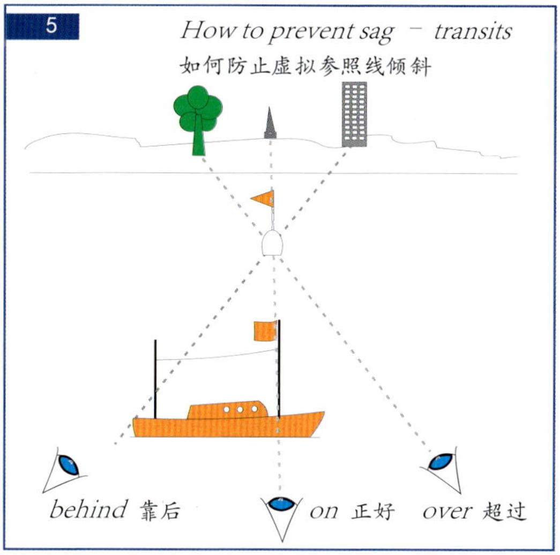

is to sail the first beat, before the start, against a friend who goes another way. Don't miss the start though!
  针对风和潮汐条件制订航行计划但随时准备做出调整，一个窍门是在起航前请一个朋友和你分别沿两个方向起航，比较效果后决定战术。但千万别错过起航啊！
- Get a good start. Very bad start? – go across the back of the fleet on port until you find clear wind. The wind you get as you cross behind the fleet on port, although 'dirty', is lifted.
  争取领先起航。如果起航就落后怎么办？用左舷航行从船队后面穿过直到你找到干净的风。驶过船队后面时的风虽然不太干净，但也足够推动你前进。
- Clear air, clear air, clear air.
  干净风！干净风！干净风！
- First 100m go for boatspeed – keep your lane.
  出发后头100米要提起速度——保持航线。
- **WORK VERY HARD ON THE FIRST BEAT!**
  首个迎风段要使出浑身解数！
- Look out for the first windshift. Be far enough ahead to use it. **WINDSHIFTS REALLY COUNT!**
  时刻注意风摆。保持一定的风夹角以随时利用风摆。**风摆确实很要命！**
- When ahead stay between the bulk of the fleet and the first mark.
  保持在大部队里直到一标。
- Be prepared to duck boats – sail your own race.
  时机成熟就破浪前行——走自己的路。

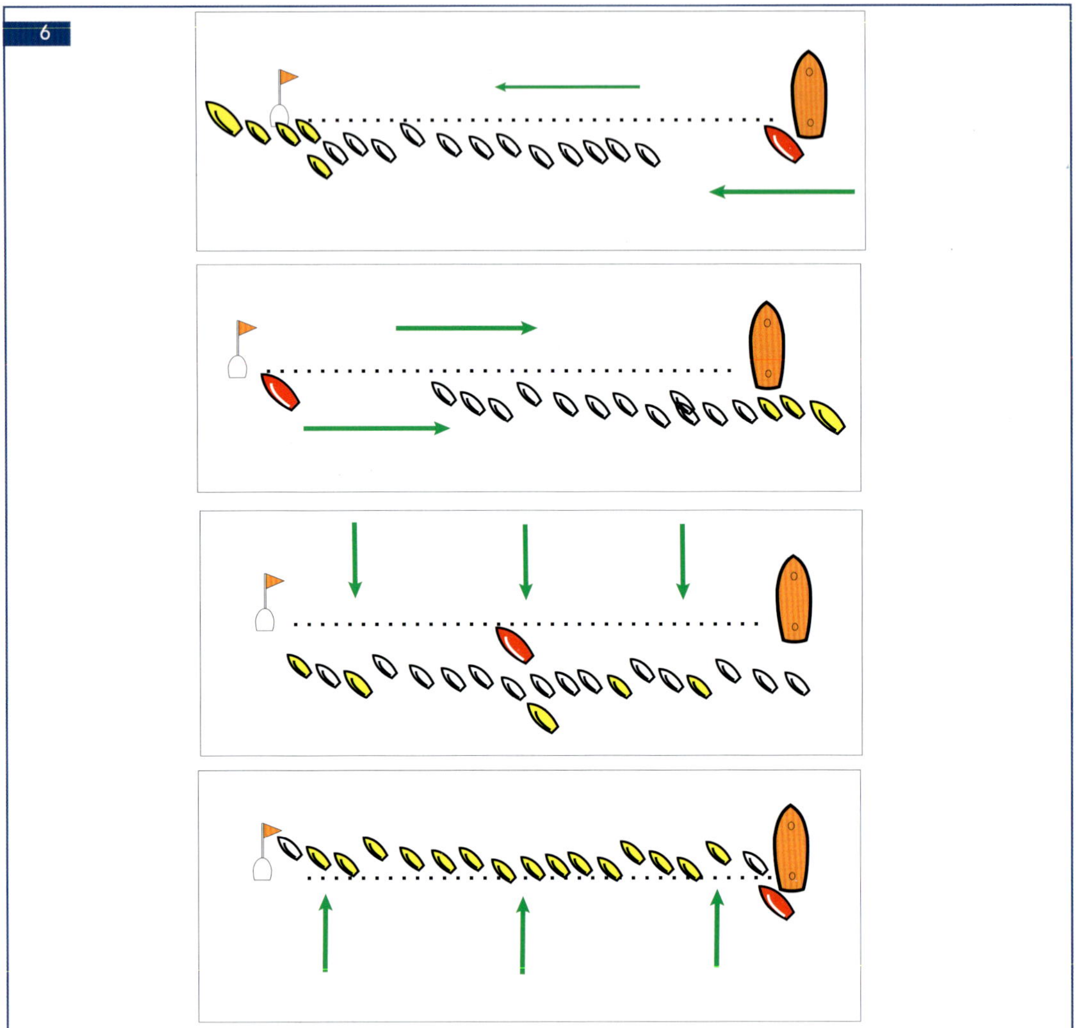

The green arrows show the direction of the current. The red boat is being smart.
绿色箭头表示水流的方向,红色船的选择正确

- Get your head out of the boat.
  探出船外随时观察。
- Don’t go to either layline. Work the side of the beat that suits your plan.
  不要靠近任何一侧的基准线，沿着你计划好的迎风航线前进。
- If you believe the right side is the better side (perhaps there is more wind) and the fleet goes left then only be more to the right than most of the fleet, i.e. be conservative.
  如果你认为右侧更有利（可能风更大）而大部分船都走左侧，你就坚定地在更右侧航行，做个不随波逐流的坚定派。
- Check your plan by coming back to the sweet spot – the middle (ish) if you can.
  航行到舒服的位置时，检查自己的计划——尽量在航程中点进行。
- In general in a big fleet the best advice is to come into the first mark on starboard.
  总的来说如果大批船只比赛，最好是右舷绕一标。
- But don’t hit the starboard layline too early.
  但不要过早进入右舷的基准线。
- Think ahead to your strategy on the next leg.
  在进入下一个航段之前确定好战术。

Windshifts 风摆

On a beat of 200m two boats set off from the leeward mark (Figure 7). One goes on a 9-degree lift while the other goes the other way on a 9-degree header. Halfway up they both tack just as a windshift happens. The one on the lift gets another 9-degree lift whilst his unlucky competitor once again gets the 9-degree header. By the windward mark the first boat has a 100m lead!
在一个长度200米的迎风航段中，两条船同时从下风标出发（图7）。左边的船比标准迎风角高9度航行，右边的船比标准迎风角低9度航行。走到一半航程时同时转向，恰好风摆发生了。左边的船可以再向上风偏转9度，而右边那条倒霉的对手却要再向下风偏转9度。这样左侧船到达上风标时已经领先了100米！
The orange boat is the unlucky one who catches two bad 9-degree headers while the blue boat gets two 9-degree lifts. The black tracks are what would happen if there were no windshifts.
橙色的船很不走运，必须向下风偏转两个9度。而蓝色船却可以向上风偏转两个9度。黑色的线表示没有风摆时的航迹。
This shows the importance of windshifts and, while you would be very unlucky to be as badly out of phase with wind as the orange boat, 9 degrees is half of one division on a tactical compass!
这说明了风摆的重要性，如果你像橙色船那样被风摆所累，9度只是一半的损失。
No amount of boatspeed will make up for being on the wrong side of a bad windshift, so how do we recognise them?

7

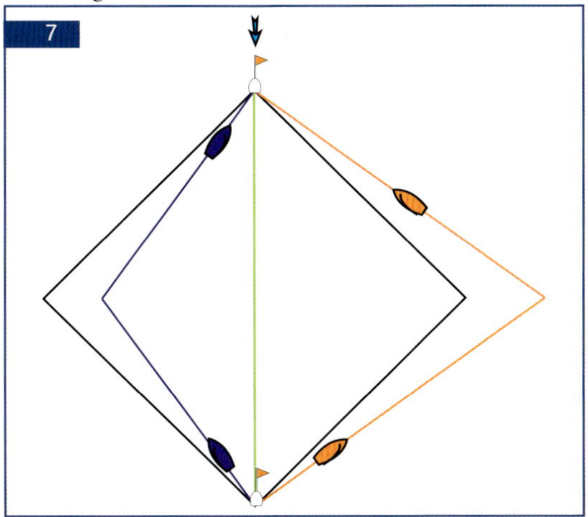

即使你提高船速也无法弥补在风摆中选择了错误航线的损失。那我们如何识别风摆呢？

- Look at other boats. Those further to windward than you will get the wind change first and you can be ready to react. Boats in line with you will appear to go backwards when you are on a lift and appear to go forward of you when you are on a header.
  观察别的船：上风的船会先遇到风向变化，你可以做好准备应对。当你遇到上风摆时，和你同航线的船会逐渐落后。当你遇到下风摆时，和你同航线的船会逐渐赶上来。
- Your boat will slow down and stop heeling as you encounter a header. In a lifting wind you will be able to head up without the boat slowing.
  如果遇到下风摆，你的船速会降低并减少倾斜。遇到上风摆时你可以走向上风而不会降低船速。
- In a header your sail will back in a big shift but before that the telltale on the windward side of the sail will drop.
  遇到下风摆时帆的角度会明显改变，在此之前上风侧的风向线会垂落。
- Your wind indicator will change direction.
  风向标会改变方向。
- Above all, your compass will show a change in your heading.
  你的罗盘会显示航向的变化。

COMPASS 罗盘

Compasses are useful all round the race course but especially on the beat. They are really easy to use. Buy a tactical compass and it will have numbers on it. Sail on each tack for a while and you will find the magic number. If it is 12 on starboard then it will be 2 on port. They are always 10 apart – 4/14, 8/18 and so on. Write this number on your boat. When the number goes up on starboard you are on a header. On port the number goes down when you are being headed. Draw a minus sign on the port side of the boat and a plus sign on the starboard side. Sail your boat and when you feel you are on a header take a look at the compass as confirmation of the fact – don't sail looking at it all the time!
整个比赛过程中罗盘都很有用，特别是在迎风段，使用起来很容易。左舷和右舷各航行一段你就可以发现一些魔法数字。如果右舷航行的数字是12，那么左舷就是2。两个数字的差值永远是10比如4/14，8/18等。把这些数字写在船上。如果右舷航行时数字在增加就意味着遇到下风摆，如果左舷航行时数字下降也意味着有下风摆。在船的左舷画一个减号，右舷画一个加号。如果你感到了风摆就看一下罗盘确认一下——但不要总是盯着罗盘！

Types of windshift 风摆的种类

Oscillating – The wind shifts either side of its average position. The timescale for the shifts is often consistent and can be tracked by sailing upwind while making a note of when the shifts happen. Remember though that when going downwind the shifts will be further apart because you are travelling with rather than against the wind. In oscillating winds it' s best to sail a little freer when you are on a lift so you get to the next lift (on the other tack) more quickly.

振动型风摆——风朝左右两个方向摆动，摆动的持续时间也基本一致，可以在迎风航行中进行记录跟踪。请记住在顺风航行时风摆可能会加剧，因为你是与风同向而行。在振动型风摆条件下，航线最好相对自由些让你更快地抓住下一个上风摆。

Windbend – wind will often follow the contours of the area it travels in. If it bends, always tack towards the inside of the bend.

弧形风摆——风通常都是沿着地形的轮廓流动。如果风向呈弧形，最好转向至弧线的内侧。

Permanent shift – where the gradient breeze is gradually shifting one way, head towards the side of the beat it is swinging to. If it' s swinging to the right, that will be the favoured side of the beat.

持续性风摆——梯度风持续向一个方向偏转。尽量在风偏向的一侧迎风航行：如果风转向右侧，就保持在右侧航线迎风上行。

Offwind 顺风航段

Tactics offwind are a little less complicated. Clearly you must keep clear air and everyone else wants to do the same. One effect of this is that there is often a large bow and few boats take the direct route to the mark. This can be exaggerated where tide has an effect. On broader reaches, on longer legs and in bigger fleets look for the option of going low immediately you exit the mark and staying low until you approach the next mark. There are big gains to be made here. But how do you know that you are on the direct line to the next mark? Look again at the way you can get a transit for the startline and use the same technique for offwind legs. As you round the first mark, look over the next mark at a feature beyond. Keep the two in line and you are on a straight-line course. Sometimes you will have to crab sideways to keep the two in line but that will indicate the presence of a current.

顺风段的战术不太复杂。因为每个人都希望得到干净风，这样会造成大家都走弧形线路，很少有船会沿直线径直到下风标。如果加上潮流的影响，这种弧形效果会更明显。如果在长距离的下横风航段中集中了很多船，你一定要尽量在过标后向下风走直到接近下一个标，这样走会相当受益。但你如何判断是否沿直线航行到下一标呢？你可以使用上面讲过的判断起航线的方法来设置顺风段航线。当你绕过一标后找到下一个标和外面的物体作为参照物，在航行中保持与这两个物体的相对关系，你的航线就是直线。有时候因为潮流产生的位移使你必须斜向航行才能保持航向。

In Figure 8 the fleet is behaving like sheep – a fleet often does! The grey boat is in the worst possible position, in the fleet' s dirty wind. The red boat has gone for clear air and will often gain lots of places.

在图8中整个船队像羊群一样前行，灰色的船是最糟糕的位置——因为它处在整个船队的脏风之中。红色船因为得到了干净风可以获得领先位置。

Rounding the leeward mark 绕下风标

Traditionally, we all round the leeward mark like boat A (Figure 9) – wide in, tight out. This is good if you are in the company of lots of boats, because you are best placed to avoid too much bad air from those in front and at the same time prevent those behind you working up to weather and preventing you tacking.

习惯上我们都像图9中的A船一样绕下风标：

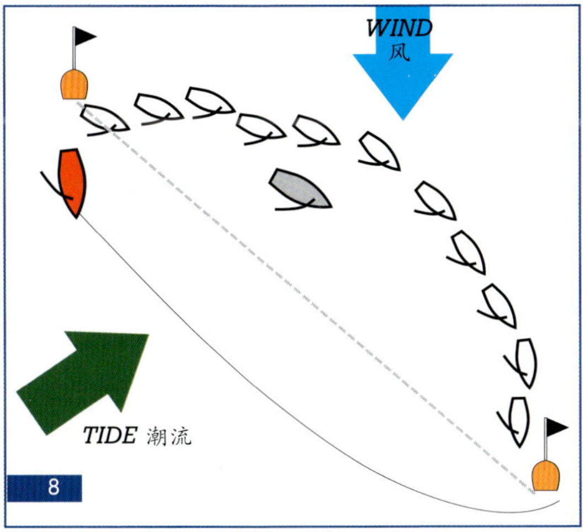

宽进窄出。这样即使你周围有很多船也可以让你避开其他船的脏风，也可以避免你后面的船赶上来阻碍你转向。

However it is worth pointing out that, in the absence of other boats, B, rounding with the same radius turn as A, but coming in close and exiting wide gets an equally good result. i.e. is as far upwind as boat A after the rounding.

值得指出的是，当周围没有其他船时，B船以和A船一样的半径绕标，但是采用窄进宽出的方式，好处是过标之后处在比A 船更上风的位置。

Amazingly, there is a more efficient way of rounding. C rounds so that the mid-point of her curve is the buoy, so she will have sailed the least distance downwind. However, this rounding should only be used when you’re well clear of other competitors!

还有更有效率的绕标方式：C船以浮标为圆心绕标，这样就减小了顺风航行的距离。但是这种方法只适用于周边没有对手的情况。

Top Ten Tactical Tips
十大战术

Tactics is about boat-on-boat manoeuvres, whereas strategy is about dealing with the elements – if there were no one else in the race what would be the fastest way around the course?

战术是关于船只之间的机动技巧，而策略则是关于和比赛有关的各类因素的——如果比赛场地没有别的船就无法确定哪一条航线是最快的。

This list of tips came from a smart group of junior

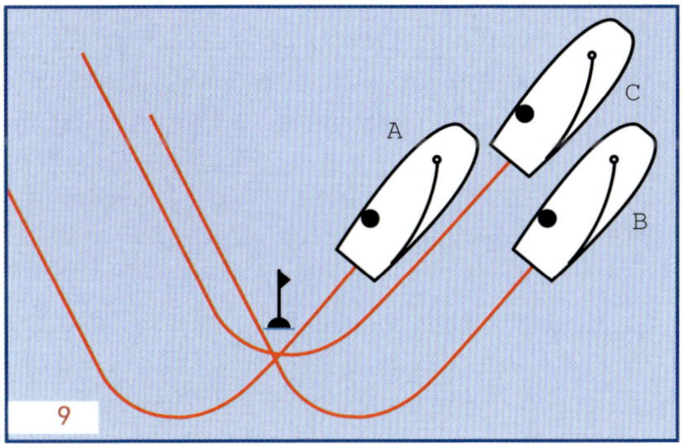

sailors who were limited to only the ten they considered the most useful – the ones to fall back on when all else fails!

这个战术列表来自一些优秀的青少年选手的总结，精简到十个最有用的——只要都做到了就不会落后！

1. Maintain clear air. 保持干净风。
2. Keep your head out the boat.
   把头探出船外。
3. Don’t be greedy – play the percentage game. Make little gains. Don’t take risks.
   不要太过贪心——有把握地进行比赛，循序渐进获得优势，不要冒险。
4. **BOGTOSS!** – pre-start checks: 赛前检查：
   B – Bias – check the line bias.
   偏角——检查起航线偏角。
   O – Observations – look around, especially for transits.
   观察——四处观察，特别注意参照线。
   G – Gusts – what is the wind doing up the course?
   阵风——航线上的风如何变化？
   T – Tide – check the tidal flow.
   潮汐——检查潮汐水流。
   O – Obstructions – for you to avoid and for the wind to flow around.
   障碍物——避免碰撞并观察对风的影响。
   S – Shifts – what is the pattern of the shifts?
   风摆——现场的风摆种类？
   S – Speed – Boat set up for the prevailing conditions.
   速度——调较好船应对各种状况条件。
5. Long tack first – there has to be a good reason not to be taking the long tack first to the windward mark.
   在迎风段航行之初最好做长距离不换舷航行，除非有很好的理由换舷。

6. If you are sailing upwind close to and parallel to the shoreline on your left-hand side, you will find there is often more wind close to that shore. The same applies if you are sailing downwind and the shoreline is to your right-hand side, but it is always something to check as this rule will not apply every time.
如果海岸在你近处的左边，平行于岸边迎风航行，你会发现越靠岸边风越大。同样的如果你顺风航行而岸在右边，也是越靠岸边风越大。但这不是百验百灵，小心观察为妙。
7. Up on starboard, down on port – if you spend most time on starboard tack upwind you are likely to spend more time on port gybe coming downwind.
迎风右舷，顺风左舷——如果在迎风段你大部分都右舷受风，那么在顺风段你可能要更多地做左舷转向。
8. Get on the lifting tack as soon as possible – after the start or on rounding the leeward mark.
在起航后和绕出下风标后尽快进行上行转向。
9. Get on the inside of an anticipatedwindbend.
尽量进到弧形风摆的内侧。
10. Take control – sheep don't win boat races!
控制好船——像绵羊一样是不可能赢得比赛。

Tide on the course
航线上的潮汐水流

Smart sailors make allowance for the tide. The grid opposite predicts what a 'STUPID' fleet would do in tidal flow A. You can use the grid to make predictions for tidal flows B, C and D.
聪明的选手会给潮流的影响留出余量。149页的表格推测了一个“笨拙的”船队面对图A的潮流如何应对。
你可以应用这个表格来计划如何应对图B,C和D的潮流。

A range of tidal flows (A-D).
面对各种潮流（A-D）

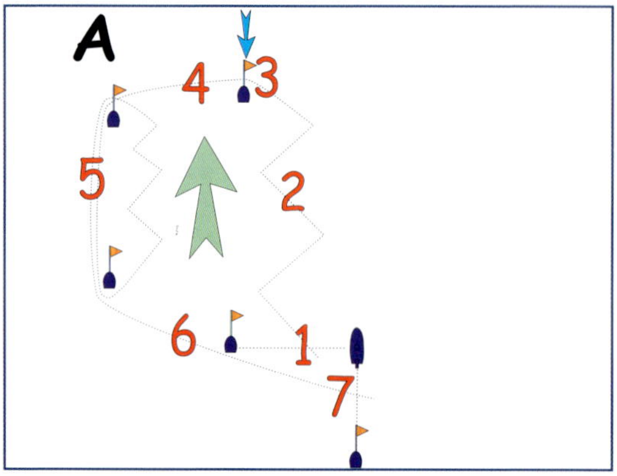

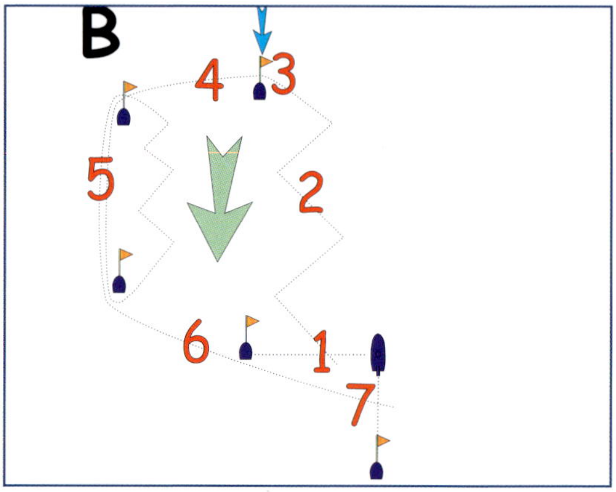

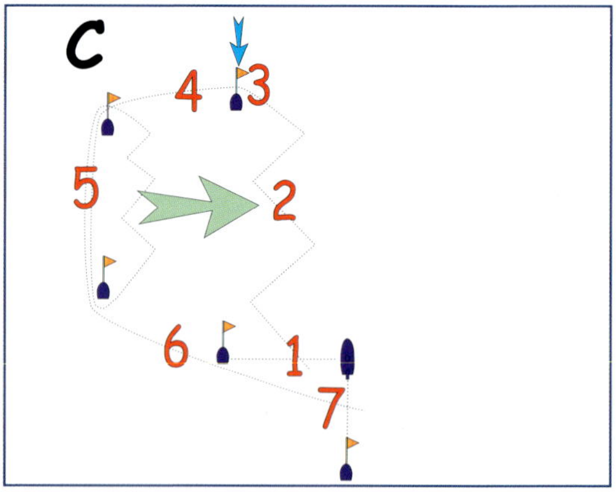

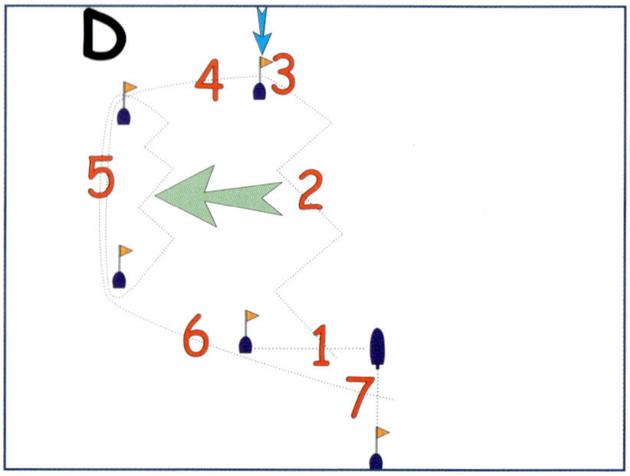

Fleets are stupid, individuals are bright – get your head out of the boat.

船队是笨拙的，但单个选手很聪明——把头探出船外吧。

Tidal Flow A 潮流A		
1	Start 起航	*The fleet will be over the line* 船队将越线抢航
2	Beats 迎风段	*There will be more waves than normal - wind against tide* 会有更多的浪,风向和浪相反
3	Windward Mark 上风标	*The fleet will overstand the laylines* 船队将超过方位线
4	Top Reach 上横风	*There will be a big bow to windward* 航线将偏向上风侧呈弧形
5	Run 顺风段	*Running downwind will be against the tide and so take longer* 顺风段船将顶流因此时间加长
6	Bottom Reach 下横风	*There will be a big bow to windward* 航线将偏向上风侧呈弧形
7	Finish Line 终点线	*There will be lots of boats at the committee boat end* 大量船集中在裁判船一端

Tidal Flow B 潮流B	
1	Start 起航
2	Beats 迎风段
3	Windward Mark 上风标
4	Top Reach 上横风
5	Run 顺风段
6	Bottom Reach 下横风
7	Finish Line 终点线

Tidal Flow C 潮流C	
1	Start 起航
2	Beats 迎风段
3	Windward Mark 上风标
4	Top Reach 上横风
5	Run 顺风段
6	Bottom Reach 下横风
7	Finish Line 终点线

Tidal Flow D 潮流D	
1	Start 起航
2	Beats 迎风段
3	Windward Mark 上风标
4	Top Reach 上横风
5	Run 顺风段
6	Bottom Reach 下横风
7	Finish Line 终点线

Masterclass 6 大师级别6
Preparing for an event 赛事准备

Competition is stressful. Sound organisation will prevent many stressful situations and increase the chances of a good result.
比赛是令人紧张的。良好的准备可以避免很多状况出现并增加获得好成绩的机会。
You may recognise the following
你应该认识到下面这些：

- Running out of time on the day so you arrive late at the start area.
  转悠的时间太长以致很晚到达起航区域。
- Forgetting your stopwatch and not having a spare.
  忘带航海表并且没有备份。
- Finding the travel lodge didn' t have your booking after all!
  到酒店发现并没有你的预定信息。
- Not having a carbine hook when one breaks.
  快挂损坏时没有备件。
- Forgetting a towel in your sailing kit.
  装备里忘记带毛巾。

So get organised!所以要周密准备!

Months before 几个月之前

- Check the events you want to compete in.
  寻找你希望参加的比赛
- Book the accommodation and ferries.
  预定住宿和船票
- Make checklists for equipment, clothing (sailing and otherwise) and spares.
  制定一个检查表，包括设备、服装（航海专用和其他）以及配件。
- Make a time plan and sequence for the day of the race.
  制定一个截止到比赛日的时间计划和流程表。

Weeks before 几周之前

- Download the Notice of Race and entry form.
  下载赛事通知和报名表。
- Enter. 完成报名。

Days before 几天之前

- Read the sailing instructions and prepare any questions.
  阅读航行指南并提出问题。
- Get the forecasts.获取天气预报。
- Look at Google Earth for the venue and likely wind directions.
  在谷歌地图上研究比赛场地和大致的风向。
- Download directions to the venue and determine travel time.
  下载旅行指南并确定旅行时间。
- Work back from the start time to determine what time you need to leave.
  根据比赛开始时间决定何时出发。

This is another case of ‘Fail to Plan and you Plan to Fail’. You will know how naturally organised you are and therefore how detailed the lists need to be. The following spares list is based on my personal experience.
有句老话说：运筹帷幄，决胜千里。你应该对自己的组织计划能力心中有数，更要知道准备工作应该多么细致。下面的备件列表来自我的个人经验。

Spares list 备件表

On water: 水上

- Length of 4mm rope.一段4毫米绳索
- Bung! 塞子!
- Carbine hook.挂钩
- Traveller shackle - will do for other applications.
  滑车快挂——也可以做别的用途。
- Chinagraph pencil and rubber for writing info on the boat.
  绘图铅笔和橡皮用于在船上写记录。
- Drink - hydration fluid is best.
  饮料——最好是运动饮料。
- Food for immediately after the race, if not during the race.
  比赛间隙和比赛后补充的食物。

Tool box: 工具箱：

Endless!!! 永远不够！

- 4mm Dyneema. 4毫米迪尼玛绳索。
- 4mm elastic. 4毫米弹力绳。
- Knife and lighter.刀和手电。
- Various shackles and carbine hooks.
  各类快挂和卡钩。
- Sif (old Jif) and rag to clean hull.
  洗涤剂和抹布，用于清洗船体。
- S/S rivets and rivet gun (needs to be beefy - some groups buy one between them - Screwfix or Machine Mart).
  S/S铆钉和铆钉枪。
- Self-bailer.排水筏。
- Waterproof tape - parcel or gaffer.
  防水胶带
- More bungs! 更多的塞子!
- Insignia cloth (same as used on sail numbers) for sail repair.
  修帆用的自粘布（与帆号的材料相同）。
- 10mm spanners for steering gear.
  10mm 扳手，用于调整舵柄。
- Phillips screwdriver. 十字螺丝刀。
- Mastgate lanyard.桅杆插槽系索。

One could go on! In truth the fleet is very friendly and will help out so some of the above is a bit OTT.
你可以出发了！其实船队是很友善的，如果你缺了任何一个备件都可以从别人那里获得帮助。

Masterclass 7 大师级别7
Dave Cockerill's guide for parents 给家长的建议

What can racing do for your youngster?
比赛能给年轻人带来什么？

Sailing is a brilliant sport. To succeed at sailing you need the kind of skills you need to be successful in life:

帆船是一项精彩的运动。要赢得帆船比赛所需要的技巧和能力，也可以帮助你在生活中获得成功。

- **Confidence –** if nothing else the confidence gained by being responsible for your own actions and for a vessel in a hostile environment and most often coming back alive! There aren't even any roads to navigate on! Some parents are unlucky enough not to get on the water. If they only knew the things their child was going through at times!

  自信——只有当你为自己的行为负责并且操纵帆船完成了竞争激烈的比赛，才能获得自信。在海上根本没有路，全凭自己寻找决定。有些不幸的家长从来没有到水上体验过，他们只知道一些孩子们已经玩腻的事情！

- **Planning skills –** goal setting is a high level skill. Even looking ahead six months to decide what events to attend is an experience worth having.

  计划能力——设立目标是非常高难的技能。提前六个月选择想加入的赛事也是值得体验的经历。

- **Making friends –** you have to help each other in this sport. You have common experiences, often ones well worth reliving together (those waves were as big as bungalows!), and you go away together.

  广交朋友——帆船运动中大家必须彼此帮助。你拥有一些基本知识，值得与大家一起分享体验（比如对大浪的经验），然后大家一起练习。

- **Physical prowess –** the open air if nothing else. Those who think that sailing is about fluffy white clouds, blue sky and pink gins have never tried dinghy racing.

  强健体魄——尽情呼吸新鲜空气！那些认为帆船意味着悠闲的白云和蓝天以及杜松子酒的人一定没有尝试过小帆船竞赛。

- **Mental ability –** toughness, making connections, seeing the bigger picture, assertiveness, playing a percentage game. It goes on and on. I'm often told that sailing has had a positive effect on an individual's schoolwork. Rarely have I heard the opposite despite the times homework is done in the back of a car on the way to an event.

  坚强意志——坚韧不拔，掌握规律，高瞻远瞩，自信果敢，步步为营。帆船的进步无止境。我经常会了解到练习帆船对提高学习成绩有积极的作用，很少听到练习帆船的负面因素，最多也就是为了赶去参加比赛而在车上赶写作业。

The commitment 投入

I have been a squaddie parent, following my son around and eventually racing a Topper myself because he was clearly having lots of fun. It all started in a small way – club race, local regatta and then local Open Meeting. You meet other parents; share a great experience or two and suddenly you're at the National Championships in some remote corner of the UK for your

holidays. The funny thing is I found myself having fun and enjoying the progress he was making.
我曾经是一个帆船选手的父亲，陪着我儿子四处比赛，在他对比赛的热情影响下最终我也参与了Topper比赛。开始总是很初级的——俱乐部比赛，地方的杯赛和公开赛事。你会碰到很多家长，大家一起分享经验感受，突然有一天你会在一个遥远的地方参加全国锦标赛。令我感到兴奋的是我开始享受比赛并且为儿子所获得的进步而快乐。
Here it gets tricky. There is a difference between enjoying your child's progress and living through them. One attitude supports what they are doing willingly, the other expects results from what you have done. The worst thing I ever heard was a child who was scared to go ashore at a windy event because "Dad will shout at me". I nearly resigned that day as National Coach because I felt the parent's attitude stemmed from the seriousness of it all. A seriousness I thought I might be adding to. There is plenty of pressure on sailors to do well from within, from peer pressure, from wanting to do well for coaches and yes for wanting to do well for parents. Too much pressure diminishes performance. As a coach I try to remove pressure. Looking at the long view is important. How good were they twelve months ago? How good will they be in twelve months time? Less pressure means better results and more fun.
事情的发展变得复杂了，享受孩子获得的进步的那一刻和一直陪伴他们成长是有区别的。一种观点认为只要孩子们愿意做出努力，就一定会获得结果。我遇到的最糟糕的事情是孩子们在大风天战战兢兢的被迫下水，原因仅仅是“如果不下水，爸爸会对我吼叫”。当时我差点就辞去国家级教练的职务了，因为我发现家长们太过于看重结果。有一件事我必须严肃地跟大家说，对于帆船选手来说，太多的压力来自于同伴竞争，来自于想在教练和父母面前表现出色，过分的压力会影响发挥。作为一个教练我总是试图为孩子们减压，重要的是着眼未来。一年前他们的水平如何？一年之后他们等有多大进步？压力越小成绩越好，乐趣也越多。

Fun 乐趣

Fun is the most important thing. It is pointless coaching a sailor who is not having fun. All that effort will be wasted if they don't enjoy sailing, because they will move on to other activities. We lose too many great young people to the sport because they are put under too much pressure. It's a sport for life, not just for teenagers!
享受乐趣是最重要的。如果一个选手毫不愉快，训练就变得毫无意义。所有的努力将会付诸东流，因为他们会转而从事别的运动。太多优秀的年轻人由于背负太多压力而选择离开。帆船是终生从事的运动，不仅仅是少年时期。

Support before and at the event 赛事前和开始后的支持

As your child gets older you will be able to extend the range of things they can do themselves. Involve them in the planning progress, expect them to prepare and rig their own boats but do be there to support their efforts. They are young and will make mistakes.
随着孩子年龄增长，你可以让他们做更多的事情，包括做比赛计划，准备和装配船只但一定陪伴他们以提供支持。孩子们总会犯错误。
I quickly recognised (are you listening Adam?) that my son needed space when he came ashore. The last thing he needed was involving me in what happened in the race even though I was keen to share the experience. The stories might come out in the car on the way home, if he wasn't asleep! Certainly they would come out over the course of the next week. Despite that he would never ask for my advice - what did I know? When I thought there were things he needed to know I would prime my brother or another parent who would make the suggestion on my behalf. Equally other parents primed me and it all worked very well.
我很快意识到（亚当你在听吗？）我的儿子上岸后不想被打扰了。他允许我参与的最后一件事是打听赛事消息，虽然我很急切地想和他分享比赛经验。如果在回家的车上他没有睡着还是愿意和我分享些比赛趣闻的。下一周他可能又会出现在下一个比赛中，但他已经不愿意听取我的建议了。如果我觉得一定要告诉他点什么，我会委托我弟弟或其他的家长代我转告，这样的效果也不差。

Oddly enough I stopped watching through binoculars because his results seemed to get better when I didn' t know what was going on!

说来也奇怪，我不再通过双筒望远镜来观察他了，之后他的成绩越来越好。

Coaches 教练们

Coaches are great people! We love what we do but it can be stressful and help is welcomed. I like to have a parent in the coach boat with me. It makes me a far more effective support boat and I do need someone to lay marks! There are two rules however:

教练们是些了不起的家伙！虽然压力很大，但我们热爱这份工作也欢迎各种帮助。我喜欢请一位家长上教练船，这样让我可以更有效地做好支持工作，同时家长也可以帮助我布标。但这有两个规矩：

- only one voice should come out of a coach boat and that' s from the coach.
  在教练船上只有一个人可以喊话，这就是我。
- you must not mention your child (biologically impossible of course!).
  你不能只盯着自己的孩子（在感情上不太可能！）。

If you decide to employ a coach and your youngster is already in a squad then it is a good move, as well as professional courtesy, to ask the extra coach to contact the squad coach who will know the areas the sailor needs to develop next.

如果你决定把一切都交给教练而你的孩子已经在训练队伍中，你最好通过其他教练来询问带队教练（这也是一种职业礼貌）孩子们下一步的发展计划是什么。

And finally - silly games 终结篇——趣味游戏

Game 1: Climbing The Mast.
游戏1:爬桅杆

Just in case this is all getting too serious···
The best two non-sailing games have long-established rules.
为了让帆船不过于严肃，有两个非航行游戏流行已久。

Game 1: 游戏

CLIMBING THE MAST 爬桅杆

1. Take all gear off the boat except the mast, daggerboard and (old) sail.
   把船上除桅杆、稳向板和一面旧帆的其他设备拆掉。
2. Wrap the sail tightly round the mast and tie it off.
   把帆卷在桅杆上并捆好。
3. Have two people stand chest deep in the water, one holding the bow and the other the transom.
   请两个人站在齐胸深的水里，一个固定住船头，另一个固定住船尾。
4. Attempt to climb to the top of the mast before the boat falls over.
   爬上桅杆顶并避免船身倾倒。
5. Prove your achievement with a photograph.
   摆好姿势拍照。

Game 2: Maximum Number of People on a Topper.
游戏2:一条Topper最多能装多少人?

Game 2: 游戏二

MAXIMUM NUMBER OF PEOPLE ON A TOPPER
一条Topper能装多少人

The official record is 17 (see photo opposite). This particular group in Dubai are sure they had 18 on the boat but I can only see 17 so 17 it is.
正式的纪录是17个人（见对面照片）。这是一个在迪拜的队伍，他们确认上了18个人但我在照片上只看到17个，所以记录只能算17人。

Can you do better?你能做得更好吗?

1.Remove all gear from someone else’s Topper. (You wouldn’t want to use yours would you!)
找一条别人的船（你不会愿意用自己的船吧？），拆掉所有装备。
2.Put it in waist deep water.
把船放在齐腰深的水里。
3. Get as many people as possible on the boat.
尽可能让更多的人上船。
4. The boat is allowed to go under water but not on the bottom (no cheating!).
船身允许沉下水面但不允许触地(不许捣鬼!)。
5. The boat must be afloat for 10 seconds.
船必须浮起十秒钟。
6. Prove your achievement with a photo!
摆好姿势拍照!

OTHER GAMES 其他游戏

How many different ways can you capsize a Topper? Here’s a start: The Pitchpole!
有多少种方法可以让Topper翻覆？从这个开始：前后颠簸纵摇翻覆!

黑版贸审字 08-2016-109号

内容简介：
本书用专业的视角和通俗的语言，介绍了驰名世界的Topper小帆船的构造特点和使用技巧。初学者通过阅读本书并进行实践练习，可以掌握基本的帆船驾驶技能，并逐步提高到参加比赛和获胜的水平。作者出身中学老师并且有近三十年的帆船教练经验，在本书中呈现了系统而深入的Topper小帆船训练方法。
本书适合青少年及成年帆船爱好者阅读，也是供帆船教练使用的一本出色的教学参考书。

图书在版编目（CIP）数据
玩转TOPPER / (英) 戴夫·柯克瑞尔
(Dave Cocherill) , (英) 约翰·凯格 (John Caig) 著；
王欣译. -- 哈尔滨：哈尔滨工程大学出版社, 2017.1
ISBN 978-7-5661-1434-1

Ⅰ. ①玩… Ⅱ. ①戴… ②约… ③王… Ⅲ. ①帆船运动—青少年读物 Ⅳ. ①G861.4-49

中国版本图书馆CIP数据核字(2016)第319668号

选题策划 史大伟
责任编辑 史大伟

出版发行 哈尔滨工程大学出版社
社　　址 哈尔滨市南岗区东大直街124号
邮政编码 150001
发行电话 0451-82519328
传　　真 0451-82519699
经　　销 新华书店
印　　刷 哈尔滨市石桥印务有限公司
开　　本 787mm×1092mm 1/16
印　　张 10
字　　数 212千字
版　　次 2017年1月第1版
印　　次 2017年1月第1次印刷
定　　价 80.00元
http://www.hrbeupress.com
E-mail:heupress@hrbeu.edu.cn